Mao Tse-tung and Education

Mao Tse-Tung and Education

His Thoughts and Teachings

BY *John N. Hawkins*

LINNET BOOKS 1974

Library of Congress Cataloging in Publication Data

Hawkins, John N
Mao Tsê-tung and education.

Bibliography: p.
1. Mao, Tsê-tung, 1893- 2. Education—Philosophy.
3. Education—China (People's Republic of China, 1949-)
—History. I. Title.
LB775.M35632H3 370.1'092'4 73-13933
ISBN 0-208-01222-2

First published 1974 under the imprint Linnet Books
by The Shoe String Press, Inc.
Hamden, Connecticut 06514

Printed in the United States of America

To Noel and Kay

CONTENTS

PREFACE

THE WRITING OF THIS BOOK has at least in one way been like the Chinese revolution: essentially a collective effort. Although the similarity ends there, it is important because without the help of many people the task of collecting, translating, sorting, and compiling materials on Mao's educational thought would have been immensely more difficult.

Major credit in this study must be given to the hundreds of students, teachers, and educational officials in the People's Republic of China who during my visit in 1971 tolerated what must have seemed to be endless questioning on China's educational system and Mao's thought. Thanks must also be given to the Chinese Association for Friendship with Foreign Countries which was instrumental in allowing a visa to be issued for my visit. My trip would have been far less fruitful without the consistently helpful advice and guidance of my two traveling companions, Tzu and Shen.

The bulk of the research for this project was completed in the United States. The librarians and staff of the East Asian sections of the Library of Congress, Columbia University Library, University of Chicago.Library, and Vanderbilt University Library all helped significantly in locating individual documents by Mao not available in the usual collections.

In Nashville, I would like to particularly thank Stewart E. Fraser, Director of the International Center at George Peabody College for Teachers for initial stimulation, encouragment, and guidance throughout the course of research and writing. I would also like to thank Howard L. Boorman, Director of East Asian Studies at Vanderbilt University for valuable criticism of the manuscript. Other members of the faculty of both schools, particularly Professors Robert M. Bjork and Charles F. Delzell, helped me to make sense of the materials on Mao's educational thought by opening new avenues of analysis and providing me with a critical forum. My fellow doctoral students served as another source of invaluable support by criticizing in a much less restrained manner my ideas and interpretations of Mao's educational thought. Special thanks must go to Ma Shih-tsun of Vanderbilt University's Chinese language program who patiently straightened out my often garbled translations of Mao's articles and excerpts on education.

There is one person who has had a hand in virtually every aspect of this study. Judith A. Takata aided in the initial research, translation of Japanese materials, and editing of the final manuscript. There is little I can say to express my feelings for her numerous contributions.

I would finally like to thank George Peabody College for Teachers for providing me with generous financial assistance through the National Defense Education Act during my program of doctoral study.

INTRODUCTION

FOR OVER FIFTY YEARS the Chinese Communist Party has been engaged in revolutionary struggles that have seen that organization grow from a small band of conspirators in Shanghai in 1921 to a supreme leadership position over the most populous nation on earth in 1973. The road to power was not an easy one. It began in the cities, led to the mountains of South China, traced its way tortuously on the "Long March" to the caves of Northwest China, and finally returned to the cities and Capital in 1949. It left a trail of immense suffering, broken dreams and lives but has ended—at least for the present—on a note of hope for the Chinese people.

Throughout this remarkable story the role of Mao Tse-tung has been preeminent. Since 1935, when Mao ascended to the top leadership of the Chinese Communist Party, he has exerted enormous influence over the reorganization and political development of modern-day China. His ideas, policies, and "thoughts" have formed the basic structure of virtually every sector of Chinese society including military strategy, political and economic affairs, and perhaps most importantly, educational policy and practice. This is not to say that Mao has had an easy task. Despite the overwhelming image he projects, Chinese society and the power structure have exhibited a surprising degree of pluralism. More than once Mao found himself in opposition even with his colleagues in the Party he helped to create. His policies were not mechanically adopted and put into practice, and many times he had to push for his programs with all the political skills at his disposal. At other times he has resorted to outright violence and revolution. Seldom, however, has he been indecisive.

While Mao looms tall in historical perspective, little is known specifically about his role in the shaping of educational policy and practice in China. Yet it is precisely in the area of education that Mao may have the most lasting influence. Mao is one of the few major political figures who began his career as a school teacher and has himself expressed a desire to be remembered simply as a teacher.[1] He has viewed education in the broadest possible context and like his traditional counterparts has ascribed to education the power to transform both man and society. Through formal and informal educational efforts Mao has sought to mold a literate society capable of staffing and maintaining a growing agricultural and industrial nation which would remain politically and ideologically dedicated to socialism. The enormity of such a task is evident. Yet the degree of success thus far is such that China's educational system has become a model for several developing countries (most notably Tanzania) and has even attracted the interest of several American educators. In general, Mao Tse-tung's educational thought has been a major factor in the attempt to unify, develop, and strengthen the People's Republic of China. In a larger sense Mao's approach to education is crucial to the eventual emergence of the "new socialist man."

There are several areas of concern in this study. The primary objective is to derive from the writings of Mao Tse-tung a representative and coherent collection of his thoughts on education. Seldom has Mao devoted a major work to the problems of education, but contained within his numerous writings are several lengthy sections related to a variety of educational issues. Collectively they present a broad outline of Mao's approach to education. More specifically, Mao's analysis of the basic aims, goals, and principles of education are examined as well as problems related to the structure and organization of both formal and informal education. Mao's writings range over a period of fifty-five years and were naturally influenced by changing historical conditions. An attempt has been made to provide the relevant historical background, but this effort was necessarily limited by a desire to focus primarily on pedagogical issues.

It is hoped that this study will be useful for educators, students, and laymen interested in educational issues in general and Chinese education in particular. At the very least it should reveal the role of Mao Tse-tung as an architect of one of the most unique and provocative approaches to education in this era.

Part I

Philosophical and Historical Background

1 Marxism, Leninism and Education

. . . Without revolutionary theory, without historical knowledge and an understanding of the concrete movement, it is impossible to lead a great revolutionary movement to victory. The theories of Marx, Engels, Lenin, and Stalin can be applied to the whole universe. Their theroies are not to be looked upon as dogma but as a guide for action—Mao Tse-tung. ["On the New Stage (November, 1938)," in *The Political Thought of Mao-Tse-tung*, ed. by Stuart R. Schram (2nd ed.; New York: Praeger Press, 1969), p. 171.]

SINCE THE SUMMER OF 1920 Mao Tse-tung has considered himself ". . . in theory and to some extent in action, a Marxist . . . ."[1] This fact has considerable importance for any analysis of the development of Mao's educational thought. It is difficult to say with any degree of precision exactly with which Marxist and Leninist writings Mao is familiar but he has certainly been exposed to the major works and, more important perhaps, to the pedagogical advice resulting from the Chinese Communist Party's long period of association with the Soviet Union. This chap-

FIG. 1. A people's Liberation Army soldier studies Marxism-Leninism.

ter will briefly discuss the main tenets of Marxist-Leninist educational thought, trace its development in the Soviet Union, and examine the route Marxism took to China. It is against such a background (and that of Chapter Two) that an extended discussion can begin of Mao Tse-tung and education.

Marxism-Leninism and Education

The distinguishing feature of Marxism as a philosophical school is its particular brand of materialism—historical and dialectical materialism. It is this structural framework that provides a basis for the Marxist epistemology and general world-view from which, of course, pedagogical concepts arise.[2] In its most fundamental sense, this brand of materialism is based on the recognition of the existence of nature separate from man's consciousness. However, at the same time man is part of nature and acts to change it, thus changing himself. Marxists believe the question of the relation of the human mind to material being is the fundamental question of all varieties of philosophy. Marx said: ". . . the idea is nothing else than the material world reflected by the human mind and translated into forms of thought."[3] This commitment to materialism is the distinguishing feature of Marxist educational theory.

The addition of the concept of dialectics to materialism sets Marx apart from earlier dialecticians and materialists. Although Marx and Engels drew much from the dialectical thought of Hegel, they disagreed completely with his theory of the relation of thought to matter. Whereas Hegel sought to put thought before matter, Marx and Engels drew the opposite conclusion. As expressed by Lenin:

> Materialism and idealism differ in their answers to the question of the source of our knowledge and of the relation of knowledge to the physical world . . . the question is decided in favour of materialism, for the concept matter, epistemologically implies *nothing but* objective reality existing independently of the human mind and reflected by it.[4]

By breaking with the two great bodies of tradition which have most influenced Western education (Greek dualism and the Hebraic-Christian tradition), Marx's materialism set a unique pattern for later Marxists including Mao and is continually reflected in Mao's educational writings.[5]

The second aspect of Marx's thought important for education is the concept of the unity of theory and practice. Marx believed all knowledge (all sciences including the most abstract) came into being in response to the requirements of man's practical life. Lenin said: "The standpoint of life, of practice, should be first and fundamental in the theory of knowledge."[6] Thus, unlike earlier materialists, Marx included practice in the theory of knowledge and viewed practice as the basis and purpose of the cognitive process. It follows that knowledge can only be truly attained in man's relation to his environment, especially his labor. With the emphasis on practice, it becomes possible for man not only to know the world but also to change it. The constant interaction of theory with practice (theory enriched by practice and practice guided by theory) therefore makes possible the conditions for society's material and technical progress.

What then constitutes the act of cognition? Lenin wrote:

> Cognition is the eternal, endless approximation of thought to the object. The reflection of nature in man's thought must be understood not "lifelessly," not "abstractly," *not devoid of movement, NOT WITHOUT CONTRADICTIONS but in the eternal PROCESS of movement, the arising of contradictions and their solution.*[7]

Marx was careful to point out, however, that the reflection of the objective world in man's consciousness (cognition-thought) is not to be understood as a single act, but rather as comprised of many aspects and steps. Beginning with sensory perception, moving to abstract thought (a qualitative leap), and concluding with practical action represents the movement of knowledge.[8] Out of this primary relationship of man to the material world arise all social relationships and institutions, including the educational system, which comprise the superstructure of society. This is best summarized in this well-known passage from Marx:

> In the social production that men carry on they enter into definite relations that are indispensable and independent of their will; these relations of production correspond to a definite stage of development of their material powers of production. The sum total of these relations of production constitutes the economic structure of society—the real foundations, on which rise legal and political superstructures and to which correspond definite forms of social consciousness. The

> mode of production in material life determines the general character of the social, political, and spiritual processes of life. It is not the consciousness of men that determines their existence, but on the contrary, their social existence determines their consciousness.[9]

It is particularly difficult to find in the immense body of literature by Marx and Lenin specific proposals for educational reform which could be reconstructed to form a genuine theory of education. What Marx and Lenin had to say about education is scattered throughout their writings and does not form a coherent whole. Certain primary orientations, however, do stand out and these can be identified as representing three categories: education and social class, polytechnical education, and education and social change. These three educational problems will be examined in the light in which Marx and Lenin viewed them and will be seen as representing what could be termed a Marxist-Leninist approach to education. These are certainly the kind of problems with which most societies are faced and with which Mao struggled for over thirty years.

The problem of education and social class has wide implications in a practical sense. Admission policies, course and text content, as well as teacher recruitment all hinge on the manner in which the educational system relates to the various strata of society. One can speak of universal education, democratic education, or simply public education, but the question of who comes to school and whom the school primarily serves is one which must be faced eventually. Marx clearly stated his view when he emphasized that there can never be "universal" or "free" education as long as social classes continue to exist. Educational policy and practice will always favor one class or another and, of course, in the democratic societies of the West that class to Marx was the bourgeoisie.[10] Lenin, perhaps put it most succinctly:

> The more cultured was the bourgeois state, the more subtly it deceived, asserting that the school can remain outside of politics and thus serve society as a whole. In reality the school was wholly an instrument of class domination in the hands of the bourgeoisie; it was permeated throughout with the spirit of caste; and its aim was to give to the capitalist obliging serfs and competent workers.[11]

Education here is seen as simply a reflection of the politics of whatever class happens to be in power. To suggest that education and politics can be separate is, according to Marx and Lenin, ". . . a lie and an hypocricy . . . ."[12] With the success of the October Revolution in 1917 it was specifically stated that the school would be converted from an instrument in the hands of the bourgeoisie to one in the hands of the proletariat. According to Lenin the school must become ". . . not only the conductor of the principles of communism in general, but also the conductor of the ideological, organizational, and educational influence of the proletariat . . . ."[13] This point was hammered home many times during the early period following the Bolshevik victory, and the position that education is dominated by social class held firm in the Marxist-Leninist approach to education.[14]

The question of polytechnical education is one which embraces the entire organizational structure of the school and particularly the curriculum program. What does one do about the relationship between liberal arts education and vocational education, mental and manual labor, and questions of theory and practice? These are all problems Marxists have discussed under the rubric of polytechnical education. A brief and initial discussion of this question is contained in point ten of Marx's ten-point program for communism (*The Communist Manifesto*): "10. Free education for all children in public schools. Abolition of child factory labor in its present form. Combination of education with industrial production, etc."[15] It is ironic that Marx gained his insight into the education of the future by observing the factory reform acts of 1864 in England. A section of the acts required that the factories and the parents allow children under the age of fourteen to receive elementary instruction while they work. Marx noted, as did the factory inspectors, the interesting phenomenon that the children who received half-day instruction and worked the remaining half were performing at least as well and in some cases at a higher level than those children of the bourgeoisie who attended school fulltime. Marx's conclusion was:

> This can be accounted for by the simple fact that, with only being at school for one half of the day, they are always fresh, and nearly always ready and willing to receive instruction. The system on which they work, half manual labor and half school renders each employment a rest and a relief to the other . . . . It is clear that a boy who has been at school all the morning, cannot . . . cope with one who comes

> fresh and bright from his work . . . . From the factory system budded . . . the germ of the education of the future, an education that will . . . combine productive labor with instruction and gymnastics, not only as one of the methods of adding to the efficiency of production, but as the only method of producing fully developed human beings.[18]

Thus, Marx's program for future education—socialist and communist education—was summed up later in the same work: " . . . there can be little doubt that when the working-class comes into power . . . technical instruction, both theoretical and practical, will take its proper place in the working-class schools."[17] The relationship between mental and manual labor Marx is discussing here became one of the most important pedagogical principles held by Marxists and has been at the root of Marxist discussions of individual differences in intellectual ability, specialization versus nonspecialization, and other pedagogical problems related to the particular mechanics of instruction, curriculum, and learning. Polytechnical education has been variously interpreted by both Marxist and non-Marxist educators and the experiences of the Soviet Union and China continue to reflect this difficult to define concept.

The Marxist conception of education as a force for social change perhaps seems paradoxical in view of the deterministic philosophy underlying Marxism-Leninism. But both Marx and Lenin have stressed the importance of viewing the role of the superstructure in a dialectical manner, that is, as having an impact on the economic base. The earlier writings of Marx particularly stressed the importance of education, even bourgeois education, in transforming man and society. While Marx never reached the heights which Mao does in applying to education powers of social change, he did consider it one of the more important dynamic agents in society. Thus he was able to write: "The materialist [mechanical materialist] doctrine of the change of circumstances and education forgets that circumstances are changed by men and the educator must himself be educated . . . ."[16] Under communism there is no question for Marx about the liberating role of education, but even in class society state-controlled education can have a transformational effect on the individuals living in that society.[19] With the establishment of socialism we see Lenin also asserting that while the economic base determines the basic form and structure of the educational system it in turn acts as a force to realign the material base and in this way transforms the basic elements of society.[20]

The three educational problems discussed above and developed by both Marx and Lenin received their first practical attempt at solution with the establishment of the Union of Soviet Socialist Republics in 1917. A firm consensus was never reached, but the relationship between Soviet social, political, and economic realities and the theoretical propositions of Marx and Lenin provides a historical comparison with similar experiences in China.

The Development of Soviet Educational Theory and Practice

The educational history of the Soviet Union ranges over a sixty-year period characterized by twists and turns in both theory and practice. It is an extremely complicated subject and can only be briefly examined here. Yet it is essential to understand the historical background of this period, particularly considering that from 1923 with the arrival in Canton of Borodin to 1960 with the withdrawal of Soviet technicians from China the Chinese Communist Party and Mao Tse-tung have at least been exposed to the ideas and experiences of the Soviet Union including (especially in the period 1950 to 1960) their pedagogical policies. Given such a long span of time some sort of periodization becomes necessary. Several schemes have been proposed and Soviet scholars have designed one of their own.[21] All such schemes have a useful rationale and simply serve to render a complex and confusing subject more manageable. In the following discussion, Soviet educational history has been divided into three periods: (1) the period of experimentation—1917-1925; (2) the period of retrenchment—1926-1945; (3) the period of reform—1946-72.

Period of Experimentation: 1917-1925

When the Russian communist party came to power in 1917 it inherited a traditional educational system in all senses of the word. At the primary level education was limited to the elite, and at the secondary level classical education prevailed characterized by rote drill and learning, authoritarian classroom procedure, and emphasis on grades and examinations. Nevertheless, liberal undercurrents existed. Some educators were familiar with the concept of child-centered education, and curricular reform was underway to redirect subject matter to the needs of modernization. Early Soviet educational reformers simply superimposed the basic philosophical principles of Marx, Engels, and Lenin on the reforms already underway.[22]

The general goals and aims of education in this early period of experimentation were coached by Soviet educators in Marxist terms: "The long range objective of Marx and Engels was to provide through the educational system for the harmonious, all-round development of every individual [under communism] to train everyone to the limits of his capacities."[23] Lenin very quickly accepted Marx's analysis of polytechnical education and recognized it as a medium whereby mental and manual labor could be unified as would theory and practice. But he also recognized that the first priority in a society like Russia was the problem of illiteracy. Thus, an early draft of Lenin's program for education stressed both the need for technical as well as general education.[24] The report finally issued in 1918 by the first commissioner of education, Lunacharski, contained seven basic principles: (1) labor as the basis of teaching and education; (2) "early fusion of productive labor and academic instruction"; (3) polytechnical education, meaning all-round development of the individual; (4) the school as a productive commune; (5) manual labor as a part of everyday school life; (6) productive, creative, and artistic endeavors; (7) emphasis on the child as a "social creature."[25] In short, Lunacharski viewed the school as a collective unit carrying out both productive and pedagogical tasks.

This idealized plan underwent early modification as the realities of Russian society forced compromises. Unified labor schools for both factory and peasant youth were established, and literary programs were enthusiastically embarked upon, but compulsory education was an impossibility because of the utter lack of facilities.[28] Lenin also realized in 1919 that the new state would have to rely upon the old bourgeois intellectuals and technicians and that this represented a contradiction with regard to the goal of working-class leadership.[27] In any case, the way was clear for the experimenters and experiment they did.

Initial approaches by such pedagogues as Shul'gin stressed the deterministic view of nonintervention; that the child should be allowed to unfold freely. Shul'gin also put forth the idea of the "withering away of the school": "In my opinion, there will be no school in the future communist society. The child will go immediately into social work . . . we will all be pedagogues. The child will go directly from social work to industrial work, and from there to the library, where he will find answers to all the questions which interest him."[26] With ideas such as this in vogue plus the theories of Marx and Engels Soviet educators began to search for methods. It was at precisely this time that the "progressive" movement was underway in the United States and it was only natural that educators from both countries became very interested in each others work. Progressive educators in the West were particularly fascinated with events in the Soviet Union where they saw for the first time the possibility of their ideas and concepts being realized on a nation-wide scale. In the 1920s there was a great deal of exchange between progressive American educators and their Soviet counterparts. During this period, Soviet educational policy, and to some extent practice, revolved around goals of instilling cooperative behavior patterns, stressing versatility in skills and knowledge, developing political socialization to socialist ideals, attacking customs and conservative family ties, and emphasizing extracurricular activities and youth clubs.[29] While traditional practices continued to operate in the rural areas, the cities became centers of experimentation and reform. Curriculum models such as the "complex method" were introduced along with programs of collective study, current problems, and individual study or self-study (replacing the earlier rote and recitation method). The traditional "teacher-centered" classroom gave way to the "student-centered" classroom, and the teacher was described as: "an organizer, assistant, instructor, and older comrade, but not [a] superior officer."[30] Teachers were to be called either comrade or by their first name, and if a teacher was not living up to stated socialist ideals and values students were encouraged to rebel against them. In addition, pupil self-government of the schools was stressed, as were youth organizations. These groups were in fact quite decentralized with a great degree of autonomous control.[31]

Perhaps the most articulate and important Soviet educator for this period was A. P. Pinkevitch, President of the Second State University of Moscow in the 1920s. Pinkevitch experimented and worked with the Dalton Plan, the project method, standard tests and measurements, and was familiar with the writings and ideas of such Western educators as John Dewey, Bertrand Russell, and Paul Monroe. Pinkevitch stressed the importance of pedology for educators; that is, utilizing the fields of physiology and psychology to understand child growth and development. According to Pinkevitch the aim of education was not knowledge, rather, knowledge should be the product. The aim was to link the school with social life. Co-existing with Pinkevitch's progressive educational ideas were his beliefs as a Marxist. He was a devoted materialist and committed to the concept of class education as developed by Marx.[32] He was also aware of the existing seeds of the old order particularly in the area of morals and values, and consequently saw the need for the development of youth groups such as the Union of Communist Youth (Komsomol). With regard to Marx's concept of polytechnical education Pinkevitch viewed the role of labor in the school in neither an economic nor utilitarian manner but as a means to instill in the child the feeling that he is a member of a laboring society and to teach the positive role of labor. Educators should work for: ". . . an organic integration of labor with the scientific, artistic, and social work of the school."[33] While educators such as Pinkevitch were remaining open to international influences, particularly from the West, others such as Anton Makerenko were more critical of what they considered a "worship the West ideology" and a conservative trend began to slowly build.[34]

As the Soviet Union entered a critical period of economic growth the educational work of people such as Anton Makerenko appeared more in line with the realities of Soviet society. Makerenko's engineering project with war orphans had been making steady progress. Lenin's death in 1924 and the rise of Stalin throughout the 1920s (especially his defeat of Trotsky in 1928) led to a retreat from the progressive practices of Pinkevitch and others. The "complex method" and the Dalton Plan were abandoned in favor of specialization and in-depth learning.[35] Stalin downgraded the role played by the deterministic forces of history and instead emphasized the interventionist role of the Party in all social affairs including education. Economic needs required strict organization of all facilities and by 1926 the retrenchment was underway.[36]

Period of Retrenchment: 1926-1945

The movement away from experimentation did not proceed quickly. Opposing views of educational theory and methods vied together for a period of about five years until the 1931 educational decrees (explained below). On the experimental side, concrete programs began to emerge: e.g., thematic organization of the curriculum; relating school to society; combining schools with factories and vice versa; encouraging student participation in decision-making; practicing decentralized decision-making; aiding minority education and coeducation.[37] With the introduction of the first five year plan (1928) the objections voiced to these kinds of practices were largely silenced as the country's revolutionary zeal was rekindled. However, at higher levels forces were at work which would eventually negate these programs and substitute a more rigorous, traditional approach to learning. The struggle between Stalin and Trotsky came to a head in 1926 and by 1928 Trotsky's position on industrialization and education was defeated (a position which favored industrial expansion but was not hostile to the experimental educational programs). Although Stalin eventually accepted much of Trotsky's economic program by 1931 the death knell had been sounded for the progressive educators.[38] In 1931 the Central Committee of the Communist Party of the Soviet Union (hereafter CPSU) issued a decree which reversed all the experimental programs discussed above. Western ideas were denounced and conventional learning stressed. The "complex method" was dropped in favor of traditional subject groupings, recitation and rote learning were reemphasized. The labor element of education was thoroughly repudiated and factory-run schools and school-run factories were closed. Grades and examinations received a new emphasis, and teachers again became the center of the classroom with the consequent result that the youth groups were either disbanded or brought under control.[39] The reorganization of education became complete when in 1931 the Director of the Marx-Engels Institute for Pedagogy, V. N. Shul'gin found his ideas under attack and his institute closed.[40] New educational spokesmen such as Kalinin set the tone by suggesting that subject matter was more important than labor and politics, teachers should be respected and students obedient, and economic production and highly skilled personnel should have priority over general educational goals.[41] With the coming of the second world war the requirements for heavy industry and war production necessitated even more emphasis on skilled labor and technicians as well as scientific research and development. Under these conditions there was no room for experimental tampering with the educational system.

What elements, then, constituted the educational system of this period? What happened to such concepts as polytechnical education and education for the proletariat? In general, the primary characteristic was that of centralization. Instead of decentralized planning at the local level, the 1931 decree moved educational policy and planning to Moscow. In addition, at the local level, the lecture method was reintroduced, specializations stressed, inflexible curricula adopted, standardized examinations and texts reappeared (all of which had been previously criticized as bourgeois), and pedology rejected in favor of "training."[42] Polytechnical training of the experimental period (emphasizing all-round development of technical and academic skills) was heavily criticized for hindering the development of general education and high level academic skills.[43] Polytechnical education at the elementary, secondary, and higher levels all but ceased in its previous form and instead: "polytechnism was reinterpreted to mean the study of the scientific subjects upon which industry is based, such as mathematics, physics, and chemistry."[44] Polytechnism also came to mean highly skilled technicians coming to the schools to lecture. However, students and teachers were not allowed to participate in productive labor and productive labor was eliminated as part of the curriculum.

The effect of these reforms on the social class composition of the schools was correspondingly dramatic. With the raising of standards and the reorganization of the curriculum emphasizing the sciences, students of working-class or peasant background were at a disadvantage when competing with students less culturally deprived. In 1940, tuition fees were reintroduced for the last three grades of secondary school and all of higher education and this was another factor in limiting education to families in higher income brackets. The entire period (1926-1945) represented in some ways a reversion to Tsarist educational policies and particularly methods. While the course content was commensurate with the needs of modernization, by the beginning of the second world war there was little to distinguish the Soviet classroom at whatever level from that which existed in Tsarist Russia. With the German surrender in 1945 another significant period in the history of Soviet education began.

The Period of Reform: 1946-1972

During the war years Soviet education was disrupted to such an extent that this period becomes particularly difficult to discuss. Eighty-four thousand educational institutions were destroyed by the Nazis, twenty-five percent fewer students attended school as a whole and at the secondary level alone attendance was cut almost in half. Educational policy during the war was dominated by patriotic and nationalistic considerations.[45] In 1946 the fourth five-year plan was adopted and it seemed as if educational policies were going to be geared along even more conservative lines. A dual system was clearly visible at this time with a heavily academic track for one sector of Soviet society and vocational education for the majority of the rural peasants and the working-class. In the academic (ten-year) track there was virtually no integration of mental and manual labor and the concept of polytechnism again assumed a different meaning.[46] Instead of integrating productive labor into everyday school life polytechnical education came to mean some form of technical education offered as a specific course. The result in many instances was that graduates were strong in the traditional academic sense but were technically illiterate.[47] This state of affairs prompted a discussion among educators aimed directly at resolving the problem of general education versus technical education.

The question of defining polytechnical education was again taken up with great zeal. Educators pondered proposals to incorporate some form of technical education into the regular curriculum, to teach it as a separate subject, or (harking back to the experimental stage) to establish school-run factories and factory-run schools.[48] The nineteenth congress of the CPSU (1952) was the last in Stalin's lifetime and contained the first criticisms that secondary education was too academic. It was formally suggested that a revised form of polytechnical education be reintroduced. The need for highly trained technicians and engineers which existed in the post-experimental phase had been met and the need now was for middle and auxillary rank personnel to maintain a growing industrial base.[49] Another factor in the move for providing more practical training for more people may have been the dissatisfaction on the part of working-class youth with their limited educational opportunities and the opinion among some that schooling was a waste of time.[50]

By 1958 Khrushchev had consolidated his power and issued a thesis on secondary school reform. An eight-year "labor polytechnical school" was established which was compulsory for all, thus, eliminating the previously existing dual track. Productive labor became an integral part of the curriculum culminating in an intense form of vocational education in the final years to prepare the vast majority for the work force. Those students who engaged in two years of productive labor in society were given priority for entrance to institutions of higher education (roughly eighty-percent were chosen from this category). However, many problems were encountered in implementing this reform: criticism from professional educators with what they viewed as a lowering of academic standards, lack of teacher training, and resistance from production managers who did not want students disrupting their production plans. In addition, there was a fair degree of student apathy because of the general inability of the reform to achieve expectations.[51]

The result was that this policy came under attack in the early 1960s so that with the fall of Khrushchev in 1964 a "reform" of the 1958 "reform" took place resulting in a kind of mix of the retrenchment policies of the thirties and forties with the reform policies of the fifties. The eight-year secondary school was again replaced with the ten-year unified program which, however, contained some form of polytechnical education. The two-year work moratorium was declared to be optional.[52] Other post-1960 reforms included: individualized counseling, job counseling, sociological polls, attempts to reduce wastage and repeaters, etc. In the area of curricular reform a 1969 proposal suggested raising the quality of the lower level grades to allow for independent research at the upper levels. Hours of instruction were increased and new methods were also introduced to program primary and secondary education to handle larger quantities of information.[53]

In conclusion, one obtains a view of Soviet education as moving between the dual forces of a complex but vague educational philosophy (that of Marx, Engels, Lenin, and Stalin) and that of economic necessity. The educational history of the Soviet Union has traced a path from the experimentation allowed by the egalitarian ideals of Marxism-Leninism to the practical programs of economic construction, and finally to a seemingly compatible mix of the two. This wealth of experience was not lost upon the Chinese and, as will be seen in Part II, the programs and policies of Mao Tse-tung will at different times appear in striking contrast and similarity to those of the Soviet Union.

Marxism and China

It is difficult to say when socialist ideas and concepts were first introduced to China. Chinese students were studying in Europe in the 1870s and some may have come into contact with socialist currents at that time, but the first reference to parties representing the interests of the poor and disadvantaged was made by the famous translator of Western works, Yen Fu, in an essay written in 1895.[54] Other references appear in the writings of one of the 1898 social reformers, K'ang Yu-wei, but neither Yen's nor K'ang's writings were widely known in China. It was not until 1903 that the terms socialism and capitalism first appeared in the writings of Liang Ch'i-ch'ao, a follower of K'ang Yu-wei. Liang was probably introduced to the literature while in Japan following the failure of the 1898 reforms in China.[55] Liang also introduced the first books on socialism by translating Japanese studies of socialist thought.[56] At the turn of the century (1905-1907) Liang Ch'i-ch'ao and Sun Yat-sen continued the discussion of how to modernize China and of such ideologies as socialism in their Kuomintang party journal *Min-pao*.[57]

Somewhat later (1907-1917) Lenin and other Russian communists were discussing the revolutionary role of non-European, basically agrarian societies including China, and reached the conclusion that in terms of possessing a revolutionary proletariat they were essentially backward. Lenin, however, did feel that in countries such as China the bourgeoisie represented a progressive force with which local communists could ally.[58] The October, 1917, revolution in Russia carried with it the expansion of socialist and Marxist-Leninist ideas to the non-European world, and in 1920 Asian delegates (e.g. M. N. Roy of India) attended sessions of the Second Congress of the Communist International.[59]

In China the October Revolution had a terrific impact on reform-minded intellectuals. Men such as Ch'en Tu-hsiu and Li Ta-chao were especially influenced although in different ways. Both advocated reform for China (following the 1911 revolution of Sun Yat-sen which overthrew the Ching dynasty) but while Ch'en was an avid admirer of the West, Li was an equally avid nationalist. In 1918 Li wrote an article in the influential journal *Hsin ch'ing-nien* in praise of the Bolshevik victory in Russia but followed this with another article devoted to his views on Marxism (1919) which in fact revealed that he had little knowledge of the subject.[6] Li Ta-chao also established the Society for the Study of Marxism at Peking University in 1918 for the purpose of academically examining the basic principles of Marxism. In September of the same year Mao Tse-tung traveled to Peking as a youth and met both Ch'en and Li and participated in the study group.[61]

At this time (1920) Chinese socialists had little understanding of the positions taken by the Comintern in Moscow and generally read Marxist tracts on their own and founded study groups where possible. In February of 1920 a Soviet agent of the Third International (Voitinsky) went to Peking and met with Li and Ch'en. Through them he gained a hearing with Sun Yat-sen and the idea of organizing a revolutionary party was discussed. Finally, in July of 1921 the Communist Party of China (hereafter—

CCP) was established and among its founders was a young Hunanese by the name of Mao Tse-tung.[62]

As connections between Moscow and the new CCP grew stronger the availability of Marxist texts, programs, and policies likewise increased. In 1922, for the first time, Chinese representatives traveled to Moscow to attend the Congress of the Toilers of the East. There they also became more fully aware of the official Comintern position on non-European revolutionary parties. While there was considerable disagreement among Asian revolutionaries on questions of alliance with the bourgeoisie, Comintern policies were followed faithfully in China up to 1927 when the CCP suffered a disastrous setback.[63] However, by that time Marxism had found its way to China and CCP leaders such as Mao were able to begin the long, arduous task of adapting it to Chinese realities.

2 Elements of Educational Thought in Traditional and Republican China

China is one of the largest countries in the world, her territory being about the size of the whole of Europe. . . . From ancient times our forefathers have laboured, lived and multiplied on this vast territory. . . . Throughout the history of Chinese civilization its agriculture and handicrafts have been renowned for their high level of development. . . . During the thousands of years of recorded history, the Chinese nation has given birth to many national heroes and revolutionary leaders. Thus the Chinese nation has a glorious revolutionary tradition and a splendid historical heritage—Mao Tse-tung. ["The Chinese Revolution and the Chinese Communist Party (December, 1939," *SW*, II, 305-307.]

IT HAS REPEATEDLY been pointed out that Mao Tse-tung and his educational thought must be viewed in light of the two great traditions which most influenced his intellectual development. One such tradition (European Marxism) has been examined in the previous chapter. In this chapter the main tenets of Chinese educational thought will be discussed both for the traditional and Republican periods. Mao is at once both a Marxist and profoundly Chinese. Much of his earlier schooling consisted of a form of learning not dissimiliar to that which had existed since the Han dynasty (202 B.C.-220 A.D.). On the other hand, he experienced the early stages of the transformation which began to take place in China's educational system following the 1911 revolution of Sun Yat-sen. This included, of course, the introduction into Chinese education of Western subject matter as well as educational structure. The question is also raised as to whether Mao and other Chinese communists are simply Confucians in Marxist garb. One noted scholar of Chinese history suggests that whatever the similarities, Marxist notions of class struggle are not consistent with Confucian harmony nor is the Marxist emphasis on movement and process at all similar to Confucian permanence.[1] This is not to say that there is a lack of intellectual continuity. The rise of Chinese communism provided intellectuals with the opportunity to reject traditionalism without completely accepting the West. Thus freeing themselves from dependence on both cultures they were able to choose acceptable elements from each with discretion. Mao Tse-tung and the Chinese Communist Party do not take China's traditional culture and thought lightly. The intense program since 1949 to reeducate intellectuals reflects this concern.[2] Yet, many of the concepts of Chinese traditional thought (particularly those associated with neo-Confucianism) are not contradictory to those of Marx, Engels, and Lenin.[3] An examination of the main elements of Chinese educational thought in the traditional period and Republican period should serve to clarify or at least bring into focus the impact of these historical periods upon Mao Tse-tung and Chinese pedagogical thought in general.

Traditional China

The intellectual foundations of China have characteristically been associated with a brief historical period during the latter part of the Chou dynasty (500-200 B.C.). This period has popularly been termed the "golden age" of philosophy in China, for it was at this time that the major philosophers and thinkers who came to dominate traditional Chinese intellectual, and eventually educational thought, lived and worked.[4] Thinkers as diverse as Confucius and Lao Tzu are purported to have vied with each other intellectually during this period. In any case, it was at this time that the basic foundations of Confucianism, Taoism, and the later development of Legalism were formed thus providing the primary groundwork for future Chinese cultural development.

Although Confucianism was eventually to triumph as the predominant intellectual strain in Chinese thought, the traditions of Taoism and Legalism made important contributions in this early period. When Confucianism was declared the state philosophy during the Han dynasty (202 B.C.-220 A.D.), there was already a mixture of Taoism (particularly the *laissez faire* attitude toward economics) and Legalism (bureaucratic organization and administrative control) resulting in the fact that Confucianism became a useful tool of the traditional state but never totally its master.[5]

The moral code permeating Chinese education from the time of Confucius to the Ch'ing dynasty consisted of a set of codes regarding social relationships such as those between parents and children, brothers and sisters, and subject and emperor. The proper harmony among these relationships resulted in the individual expression of *jen* (benevolence) toward mankind. This concept of benevolence and harmony became a universal ideal for the Chinese. It extended even to the realm of science and other practical subjects (i.e., astronomy, agriculture, artistry, and manufacturing) which emphasized the *tao* or way of nature which was harmonious and in balance.[6] Because the codes involved social behavior they could be taught, and Confucianism particularly emphasized the power of education to improve society and citizenship in both an intellectual and moral sense.[7] By providing a model which people could emulate, education could transform society. The model had two main functions before the innate goodness (*jen*) of man could be brought forth. It must first "provide peace and prosperity" and second "provide moral training and education."[8] Thus, the rationale was provided for considering education as a primary goal of the just society; Confucius went so far as to suggest that "in education there should be no class distinctions" (*yu chiao wu lei*) thus laying the theoretical groundwork for a broadly based educational system.[9] Later thinkers including Hsun Tzu and Confucius's disciple, Mencius, also attributed great importance to education and its ability to transform people and society. In the former, man was not viewed as being innately righteous or benevolent but inherently depraved. Nevertheless, to bring about an orderly society Hsun Tzu believed that only education could provide man with the customs and habits necessary to counteract his essentially negative character. Mencius on the other hand expanded on the idea of innate goodness held by Confucius and suggested that all men intrinsically contained as part of their human essence four qualities: (1) *jen*—benevolence; (2) *yi*—righteousness; (3) *li*—propriety, customs, ritual; (4) *chih*—wisdom.

If a person has not come into harmony with his inner wisdom and *jen,* then it is possible that this can be brought forth through formal education.[10] The basically essentialist philosophical position of Hsun Tzu contrasted with the philosophical idealism of the Confucian thinkers, but both agreed on the great potential and force of education.

Early Chinese epistemology suggests an interesting mixture of idealism and pragmatism.[11] This mix was expressed during the Chou dynasty by the phrase *te-hsing*. The *te* referred to the practice of that which was innate. Innate knowledge, and the practical application of it once brought forth, characterized early Confucian epistemology.[12] Another way of explaining this development suggests that Chinese thought during this period considered two realms of reality: the inner (*nei*) and the outer (*wai*). The inner realm was set by nature and the outer realm could bring forth and determine the practical aspects of the inner. Harmony and gentleness characterized the former while discipline was associated with the latter. During the height of Legalist influence (Chin dynasty—221-207 B.C.) the concept of the inner realm was totally abandoned, the rulers preferring to rely on outward discipline and in some cases brute force to affect men's minds. Although the Legalists did not persevere, the imprint which they left upon Chinese concepts of knowledge and action is significant.[13]

The relationship between knowledge and action in the Chou period was not abstract but concrete and factual. The good society according to Confucius was not an abstract construction arrived at by deductive reasoning in the manner of Plato's *Republic*. To know this society one had to know the facts about it thus providing a very practical orientation to future educational and philosophical discussions. In the more abstruse language of Confucius: ". . . shall I teach you what knowledge is? When you know a thing, say that you know it; when you do not know a thing, admit that you do not know it. That is knowledge."[14]

What were the implications of this brand of philosophy for teachers during the Chou period? What teaching methods were to be employed? According to the *Book of Rites* (*I Li*) education was not a procedure involving memorization (as it later became) but stressed the concept of unfolding knowledge (*nei-tse*) from within: "We are told that learning should proceed from the easy to the difficult, from the coarse to the fine; that transition from one step to another should be gradual rather than sudden; and that great things should be accomplished through the accumulation of many small things."[15] Students were to be encouraged to solve problems and not simply memorize the content of the texts: ". . . if of the four corners of a thing I [Confucius] have shown and explained one corner and the scholars do not find for themselves the other three, I do not explain further."[16] In line with these principles teachers were to be models and guides, and students were expected to think analytically at least to the extent necessary to solve philosophical and logical problems.

Intellectuals or scholars during the Han dynasty assumed a new role as government advisers and officials. It was during this period that the scholar-officials grew to become the dominant social force in government. When Confucianism was decreed to be the official ideology, state universities or academies consequently were established along with a competitive civil service examination which in turn served as a catalyst for whatever education existed at that time. The establishment of the examination system insured the continual reproduction of the scholar elite as a segment of the ruling group.[17] Thus, the Chou and Han periods set an intellectual pattern which was to dominate and define educational theory and practice until the next major period of intellectual change during the Sung dynasty (960-1279 A.D.).

The Sung period represented in some respects a Confucian revival as ideas formulated over a thousand years previous were reaffirmed and discussed anew. Movable type was invented during the Sung, and this facilitated the widespread use of books and thus provided an impetus to educational development. Academies were established and urbanization created a desire for new ideas. Sung thinkers discussed with more rigor earlier Confucian ambiguities such as the relationship between abstract principles and material force (*li* and *ch'i*). The epistemological problem as to which is primary was not clear from the early Confucian texts and later discussions, but when pressed the Sung philosopher and neo-Confucian, Chu Hsi, finally assumed a basically idealist position: "Fundamentally, principle and material force cannot be spoken of as prior or posterior. But if we must trace their origin, we are obliged to say that principle is prior."[18] We see here perhaps a departure in the Confucian theory of knowledge. There was an undeveloped form of materialism in the writings of Confucius (e.g., *Ta-hsueh* [*Great Learning*]), particularly his reference which states: "Wishing to rectify their mind . . . they first extended to the utmost their knowledge. Such extension of knowledge lay in the investigation of things. Things being investigated, knowledge became complete."[19] The emphasis on the investigation of "things" or elements of the material world also existed in the writings of the neo-Confucians, but a corresponding importance was attached to innate principles which existed in the mind. Wang Yang-ming of the Ming period (1368-1644) furthered this idea by suggesting that not only did basic principles exist in the mind but in the universe as well. Yet, the clear idealism expressed here did not particularly affect the practical orientation of the educative process. Both Chu Hsi and Wang Yang-ming continued to stress the unity of knowledge and action and maintained that only by correctly combining the one with the other could knowledge by attained: "knowledge is the beginning of action; action is the completion of knowledge."[20]

With the new Sung emphasis on learning and knowledge an educational system was designed to prepare students for the more specialized civil service degrees. The idea of education as a social change agent and the belief that correct knowledge could transform human society represented another strong trend during the Sung.[21] A Sung general and statesman (Fan Chung-yen) became the first to propose a set of educational reforms for the Imperial government. Fan proposed the establishment of a national school system from the district level to the capital. The purpose of this proposal was to facilitate training of civil servants with respect to the examination system. It can not thus be viewed as an attempt to broaden the base of public education for the sake of education *per se* but the reforms were in any case a significant pedagogical development.[22]

During the Ch'ing dynasty (1644-1912), which preceded the formation of the Republic, many scholars were rejecting some of the idealism of the neo-Confucians, thus opening the way for a more scientific approach to examining questions of knowledge and learning. They stopped short, however, of developing the inductive empirical scientific method of Western thinkers of this period and preferred to proceed from general principles (*li*) to the particular aspects of problems (*shih*). Against this background education became more involved with problem solving while retaining the philosophical idealism of Confucianism. The educational model which prevailed at this time began to depart from the former "amateur" ideal to one in which the scholar was more concerned with form (an example would be the prominence of the "eight-legged essay" or *pa-ku* style of essay writing).[23]

As the West and Japan began to threaten the centuries old internal solidity of the Chinese scholar class, it became apparent that in order to preserve some semblance of Confucian values and norms concessions would have to be made to bring about a revitalized educational system more conducive to the needs of modernization. From 1860 to 1905 the aim of education was shifted from one which emphasized the reproduction of a scholar class, well-trained in the classics to a new aim which subscribed some importance to Western learning. Organized schooling took the form of the *shu-yuan* or provincial colleges and the *Kuo-tzu-chien* which constituted a national college in Peking. Local education was left to the villages and families or clans who engaged tutors privately to work with promising students. Modernization of the school system took place only at the top where some selected Western-style technical schools were established primarily for the purpose of training military personnel.[24] With the defeat of the Chinese in the 1894-1895 Sino-Japanese war further reforms were attempted and more Western subject matter was introduced into the curriculum. When it became apparent that Confucianism and other Chinese traditional views of the world were no longer satisfactory to meet the needs of a vastly changing world, traditional Chinese society and its educational philosophy entered a period of decline from which it was never to recover. In 1911, a movement led by Sun Yat-sen succeeded in toppling the last dynasty of China and a period of uncertainty ensued during which the Chinese searched for new social, political, and economic forms while not entirely desiring to discard all the old ones.

Republican China

When Sun Yat-sen's haphazard 1911 revolution was realized the social fabric including the educational system was already tearing at the seams. As a result of the Sino-Japanese war (1894-1895) and the later abolition of the examination system (1905), educational thought and practice in China began to undergo significant change in response primarily to external demands. By 1905, a large number of Chinese had traveled to and studied in Japan, and their pedagogical impact upon returning was profound. Chinese education became almost a carbon copy of the Japanese model both in structure and content. Lower and upper primary schools were established along with lower and upper middle schools. The middle-school curriculum was departmentalized (arts and sciences) and the general curriculum followed the Japanese pattern (classics, history, geography, morals, sciences).[25]

Following the establishment of the Republic in 1911 educational reformers were convinced that one result would be a complete restructuring of education. In fact, there was little change in the content of educational theory and practice despite the efforts of the new Minister of Education, Ts'ai Yuan-pei. Attempts were made to break away from the centralization inherent in the Japanese model of education but to no avail. Moreover, the president, Yuan Shih-k'ai, began to issue decrees urging the reestablishment of Confucian learning and ethics, and finally in 1913 restored Confucianism to its previous position as the official ideology. His overthrow and death in 1916 ended this attempt to reconstruct the past.[26]

Chinese education began to exhibit the pattern of reflecting the current domestic and international political situation. As relations with Japan became more strained Chinese educators began to look for alternative models. From 1915 to 1928 a series of conferences were held in China which gradually changed the character of Chinese education from a centralized system patterned after the Germans and the Japanese to one more similar to the American model. Several factors were involved in this shift. Following the Japanese Twenty-One Demands in 1915 (an attempt by the Japanese to gain economic and political advantages in China) many Chinese educators became disenchanted with Japanese society and politics. In addition, numerous Chinese had studied in the United States and returned very impressed with the American system of public education. Prominent American educators such as John Dewey and Paul Monroe had been touring China and they carried with them the spirit of the progressive movement then underway in the United States. By 1922, leadership in educational matters passed to American-trained Chinese, and the government sanctioned the adoption of a basically American style educational system. Students were encouraged to "learn by doing" and a generally progressive attitude spread among Chinese educators. Minority education, peasant, and worker education were all encouraged as well as the general ideal of serving society rather than the nation.[27] Another characteristic of this period, partly a result of the new emphasis on decentralization, was the lack of direction and support of the Ministry of Education. The previous paternalism of the central government toward students studying at home and abroad disappeared and both educators and students experienced a new independence.

In 1925 political events again brought about a shift in educational policy and practice. In the middle of May, a Chinese labor union representative was killed by the Japanese at a Japanese-owned mill in Shanghai. The protest which followed resulted in the death of ten more Chinese, this time at the hands of British controlled police in the International Settlement.[28] Patriotic Chinese were outraged and the power and influence of the Kuomintang (KMT Nationalist Party) led by Chiang K'ai-shek began to grow. The increase in nationalism and the strength of the new revolutionary government following the Northern Expedition in 1926 (which destroyed or neutralized the influence of regional warlords) all combined to significantly shift educational priorities in a different direction.

At an educational conference held in Tai-yuan in 1925, educators suggested that the primary and secondary school curriculum be changed to include a strong nationalistic ingredient. It was further suggested that military training for both boys and girls be reintroduced into the curriculum.[29] Textbooks, particularly history texts, were revised to include episodes stressing previous humiliating events in Chinese history and urging students to be more patriotic toward the motherland. The experimental programs launched during the period 1916 to 1925 were abandoned and the progressive educators were held responsible for the unorganized and chaotic state of the educational system.[30] With the increased strength of the KMT in 1928, a more rigid German model of education was followed which included strict control over the schools and student organizations. The KMT had established a secret police system to control student and faculty activities, and party ideology became one of the more important ingredients in the curriculum particularly at the university level.[31]

As full-scale war erupted between Japan and China in 1937 and conflicts between the KMT and the Chinest Communists increased (finally developing into nation-wide civil war in 1946) social conditions were chaotic at best and the power of the government over education as well as other areas of society weakened and declined. The KMT retreated to those cities which were not harassed by the Japanese and adopted a more pro-Western stance which again affected the educational system. Where the KMT did have control of education, nationalism and patriotism remained the primary content of the curriculum and students continued to be divorced from the realities of agricultural and rural life.[32]

The most striking characteristic of modern Chinese education is the fact that it developed basically as a forced response to the demands put upon China by the West, and thus from the start the West and Western ideas played a disproportionate role in the development of post-1911 Chinese pedagogical theory and prac-

FIG. 2. PLA soldiers and officers receive political education in the 1930s.

tice.[33] There were several negative results of this type of foreign borrowing. Because most foreigners lived in the large urban centers, educational facilities and teaching staff tended to concentrate in the cities with little penetration to the vast, heavily populated rural areas. In addition, undue reliance on foreign texts and curriculum content resulted in learning materials out of touch with Chinese society (e.g., Occidental features on children in story books; one Japanese text was uncritically translated from the Japanese to Chinese and copied to such a degree that the Japanese flag still appeared on the cover).[34] There was a distressing lack of subject matter on Chinese affairs. Following the decline of classical Chinese studies nothing was substituted to convey to the students a knowledge of their own people's customs and habits, particularly at the rural level.

In the 1930s and 1940s, because of the inordinate emphasis on training well-qualified scientists with high level skills there resulted a lack of technicians with middle level skills which were precisely those necessary to begin the task of reforming and modernizing China.[35] Among those students who studied abroad the majority studied some form of engineering while the least popular subjects were those involving agriculture. In short, Chinese students were receiving a rather dysfunctional academic training in terms of the developmental needs of China as a nation. Most students attempted to remain in the urban centers and utilized their degrees and credentials as steppingstones to obtaining lucrative positions in the government or general field of education.[36] Education was valued and desired primarily as a means to further one's personal career or in some way become more "clever" than the ordinary individual. It was not viewed in developmental terms as a means to increase the stability and economic growth of Chinese society.[37]

The deterioration of the educational system and the Chinese Communist's victory in 1949 heralded the advent of the first truly revolutionary break with traditional or borrowed educational forms. Traditional forms of education had already been significantly weakened as has been noted above. The experience of the new republic from 1911 to 1949 provided the Chinese with alternative educational models from which to choose. The fact that no single model worked was not surprising as external factors played havoc with Chinese society contributing to an already harassed educational system. Yet the Nationalist government from the start made little attempt to restructure education from the bottom up, preferring to concentrate its resources on university and college

Fig. 3. The Chinese Communist Eighth Route Army study on the march.

level education primarily of an urban variety. During the civil war (1946-1949) large numbers of students left these same institutions and joined up with the Red Army in the Communist-held rural areas. There they found Mao Tse-tung, who for the past twenty years had lived and worked with the Communist party in the rural regions, organizing peasants and a peasant army, and in addition organizing peasant schools and colleges. Mao had already formulated many of the pedagogical ideas that were to be instituted with varying degrees of success throughout China in the future. His writings and pronouncements on various facets of education were to form a body of pedagogical statements which eventually would lead to establishing China as a leader in worldwide educational experimentation some two decades later in the 1970s.

Part II

The Educational Thought of Mao Tse-Tung

3 Mao Tse-tung: A Biographical Sketch[1]

. . . Mao had talked for a dozen nights, hardly ever referring to himself or his own role in some of the events described. . . . he tended to talk only about committees, organizations, armies, resolutions, battles, tactics, "measures," and so on, and seldom of personal experience. . . . Later on I discovered that most of them [Mao and other communists] . . . did not remember personal details . . . . I found repeatedly that the Communist would be able to tell everything that had happened in his early youth, but once he had become identified with the Red Army he lost himself somewhere, and without repeated questioning one could hear nothing more about *him*, but only stories of the Army, or the Soviets, or the Party—capitalized. [From Edgar Snow's biography of Mao Tse-tung, *Red Star Over China*, 2nd ed. (New York: Grove Press, 1968), p. 129.]

Mao As a Young Man

MAO TSE-TUNG WAS BORN on December 26, 1893, in the village of Shaoshan near Ch'angsha the capital of Hunan province. His family shared a modest house with another family and his father had achieved the status of a middle peasant which in terms of the poverty of the Chinese countryside was not an especially comfortable position.

When Mao was five he was tutored privately in reading and writing and at the age of eight attended a traditional style primary school in his native village. Here he studied the classics and in addition familiarized himself with more popular and exciting novels such as *The Romance of the Three Kingdoms* and *Water Margin.*[2] Mao was only allowed to continue his studies for five years, and when thirteen his father determined that he should devote full time to farm work. He continued to study on his own but eventually, dissatisfied with this method, enrolled in the Tungshan Primary School in the nearby district of Hsiang-hsiang. This school was considered a modern-type institution in that Western subjects were taught in addition to the traditional Chinese classics. In 1911, the following year, Mao continued his education in a middle school in the capital city, Ch'angsha, and at the same time became involved with the republican movement led by Sun Yat-sen. He joined the revolutionary army in October but was demobilized in February of 1912 without seeing action. His experiences in the modern primary and middle schools at this time had a profound effect on his intellectual development. He came into contact with, and read the works of, modern Chinese reformers, and he heard of leaders in the Western world.[3] Upon leaving the army Mao was undecided as to a career and eventually decided in 1913 to enter the Fourth Normal School in Ch'angsha (later merged to form the First Teachers' Training School). While attending the normal school Mao's radicalism began to emerge. In 1915 and 1916 Mao participated in student activities primarily directed against Yuan Shih-k'ai, and in 1917 he became chairman of the Students Society. In the Spring of 1918 Mao graduated from the Ch'angsha normal school and began teaching a group of workers in an evening school. In the fall he traveled for the first time to Peking where he worked as an assistant librarian at Peking University and met Li Ta-chao, Ch'en Tu-hsiu, and Chang Kuo-t'ao who were actively involved in the study of Marxist theory. It was at this time that Mao first became aware of socialist currents of thought and began to read revolutionary literature.[4]

The Making of a Marxist

In March of 1919, Mao returned to Ch'angsha and assumed a position as teacher in an elementary school. The spring and summer of that year were eventful for Mao and other Chinese students. The dramatic nationalistic May Fourth Movement swept China and contributed to the growing radicalism of Chinese youth. In

Ch'angsha Mao was giving public lectures on Marxism and organizing student unions to direct strikes and boycott Japanese textile and other consumer goods. In July, he took over the editorship of the *Hsiang River Review*, a magazine of the Hunan United Students Association. Here he published his most significant article of the period entitled "The Great Union of the Popular Masses" in which he revealed many of his political and educational points of view.[5] Somewhat later in the year or possibly early in 1920, Mao read the *Communist Manifesto* for the first time. Two other books also greatly influenced him, Kautsky's *Class Struggle* and a *History of Socialism*. From this point on Mao considered himself a Marxist both in theory and practice.[6]

Early in 1920, Mao again traveled to Peking, this time to protest against the repressive activities of the governor of Hunan, General Chang Ching-yao. On his return via Shanghai he met Ch'en Tu-hsiu again and became a more dedicated Marxist. Upon his return to Ch'angsha in July, Mao organized the first communist study group in his native village of Shao-shan and at the same time became director of the primary school section of the Ch'ang-sha Teachers Training College. Toward the end of the year communist groups were founded in Shanghai, Peking, and other urban centers, and discussion began to take place on the feasibility of founding a genuine communist party. Comintern agents had already been active in Peking and Canton, and finally in July, 1921, Mao participated in the founding and first congress of the Chinese Communist Party.[7]

The entire period from 1921 to 1935, when Mao assumed direct leadership of the CCP, was one of struggle, trial, and error not only for Mao but for the entire CCP structure. From 1921 to 1923 Mao remained active in Hunan politics organizing trade unions and miners in Ch'angsha and Anyuan, establishing a self-education college and becoming secretary of the Hunan committee of the CCP.[8]

In 1923, the CCP and the Kuomintang (KMT) parties agreed to collaborate, and Mao left Hunan (where an arrest notice had been issued for him) to work for the CCPin Shanghai. In June of that year he was elected to the Central Committee of the CCP and his responsibilities in the Party increased. Mao returned to Hunan the same year where from 1923 to 1927 he began to take a deep interest, apparently on his own initiative, in the organizational and revolutionary potential of the peasantry. During this same period relations had become strained to the breaking point between the CCP and the KMT and finally erupted into a complete break between the two organizations and the virtual annhilation of the urban-based communist movement.

From 1927 to 1935 Mao became even more involved in organizing the peasantry and recognizing their revolutionary potential. A number of peasant uprisings were carried out during this period but none succeeded for any length of time. In October, 1927, Mao, now head of the All-China Peasant Association, established the first guerilla base in the Chingkang Mountains on the border of Hunan and Kiangsi provinces. From 1928 to 1935 Mao and other Party strategists disagreed on the best method of realizing the revolution and withstanding the attacks on their base by the KMT. By 1931 Chiang Kai-shek launched a series of encirclement campaigns to isolate and destroy the communist base in the Chingkang Mountains. After repeated attacks by the KMT armies, Mao's influence in the Red Army as well as the Party was on the decline and in 1934 the Party's base was threatened with destruction and the epic Long March began.[9]

Mao As Leader Of The Party

In January, 1935, Mao was elected Chairman of the Politburo of the CCP at the Tsunyi conference and from this point on retained primary leadership over the Party. His previous weakened position had been due to the predominance in the Party of factions (the "Twenty-eight Bolsheviks") holding military strategic views differing considerably from his. With the attacks of the KMT and the subsequent retreat of the Party on the Long March ended for Mao when his force, greatly reduced due to the severities of the march, arrived in northern Shensi. The basic policy of the Party at this time was to present the image of being defenders against the Japanese while at the same time being revolutionaries concerned with the re-structuring of Chinese society. With regard to the former policy the CCPand Mao urged that a second united front be established with the KMT, putting aside their differences for the time being to wage a common struggle against the foreign invader. The years 1936 to 1937 were for Mao a period in which he tried to realize the alliance with the KMT (finally established following the Sian Incident in which Chiang K'ai-shek was captured by his own men and forced to ally with the CCP) while at the same time justifying his position within his own party.[10]

Throughout 1938 Mao concentrated his efforts on the strategy of the anti-Japanese war and many of his most important military writings date from this period. Although an alliance had been

Fig. 4. Mao talks to peasants in North Shensi.

effected between the KMTand the CCP, numerous skirmishes occured between 1940 and 1949, and thus both armies were kept occupied fighting each other as well as the Japanese. In 1941 and 1942, Mao's influence and prestige greatly increased in the Party and in the areas under communist control. In addition, be began to initiate more rigorous discipline in the Party and suggested that fewer concessions be made to the KMT. As outright civil war between the CCP and the KMT neared, diplomatic maneuvers were hastily entered into between the KMTand CCP with additional attempts by the United States (Ambassador Patrick Hurley visited Yenan in November, 1944, following the recall of General Stillwell, and in November, 1945, General Marshall arrived in China as a special envoy of President Truman) to avert a final clash between the communists and the nationalists. All these efforts, however, failed and in 1946 fighting again erupted and full-scale civil war broke out.[11]

The civil war raged over north China, and by 1948 most of that area became secure in communist hands. In May of 1949 Marshall Lin Piao's troops crossed the Yangtze River and by the fall of the year the armies of the KMT had either been destroyed, captured, or had fled to the island of Taiwan. In October, 1949, Mao Tse-tung, the son of a Hunanese peasant, stood on the platform in Tienanmen square in Peking and proclaimed the founding of the People's Republic of China. Mao, whose rise in the Party had been difficult and full of pitfalls, had now been thrust into the position of leader of a state of over 600 million people.

Mao As Leader Of The State

In 1950, the newly founded People's Republic of China faced an enormous task. Every sector of society was in a critical state and in need of complete reconstruction. Land reform policy was drafted by Mao and other Party members and steps were taken to secure control over the population in general. In the field of foreign policy Mao left China for the first time in his life to visit Moscow where he successfully concluded a treaty of "Friendship Alliance and Mutual Assistance" with the Soviet government. To complicate matters the Korean war broke out in the same year and by October Chinese troops were actively engaged in the fighting. It is unlikely that Mao was anxious to join in an open conflict with the United States (or any other major power) at this time and there is some indication that he was not informed about the conflict until it was a *fait accompli*.[12]

Fig. 5. Mao studies in his cave in Yenan.

The following year a whole series of campaigns were launched by Mao to thoroughly transform the activities and intellectual orientation of both Party and non-Party personnel. Intellectuals were exposed to an extreme program of "thought reform" which basically consisted of criticism and self-criticism sessions followed by numerous confessions. The main orientation of this program was to communicate to the intellectuals the language and content of Marxism-Leninism in order to prepare them for the new role they were to play in the reconstruction of Chinese society. At the same time a broad campaign was carried out to expose and neutralize either through imprisonment or execution active "counter-revolutionary" opponents of the regime.[13]

As the Korean War terminated in 1953, Mao devoted most of his efforts to the task of re-organizing the rural areas and taking part in the general economic re-construction then underway. In January, 1953 the first Five-Year Plan was announced and the Chinese economy began to exhibit the general characteristics of a Soviet-type economy. By late 1953 the rural regions had been transformed into Agricultural Producers Cooperatives, a further step in the collectivization of agricultural production. In September, 1954, Mao presided over the opening of the first meeting of the National People's Congress which proclaimed a new constitution and established the State Council and other organs of government. In the same year, Mao and Soviet leader Khrushchev conferred in Peking in a show of Sino-Soviet unity and friendship.[14]

The two years 1955 and 1956 represented in China a period of intense economic and political activity. A new currency was issued, powerful figures in the Party were purged (Kao Kang and Jao Shu-shih), the bureaucracy reorganized, agriculture became more collectivized, "socialist reform" of private business initiated, and finally in the spring the economic program became more stabilized. In all of these activities Mao played an important role, participating in the purge of Kao and Jao and helping to formulate and launch the co-operativization movement in the countryside. In September, 1956, Mao presided over the Eighth Congress of the CCP at which time the Party constitution was revised. A significant event for the intellectuals was the announcement in May, 1956, of the Hundred Flowers policy. This represented the Party's first real "thaw" in their relationship with the intellectuals and students. However, in the early stages few dared to respond to the invitation to criticize public policy. The next major speech was given by Mao on February 27, 1957, at an enlarged session of the Supreme State Council and was entitled: "On the

FIG. 6. Mao proclaims the founding of the People's Republic of China in 1950.

Correct Handling of Contradictions Among the People." In this speech (which was not released to the public until June 10) Mao announced that a rectification campaign was about to be launched and indicated that although criticism of the Party by non-Party people should be earnest it should nevertheless be like a "mild breeze and a thin rain." It is not clear why the Party and Mao chose this time to seek criticism from the intellectuals but the Hungarian Revolt in October, 1956, must have certainly been a factor. (See chapter 7 for explanation of this relationship.) The intellectuals exercised their privilege of criticism in May, 1957, only to have it abruptly rescinded in June. The criticism obviously had gotten out of hand as some intellectuals foolishly called for the overthrow of the Party.[15] An anti-rightist campaign began and another Mao-study campaign was launched in November.

The period 1958 to 1960 is characterized by the movement known as the Great Leap Forward. This possibly represented Mao's program for future social and economic development in China and contained elements later to emerge during the Great Proletarian Cultural Revolution. At this time, Mao became convinced that China could move ahead economically and culturally at a much faster pace than previously thought possible and that in fact the entire fabric and structure of Chinese society could be transformed. He described China's people as being "poor and blank" and saw this as a positive attribute which could contribute to the development of Chinese society. In the economic sphere Mao and others in the Party urged the amalgamation of the Agricultural Producers Cooperatives into a commune structure and at the same time urged the decentralization of industry in the form of home-made factories and steel producing units. He praised the power of the masses to transform both nature and society. In the field of education a similar de-centralization took place and a renewed emphasis on worker-peasant education. The army also experienced change as a "people's militia" (*min-ping*) was formed to augment the more formal army structure. However, by December, 1958, a retreat from Great Leap Forward policies was underway. The movement had suffered some serious setbacks which unfortunately were also accompanied by a series of natural disasters. While the movement met several successful goals in terms of politicization (more people had been involved in political processes than ever before) the failures were sufficient to reduce Mao's authority in the Party hierarchy. In December, 1958, Mao resigned as Chairman of the People's Republic presumably to devote himself primarily to Party affairs. However, in August of the following year, Mao found himself under violent attack from Defense Minister P'eng Te-huai for his radical economic and social policies. Although P'eng was dismissed from his position, it was clear that Mao's position of authority had been weakened.[16]

During the years 1960 and 1961 Mao Tse-tung devoted himself to receiving foreign guests and heads of state as well as keeping abreast of the rapidly deteriorating relationship with the Soviet Union. In August of 1960, Soviet technicians were completely withdrawn from China and this development profoundly influenced Chinese social and economic efforts. In the field of agriculture and industry the Chinese adopted a more independent stance and proclaimed a priority sequence which placed primary emphasis on agriculture with light and heavy industry next in line. In September, 1962, Mao presided over the Tenth Plenum of the Central Committee and proposed both a consolidation of the communes and the launching of the socialist education movement. Neither proposal aroused much enthusiasm, but the socialist education movement began and eventually became the precursor of the Great Proletarian Cultural Revolution.[17]

The years 1964 and 1965 witnessed a further worsening of relations with the Soviet Union, and Mao attacked more vehemently "modern revisionism." In March of 1964, the People's Liberation Army under Defense Minister Lin Piao launched a "Mao-study" campaign and the famous *Quotations from Chairman Mao Tse-tung* (the "little Red Book") was published. In January, 1965, the socialist education movement was stepped up and the following month the United States began its bombardment of North Vietnam. These events and others contributed to a general state of tension among Chinese leaders; the first indication that all was not well between Mao and other communist leaders came in November when the Vice-Mayor of Peking, Wu Han, was attacked for anti-Mao activities in connection with a historical novel he had written. By August, 1966, the greatest internal upheaval yet to shake China, the Great Proletarian Cultural Revolution (GPCR) was underway. Student Red Guard units were formed, top Party leaders toppled from power, and the entire society underwent a major transformation as the economic, political, and educational sectors were reformed more in line with Mao's ideas and policies.

The GPCR raged for three years before significant stabilization set in. By 1969, most of the institutions in Chinese society were back in operation under a reformed Party and administrative structure. Mao's heir apparent, Liu Shao-ch'i, had been driven out of office and a new hierarchy emerged composed of Lin Piao (Defense Minister), and Premier Chou En-lai, and Mao's wife, Chiang Ching. Further struggles were forthcoming and in 1972 it was learned that Lin Piao had been engaged in an attempt to overthrow Mao's rule and had fled China only to die in an unexplained airplane crash. China entered a new phase of international activity in the 1970s culminating in the visit to that country of the first United States President to do so, Richard M. Nixon. The Nixon-Mao meeting in 1971 terminates for the time being a long period of estrangement between both China and the United States.[18]

Mao, who began his revolutionary career as a school teacher, union and student organizer, and communist party official will end his career as the man most responsible for transforming Chinese society, institutions, and modes of thought (which establishes his importance as an educator) as well as Sino-American relations. His role as an educator and educational policy-maker is preeminent in understanding the preponderant impact Mao Tse-tung has had upon Chinese society.

4 MAO TSE-TUNG ON GOALS, AIMS AND BASIC PRINCIPLES OF EDUCATION

Our educational policy must enable everyone who receives an education to develop morally, intellectually and physically and become a well-educated worker with socialist consciousness—Mao Tse-tung. ["On the Correct Handling of Contradictions Among the People (February, 1957)," *Four Essays on Philosophy* (Peking: Foreign Languages Press, 1968), p. 110.]

THE ROOTS OF ANY EDUCATIONAL THOUGHT may be found in the manner in which the thinker or writer comes to terms with certain fundamental pedagogical problems, among these problems may be those listed which relate to epistemology (problems of knowledge and learning), more general goals and aims of education, and the relationship of education to society. Obviously there are many more specific problems but the above serve to suggest a useful framework from which the specifics can be extracted. Mao has always preferred to speak and write more *generally* than specifically, and the quantity of his pronouncements on the goals and aims of education far exceed those statements where he deals with specific educational issues such as curriculum and instruction, administration, and teachers and students. The matter is further complicated by the fact that the Mao Tse-tung of 1917 is qualitatively different from the Mao Tse-tung of the 1920s and the 1930s; and certainly the period of the People's Republic is unique in itself. There is then a historical context that must be considered when attempting to discuss the basis of Mao Tse-tung's educational thought.

The Early Period: 1917-1927

Mao's educational writings during this most formative period of his life certainly reflect his experiences in primary school and later the middle school at Ch'angsha as well as the climate of social and political change that was sweeping China during the 1920s. He had come to be devoted to the republican cause and was enthusiastically involved in student life and political activities. Foremost in his mind was the regeneration of China and the Chinese people, but unlike other reformers who primarily stressed the need to develop a more modern form of education Mao assigned equal importance, indeed primary importance, to the need to strengthen the nation physically.

His first important article dating from this period was entitled "A Study of Physical Education."[1] Mao, of course, was reacting to the obvious lack he encountered of any form of physical education in the Chinese primary and secondary curriculum, but moreover he viewed physical development and health as a prerequisite to gaining and developing knowledge: "Physical education complements education in virtue and knowledge. Moreover, both virtue and knowledge reside in the body. Without the body there would be neither virtue or knowledge . . . hence, one can say that knowledge is acquired indirectly through physical education."[2] Mao's article suggests that one must first pay attention to general health before attempting to seek knowledge; this is perhaps an early and important indication of Mao's negative orientation toward "book-learning" which appears in a more developed and articulate form twenty years later.

By 1920 Mao had become exposed to more revolutionary ideas; he had traveled to Peking and met the most important radical thinkers of that time and was moving resolutely in the direction of becoming a Marxist and a communist. China was in a state of turmoil and cultural excitement which reached its peak with the May

FIG. 7. Students and teachers take part in daily physical exercise.

Fourth Movement in 1919, when Mao and others began to organize students, workers, and Marxist study groups. It was against this tumultuous background that Mao's educational ideas began to assume a more coherent pattern particularly his view of the relationship between formal education and society. Bertrand Russell, John Dewey, and Paul Monroe had all traveled and lectured in China (1919-1921) and their ideas contributed to the lively cultural and intellectual atmosphere of the time. All of them had something to say about education, but Russell had the most interest for Mao. Russell was an avowed socialist and his ideas appealed to the more radical Chinese students and intellectuals. Mao, however, seriously questioned Russell's ideas on the interaction between education and society and the reform of society (Chinese society in particular). Russell had indicated that socialism and communism could be achieved, at least in some case, without a dictatorship of the proletariat. The propertied classes he felt could be reformed through intensive efforts to reeducate them. Mao countered these ideas in a letter to a friend and put forth a basic Marxist-Leninist position which stated that under capitalism all the instruments of education were in the hands of the ruling class, and furthermore, they would not willingly give up their privileges thus necessitating a violent struggle. Mao seemed to think Russell naive to expect that socialism could be achieved peacefully. Mao's position on this question was of course not particularly original. It demonstrates, however, that he had accepted the basic Marxist-Leninist principle that education is simply part of the superstructure of society, and that unless the economic base is changed there is little chance that education can be anything more than a propaganda tool in the hands of the bourgeois ruling class.[3]

A further move in the direction of viewing education in a Marxist-Leninist manner is revealed in Mao's classic analysis of the peasant movement in the Hunan countryside (1927).[4] At this time Mao was active in the Chinese Communist Party. The Party had gained strength particularly in the urban areas, only to be crushed in the same year. However, Mao had devoted most of his attention to the rural regions organizing peasant associations, apparently on his own initiative, and aiding in the establishment of peasant schools. In his article published in March, Mao stressed the class nature of education in Chinese society and elaborated on the relationship between education and social class:
tionship between education and social class:

> In China education has always been the exclusive preserve of the landlords, and the peasants have had no access to it. But the landlord's culture is created by the peasants, for its sole source is the peasant's sweat and blood. In China, ninety percent of the people have had no education, and of these the overwhelming majority are peasants. The moment the power of the landlords was overthrown in the rural areas, the peasant movement for education began.[5]

#5

This assessment of education and social class has remained with Mao up to the present and represents a standard Marxist-Leninist view (allowing of course for the fact that Mao is speaking of peasants rather than industrial workers). In addition, however, there are indications that Mao regarded local initiative in establishing and managing schools as important and noted that education would have to relate to the peculiar needs of the peasantry before they would accept it as their own.[6] This is a theme that he developed in more detail later.

The Kiangsi Soviet Period: 1928-1934

The communists following the destruction of the CCP apparatus in the urban areas in 1927 were forced to withdraw to the countryside to consolidate their forces. Mao had already been active in this regard and quickly assumed a more important position in the Party. The establishment of the Kiangsi Soviet in October 1930 and the previous experience in establishing revolutionary base areas (i.e., Mao's first base in the Chingkang Mountains) provided the CCP and Mao with their first fairly stable territory within which to construct an educational system. Although this represented a short period of stability, Mao nevertheless began to think more systematically about educational problems in general and the basic goals and aims of education in particular.

A critical problem besetting the communist-occupied base areas at this time was the necessity to remain financially viable in the face of repeated armed attacks by the Kuomintang armies led by Chiang Kai-shek. This required a basic level of agricultural and industrial productivity and the close support of the peasantry. Mao viewed the continued growth and development of education as a primary means to insure a strong economic base. The idea of education for investment or education for economic construction thus appears for the first time in Mao's writings and hereafter remains an important component of his educational thought.[7]

More important, he began to formulate definite educational policies and goals while at the same time experiencing the corresponding practical difficulties that accompany policy-making.

Mao following an investigation of educational work in the Soviet areas drafted a document in October, 1933, discussing his findings and proposing changes for the future. Mao criticized the lack of work in the field of education in general and reminded Party cadres that education and culture occupy an extremely important aspect of Soviet life. Mao suggested that education has as one of its long-term goals the task of raising the political and cultural level of the masses while building a new revolutionary generation. The policy of the Soviet should be to recognize the need for and carry out a program of universal education (*p'u-ch'i chiao-yu*). Moreover, education should be compulsory and free with the specific purpose of eliminating illiteracy in the shortest possible time.[8] Mao recognized the current successes in educational work particularly the establishment of a limited number of primary schools, night schools, literacy classes, and the Soviet and Red Army University, but suggested that more effort should be expended to increase educational facilities particularly at the primary level with the principal goal of eliminating illiteracy.[9]

By 1934, some progress had been made in this respect but external conditions were quickly changing the political and social stability of the base areas. In January, the KMT armies were pressing close to the Soviet captial at Juichin and in October the Red Army and the CCP began their Long March which was to take them completely out of the Southwest and into the extreme Northwest. Mao, however, was still expressing his intense concern with the progress of educational development and drafted in embryonic form a general policy of education that was to develop more fully in the new base area at Yenan. Education was still viewed in the broad political, cultural, and economic framework Mao had stressed earlier:

> For the sake of the victory of the revolutionary war, for the sake of consolidating and developing the political power of the Soviet, for the sake of mobilizing all revolutionary forces among the people to participate in the great revolutionary undertaking, and for the sake of creating a revolutionary new era, the Soviet must carry out reforms in culture and education, get rid of the spiritual shackles imposed on the worker-peasant masses by the reactionary ruling classes, and create a new Soviet culture of the workers and peasants . . . . Where

> does the general policy of the Soviet in culture and education lie? It lies in educating the broad masses of the toiling masses with the communist spirit making culture and education serve the revolutionary war and the class struggle, integrating education with labor, and turning the broad masses of the Chinese people into people enjoying the blessing of civilization.[10]

While the experiences of the Kiangsi Soviet Period were limited to three years they did illustrate the difficulties that the CCP and Mao were ultimately going to face when their base of power eventually was expanded. Moreover, the initial outline of Mao Tse-tung's educational thought became discernible during this period.

The Yenan Period and Civil War: 1935-1949

The Yenan Period is correctly understood as being the most prolific and creative of Mao Tse-tungs's intellectual development. It was at this time that he wrote the more significant of his theoretical and philosophical writings including those relating to the goals and aims of education. Mao also came to terms with and wrote about the epistemological implications of Marxism and creativity, and learning. His writings in this respect form the theoretical framework out of which he and future educational thinkers in China would formulate educational policy and practice.

Knowledge and Learning

While Mao generally related the acquisition of knowledge and learning to practical activities (learning by doing), during this period of relative stability he addressed himself to the task of systematically and theoretically utilizing Marxist ideology to discuss at length the nature of these two endeavors.[11] By October, 1935, the Long March had ended for Mao and in December, 1936, the CCP capital was moved to Yenan. Here, in July and August of the following year, Mao wrote what were to become his major statements on the nature of knowledge and learning which also served to represent the theoretical groundwork for his educational thought.

In the first article entitled "On Practice," Mao discussed at length Marxist dialectical materialism and its implications for understanding the processes of cognition, knowledge, and learning. Mao stated that the difference between Marxist materialism and

Fig. 8. An industrial worker gives technical instruction in a primary school.

other forms of materialist thought is that Marx recognized the inter-relationship and dependence of "knowledge on social practice, that is the dependence of knowledge on production and the class struggle . . . . Man's knowledge depends mainly on his activity in material production."[12] Mao went on to stress that only through the act of producing goods does man become conscious of his relationship to nature, to other men and to himself. Mao continued noting that material production alone does not shape man's consciousness. Man is also influenced by the class struggle, his political relationships and experiences, the general and local culture—in short, his entire social milieu. But of all these factors the class struggle and the relationship of the individual to the means of production remained the most signficant determinants of consciousness for Mao.[13] On this basis and understanding of Marxist materialism Mao elaborated and developed five steps in the acquisition and the practical application of knowledge:

1. Sense perception: at this stage only separate aspects of reality are perceived and more general concepts and logical conclusions can not be drawn.

2. Conceptual stage: at this stage man has engaged in social practice to the point that images pile up in his brain, experiences are repeated enough times to necessitate a cognitive leap after which concepts are formed, thus bringing knowledge to a qualitatively different and higher level. Mao stated that one can not rely upon the first stage (empiricism) or the second stage (rationalism) but must see the interconnectedness of both and the dependence of the latter on the former.[14]

3. Application of conceptual knowledge: Mao stressed again that knowledge which remains inactive is useless; the knowledge gained in stage two must now be reapplied to practical conditions so that social change is the result: "Marxist philosophy holds that the most important problem does not lie in understanding the laws of the objective world and thus being able to explain it, but in applying the knowledge of these laws actively to change the world."[15]

4. Theory building: this stage requires that the experiences gained in the previous steps result in a general plan of action, theory or program. These theories are a systematization of the previous steps but normally contain errors; thus, this stage is also one of revision: "In such a situation, ideas, theories, plans, or programmes are usually altered partially or sometimes wholly,

because of the discovery of unforeseen circumstances in the course of practice."[16] When the theory finally accords with practice and consistent success is achieved, then the movement of knowledge with regard to that particular objective can be considered complete.

5. Adaptation to new conditions: however, the movement of human knowledge is not complete, and Mao stressed the necessity to constantly adapt to new objective conditions; this of course makes "true" knowledge difficult to pinpoint: "Marxists recognize that in the absolute and general process of the development of the universe, the development of each particular process is relative, and that hence, in the endless flow of absolute truth man's knowledge of a particular process at any given stage of development is only relative truth. The sum total of innumerable relative truths constitutes absolute truth."[17]

Clearly, Mao Tse-tung conceives the acquisition of knowledge as comprising a cyclical chain: from sense perceptions to conceptualization; back to practice and then to theory; back to practice for revision and so on. For Mao this represented an endless chain, each level of knowledge qualitatively higher than the other thus accounting for human progress.[18] In another sense Mao illustrated his flexibility with regard to materialist doctrine and thereby avoided some of the pitfalls of a more mechanical brand of Marxism. This flexibility, or more precisely Mao's ability to "alter partially or sometimes wholly" various programs, policies, and theories, is reflected in Chinese communist educational policy and practice from this point up to the present.

Mao's reliance on practice as the major vehicle leading to knowledge was stressed again and expanded upon the following month in a second important article entitled "On Contradiction."[19] In this article Mao discussed the major law of materialist dialectics—the law of contradictions or unity of opposites. According to this law all matter is constantly undergoing change, which contains both an external and internal dimension. The internal is the most significant for Mao because herein lies the contradiction; things are always in a state of change, moving in the direction of becoming their opposite. Contradictions moreover are divided into two categories: (1) universal (because all phenomena contain contradictions) and (2) particular (the specific character of matter). It is with respect to the particularity of contradictions that educational theory arises: "Man's knowledge of matter is knowledge of its forms of motion, because there is nothing in this world except matter in motion and this motion must assume certain forms."[20] Knowledge, then arises out of man's ability to recognize and distinguish the various elements of the material world. Mao reiterated the argument advanced in the previous article that knowledge moves from the particular to the general and then back to the particular, and with the completion of each cycle human knowledge advances to a qualitatively higher level.[21]

This article also lays the groundwork for Mao's later conception of the learning process. Mao notes that the particularity of contradiction is not a static process but is also represented by cyclical change. In order to be able to determine the nature of each particular contradiction (essential for transforming man and society) the individual must, according to Mao, continually study and examine all aspects of reality in a never-ending movement. As soon as one field of study is mastered, the particularity of the contradiction transforms itself to a new level and the whole learning process must be repeated at this higher level. This represents progress.[22] It is with regard to the changing nature of the principal aspect of contradictions that Mao makes a most significant statement. In keeping with materialist dialectics Mao adheres to the principle that the economic base is the primary determinant of change. He again demonstrated his flexibility in this connection by recognizing the role ideas and institutions play in transforming man and society:

> . . . while we recognize that in the general development of history the material determines the mental, and social being determines social consciousness, we also—and indeed must—recognize the reaction of mental on material things, of social consciousness on social being, and of the superstructure on the economic base.[23]

This statement not only demonstrates ideological flexibility but also lays the foundation for the theoretical importance of education.

Both articles (" On Practice", and "On Contradiction") reveal Mao Tse-tung's understanding of Marxism and basic materialist philosophical stance. Yet there are strains of traditional Chinese thought present, particularly in the general areas of the relationship between knowledge and action, the concept of multiple contradictions, and the emphasis on the transformational character of education.[24]

In a series of articles between 1938 and 1942 Mao continued to discuss and develop the concepts and ideas articulated in the two articles above. In particular, the role of ideas and their effect on both people and institutions was stressed as well as the relationship between theory and practice.[25] Mao clearly favored practical activities and studies: "Holding fact-finding meetings is the simplest, most practicable and most reliable method, from which I have derived much benefit; it is a better school than any university."[26] The Yenan Period revealed Mao's accepted epistemology and demonstrated his understanding of Marxist ideas and concepts which resulted in further statements on the goals and aims of education and on general policy formation.[27]

Goals and Aims of Education

The outbreak of the Sino—Japanese war in July, 1937, turned Mao's attention away from the more theoretical aspects of education and toward practical questions of general and specific goals and aims. The second United Front between the CCP and KMT was formed in order to resist the Japanese attack, and the primary task of the Communists was to maintain the stable base area at Yenan. In the field of education Mao perceived both specific and general goals and aims of education. Very simply stated, one specific goal of education was to propagandize and organize the resistance forces to fight the Japanese. Shortly after the Japanese attack Mao suggested that educational policy be changed to solidify the United Front in the war against Japan.[28] In a policy statement in July, 1937, Mao outlined the aim of education at this time as being to:

> Institute education for national defence. Radically reform the existing educational policy and system. All projects that are not urgent and all measures that are not rational must be discarded. Newspapers, books, and magazines, films, plays, literature and art should all serve national defence. Traitorous propaganda must be prohibited.[29]

Some of the educational reforms specified by Mao to restructure education included cutting unnecessary courses, streamlining the administration, enlarging mass education efforts in the form of remedial schools and classes, utilizing traveling art troupes, and instituting compulsory primary schools.[30] In short, the institution of education was viewed as an elaborate device to achieve very specific aims and goals.

Education in both a formal and informal sense assumed great

importance for Mao at this time. Incorrect ideas and tendencies among party and military personnel were to be rectified through "painstaking education."[31] The masses of Chinese people were to be mobilized in an all-out educational effort to transform their thought and actions.[32] Indeed, the power of education was thought by Mao to be so great that he was able to state: "We should sweep backward ideas from the minds of the Chinese people, just as we sweep our rooms."[33]

Assuming such power of the educative process Mao noted that formal education should seek first of all to instill in the students the correct ideological orientation; this became a primary goal.[34] In discussing the role of the Anti—Japanese Military and Political College of Yenan Mao reiterated the important role of political education and elaborated that the aim of education should be to ". . . cultivate a firm and correct political orientation, an industrious and simple style of work, and flexible strategy and tactics."[35] Students were to be expected to gain an understanding of proletarian ideals and ideology even if they were not from the working class or the peasantry. Mao recognized the difficulty many of the bourgeois students would have in relating to working-class ideas and expected ideological struggles to be the result. Students were further expected to be disciplined in their study, meet the local people and generally "serve the people."[36]

The goals and aims of education thus came to be associated with current practical, political, and ideological struggles, In addition, education was meant to instill in students a disciplined style of work and desire to work among the masses of people.

Education and Society: Policy Formation

Among the many suggestions and proposals between the CCP and KMT that followed the Sian incident (December, 1936) were those by the Communists and Mao in particular suggesting that educational policy be reformed nationwide to incorporate the general orientation of resisting Japan. By September, 1937, the CCP had grown increasingly disillusioned with the failure of the KMT to enact even modest reforms and Mao began to level criticism at KMT vacillation while still maintaining that a second United Front was desirable:

> In relation to the masses the Kuomintang is continuing the same practices it has followed for the last ten years; there has been no change and on the whole everything has remained

> the same for the last ten years, from the government apparatus, the army system and the policy towards civilians to financial, economic, and educational policies.[37]

The CCP and Mao increasingly subscribed to the idea that only through armed struggle could reforms be achieved including educational reforms: "[when we have guns] . . . we can also create cadres, create schools, create culture, create mass movement."[38]

The primary task, however, became that of defining and constructing a new culture against which other aspects of society (including education) would appear in relief. In 1940, in a very important programatic document, Mao outlined his vision of the kind of society and culture which should be constructed in the future. He called for a cultural revolution that would break away from the old "ignorant and backward" forms of culture and stressed that a new "national" culture was one of the goals of the CCP.[39] But what exactly was the relationship between culture and the rest of society?

> Any given culture (as an ideological form) is a reflection of the politics and economics of a given society, and the former in turn has a tremendous influence and effect upon the latter; economics is the base and politics the concentrated expression of economics. This is our fundamental view of the relation of culture to politics and economics and of the relation of politics to economics.[40]

This basically materialist view of the role of culture in society nevertheless reveals again the nonmechanical manner in which Mao understands the reciprocal role of the superstructure on the economic base. In order to attain the new culture (which was to be democratic, scientific, and mass) it was necessary for China to pass through two distinct stages: a democratic revolution and a socialist revolution.[41] A segment of the guiding force of the new democratic republic envisioned by Mao was to be the students and intellectuals.[42] They had played an important role in early modernization efforts but now needed a new orientation. Mao recalled how the period prior to the May Fourth Movement in 1919 had been characterized by a vigorous struggle between the modern school system (European and American models) and the more traditional Chinese schools (*shu-yuan*). The new schools of the 1920s and 1930s and their teachers represented a revolutionary trend, according to Mao, because they were struggling against obvious obstacles to Chinese modernization. However, this struggle remained positive only for a short while and as soon as foreign influence increased and China became internally weakened the old forms again reappeared and what new forms remained were serving non-Chinese interests.[43]

Mao, following the May Fourth Movement, viewed China as having entered a new stage of cultural revival, the leading component of which was Communist ideology. This new communist cultural trend was led principally by Lu Hsun and was described by Mao as having: ". . . made great strides in the domain of the social sciences and of the arts and letters, whether of philosophy, economics, political science, military science, history, literature, or art (including the theatre, the cinema, music, sculpture, and painting)."[44] In short, two distinct cultural periods emerge from Mao's discussion: (1) pre-1919 period characterized by bourgeois trends and (2) post-1919 period (to 1940) characterized by proletarian cultural ideological leadership. Mao reiterated that although proletarian forces were leading the new cultural movement the movement as a whole was not yet a socialist movement. The broad national trend was still viewed by Mao as being in the "new democratic" stage:

> For the Chinese revolution in its present stage is not yet a socialist revolution for the overthrow of capitalism but a bourgeois-democratic revolution, its central task being mainly that of combating foreign imperialism and domestic feudalism.[45]

The new democratic culture was "nationalistic scientific (modern), and of the masses" but it was not yet a Marxist or socialist culture. Such a culture could only appear once the economic base had been changed through socialist revolution.

The relationship between the new democratic culture and educational policy was also flexible. Mao emphasized that the aim of education during this cultural stage should be to communicate skills and practical information necessary to maintain the struggle against the Japanese as well as instilling patriotism and nationalism in the students. Even though there were obvious obstacles to overcome, bourgeois and liberal educators, journalists, and other intellectuals were encouraged to come to the base areas, particularly in the Northwest to join with the schools, to help operate and manage educational enterprises, and generally contribute to the cause of resisting Japan. In addition each base area was to establish publishing outlets for books and newspapers, distribution and delivery centers, as well as numerous cadre training schools.[46]

While the Sian incident forced the KMT to cease overt attacks on the Communists and to begin actively resisting the Japanese, the alliance in the second United Front was shaky at best. The Communist's educational policy as expressed by Mao continued to emphasize the need to establish a universal, free, and nationalistic educational system which included the armed training of students.[47] The Nationalist government was not prepared to agree to these demands, or the general political program of the CCP and it was not long before clashes between the two sides were a regular occurrence. In the face of renewed attacks by the KMT some CCP educational personnel were urging that the United Front's policy in education be abandoned and replaced with one which stressed proletarian policies exclusively. However, Mao maintained that it was still necessary to work in the United Front concept of a broadly based educational movement.[8] At the same time he began to outline proposals more in keeping with the deteriorating political situation. Propaganda organs and means of dissemination were expanded (including more schools, newspapers, literature and art, public health service, etc.)[59] and efforts were renewed to reach the peasantry educationally.[50] This resulted in a new awareness of the differences between rural and urban educational problems (which were to arise later when the CCP and Mao became leaders of the state).[50] As civil war approached and the United Front appeared doomed, Mao proposed a more critical educational policy which suggested that any new government should:

> Abolish Kuomintang indocrination in education and promote a national, scientific and mass culture and education; guarantee the livelihood of the teachers and other staff members of educational institutions and guarantee academic freedom. Protect the interests of youth, women, and children—provide assistance to young student refugees, help the youth and women to organize in order to participate on an equal footing in freedom of marriage and equality as between men and women and give young people and children a useful education. . . .[52]

The model, of course, for such an educational system was the communist school system in Yenan which evidenced a clear contrast to those existing in the Japanese-occupied areas or those under the oppression of the Nationalist secret police. Thus, while Mao and the CCP continued to officially follow the policy of the United Front, they gradually began to move in the direction of constructing an independent educational policy and practice designed to serve the interest of the approaching civil war which contained within it the possibility of nationwide victory.

Full-scale civil war finally broke out in July, 1946, and by March, 1947, Yenan had fallen to the Nationalist armies. This, however, represented a hollow and temporary victory as the Communist armies were already on the move and the loss of Yenan did not significantly weaken their position in the northwest. Even while on the march educational efforts did not cease as soldiers and others were encouraged to continue their studies on their own.[53] As the PLA began to show its strength, educational policy began to swing behind the more revolutionary political situation. In October, 1947, Mao announced that a new United Front should prevail among workers, peasants, soldiers, and revolutionary intellectuals to overthrow the Chiang Kai-shek government and establish a new coalition government.[54] As the Nationalist armies fled southward or surrendered it became clear that complete victory was in the offing. Mao announced that during this period the central task of education was to prepare for reconstruction of the country and for production.[55] In addition he ordered the PLA troops to follow a prudent policy when occupying new areas:

> Protect all public and private schools, hospitals, cultural, and educational institutions, athletic fields and other public welfare establishments. It is hoped that all personnel in these institutions will remain at their posts; the People's Liberation Army will protect them from molestation.[56]

As the founding of the People's Republic became imminent it was evident that the new educational policy would include many of the elements propounded by Mao Tse-tung earlier. The system would clearly not be a copy of either traditional Chinese or modern Western models, but more along patterns which had emerged in the Soviet Union and which at least for the near future would provide a model for the Chinese.[57]

The People's Republic of China: 1949-1973

The founding of the People's Republic of China in 1949 brought Mao from the caves of Yenan and into the position of leader of a state of over 600 million people. The obstacles facing the Chinese Communists and Mao were staggering. The economy was plagued by galloping inflation, the political structure was dysfunctional and in need of complete reform, and the educational system was unable to satisfy even minimal requirements. Internal social problems were further complicated by China's new foreign posture. One of Mao Tse-tung's first official acts was to make his first trip abroad to Moscow where, on February 14, 1950, he concluded a "Treaty of Friendship, Alliance, and Mutual Assistance" with the Soviet government. The following months and years witnessed further external and domestic complications including Chinese participation in the Korean War, thought reform movements aimed at Chinese intellectuals and internal Party disputes. Although Mao's writings (at least those which are accessible) are not nearly as numerous as in previous years before the seizure of power, sufficient information is available to assess the direction and development of his views with regard to education. The focus of the new political and social situation encountered after 1949 required some adaptation of previously articulated pedagogical goals and aims. In general, however, the basic principles formulated by Mao both during the Kiangsi period in the 1920s and the Yenan period in the 1940s were reaffirmed in light of the new situation.

Pre-Cultural Revolution Period, 1949-1965

One of the first problems Mao faced after 1949 was to communicate to intellectuals, students, and others the blunt facts concerning the relationship between the new government's political ideology and education. With a much larger and more diverse political unit to control, the flexible attitude that the CCP and Mao had taken in Yenan toward intellectuals and students now underwent change. For example, in regard to a 1955 political campaign Mao suggested that the general political situation in China required that careful distinctions be made between conflicts among the "people" and conflicts between the "people" and others.[58] Those who fell within the category "people," of course, included the natural allies of the revolution—the workers and peasants—as well as others who supported actively the cause of the struggle. This group included revolutionary intellectuals, students, and the national bourgeoisie. The critieria always included active and visible support of the policies of the CCP and Mao. Mao reiterated his position that among the people diversity of opinion and discussion should be encouraged, and coercion should not be used by the authorities to change ideas not consistent with government policy. However, he also stated that diversity should be properly balanced with a certain amount of collective effort and restraint. Those who upset this balance were clearly moving in the direction of counter-revolution and the freedoms accorded the people did not apply in those cases. During this period educational policy and practice were formulated within this delicate balance of diversity and discipline.[59]

The precise definition as to what constituted revolutionary and counter-revolutionary criticism depended a great deal on specific social conditions and was later expressed in terms of the struggle between "redness" and "expertness." The basic principles and aims of education were likewise discussed by Mao against the background of political struggle and the need to train qualified personnel for the task of economic reconstruction. The general policy which eventually emerged combined these apparent contradictory elements:

> All departments and organizations should shoulder their responsibilities in ideological and political work. This applies to the Communist Party, the Youth League, government departments in charge of this work and especially to heads of educational institutions and teachers. Our educational policy must enable everyone who receives an education to develop morally, intellectually, and physically and become a well-educated worker imbued with socialist consciousness.[60]

The relationship between politics and education has clearly dominated educational controversy at all times, but the primary aim of education according to Mao was to eventually resolve this contradiction and produce an educational mix that would result in the kind of socialist-worker-student envisioned by Mao in the quote above.

At various times, certain aspects of the red-expert, individual versus collective-effort equation were emphasized over others but for Mao the most basic ingredient continued to be politics. In 1957, Mao shifted momentarily from stressing unity in educational affairs and announced a policy of "let a hundred schools of thought contend." Intellectuals were encouraged to discuss and experi-

FIG. 9. A professional singer teaches rural children Peking opera.

ment with diverse educational ideas and were also encouraged to criticize Party policy with regard to such areas as education. The "Hundred Flowers Movement" may have been in response to events in Poland and Hungary in 1956 when Russian intervention proved necessary to quell popular discontent. It is possible that Mao felt that the Soviet Union and the respective Communist governments in Poland and Hungary had upset the balance between unity and diversity and had not allowed enough popular criticism, and he therefore sought to avoid a similar situation developing in China.[61] In any event, the movement was officially launched and the criticism Mao and the CCP had been seeking flowed in. Much of the discussion produced beneficial results in the sense that positive criticism was offered and the Party was able to make desired changes in both policy and practice. However, several instances occurred of negative criticism some of which called for the ouster of the Communist Party as the leading policy-maker in Chinese government. This was clearly beyond the bounds of the policy of diversity Mao had advocated and a campaign to tighten up the relationship between education and politics quickly followed the "Hundred Flowers Movement."[62]

The emphasis on politics or "redness" and education returned to remain as Mao's basic pedagogical position throughout the Great Leap Forward in 1958. This movement introduced possibly for the first time an educational policy more directly in line with the educational goals outlined by Mao during his days as a guerilla fighter in Kiangsi and Yenan. Mao stressed that the primary aim of education was to ". . .serve proletarian politics and be integrated with productive labor. It is necessary to make intellectuals identified with the laboring people and vice versa."[63] The task and ultimate goal of education came to be framed by Mao in terms of the contradictory but resolvable concepts of "red" and "expert." In this view, the educated members of society were to be politically aware and possess a theoretical understanding of their work as well as being technically proficient in their speciality. Mao expressed this relationship in the language of dialectics:

> The relationship between redness and expertness, between politics and work, stands for the unity of two opposites. It certainly is necessary to criticize and repudiate the tendency to ignore politics. It is necessary to oppose the armchair politician on the one hand and the practicalist who has gone astray on the other.[64]

FIG. 10. Student Red Guards participate in a political demonstration.

The role of education in society in Mao's view was to facilitate the eventual integration of political consciousness and dedication to socialism with the more conventional pedagogical goals of acquisition of knowledge.

In implementing this desire, Mao, especially in 1958, advanced the idea of establishing communes and suggested that culture and education would ultimately fall into this category: ". . . our goal is to gradually and systematically organize our industry, agriculture, commerce, culture, education and military (i.e., militia) into a great commune, making it the basic unit of our society . . . ."[65] The greatest educational task, of course, still remained the problem of peasant illiteracy. Mao suggested that the primary long range educational goal for the rural areas was to eliminate illiteracy through both formal and informal means, to ensure that each cooperative (and later commune) should have a primary school and a spare-time school and finally to attempt to establish some form of agricultural training school. Mao further reinforced his previous conviction that locally supported, self-sufficient schools were more desirable than state-funded public schools.[66] The Great Leap Forward program did not survive the setbacks which immediately followed. A series of natural disasters, shortcomings in the economic policies of the Great Leap Forward movement, and the withdrawal of Soviet technicians in 1960 all contributed to the abandonment of Great Leap educational policies in the early 1960s.

A period of retrenchment ensued during which two diametrically opposed educational lines began to emerge. For his part Mao concentrated his argument on what he considered to be one of the most basic principles of education: the integration of theory and practice. In his major statement on the origin of knowledge since his article entitled "On Contradiction" (1937) Mao reaffirmed the primary importance of practical activities:

> Where do correct ideas come from? Do they drop from the skies? No. Are they innate in the mind? No. They come from social practice and from it alone; they come from three kinds of social practice, the struggle for production, the class struggle, and scientific experiment. It is man's social being that determines his thinking. Once the correct ideas characteristic of the advanced class are grasped by the masses, these ideas turn into a material force which changes society and changes the world.[67]

Summed up in this succinct statement are many of the pedagogical assumptions which characterize a Marxist approach to education and knowledge: philosophical materialism; the relationship among politics (class struggle), production, and theory; the transformational nature of education (education for social change).

As political positions hardened in the early 1960s, Mao continued to drive home his point that the existing educational system was unnecessarily pedantic and gradually becoming divorced from the policies he had earlier advocated. While educators such as Lu Ting-yi (Minister of Education—1960s) claimed that the goal of education was to provide in-depth treatment of traditional subject matter (similar to an "essentialist" philosophy of education), Mao dismissed all such arguments as ". . . scholastic philosophy which is doomed to become extinct."[68] Mao instead took the position that too much formal education was actually harmful to the full development of individuals. He noted that schooling does not necessarily make an educated man and cited such diverse figures as Confucius, Gorky, and Benjamin Franklin as having been commoners with little formal education.[69] Undue reliance on institutionalized education, in Mao's view, led to dogmatism and lack of experimentation.[70] By the mid-1960s political events were gradually reaching a climax as Mao encouraged all schools to look to the People's Liberation Army rather than the Party for political leadership.[71] The Cultural Revolution resulted in major reforms in all sectors of Chinese society but especially with regard to education. In a corresponding manner Mao's stated aims and goals of education narrowed down to focus on problems related to the general crisis in Chinese society.

Post-Cultural Revolution Period: 1966-1973

The transformation of the entire school system during the years 1966 to 1968 required a clarification of Mao Tse-tung's thoughts on the basic principles, aims, and goals of education as well as specific policy suggestions. During this period the majority of schools at all levels were closed and the struggle between Mao and the anti-Mao factions in the Party and society took shape. The dual-track educational structure and the generally elitist character of educational policy and practice in the early 1960s resulted in confusion among educators and others as to the correct orientation toward education. In keeping with the political struggle of the Cultural Revolution Mao expressed his position on these questions in a series of short, concise statements, some of which are discussed below.

Mao has always stressed fundamental Marxist concepts as providing the framework which ultimately determines basic educational principles. As a general guideline for the eventual construction of a transformed educational system Mao's conviction that education is dictated by whatever class is in power again emerged early in the GPCR.[72] Interestingly enough, the model put forward to give educators an idea of correct educational principles was the Anti—Japanese Military and Political University of the Yenan era. About this school Mao had said that the basic principles of education included: "Correct political orientation, plain, hardworking style, flexible strategy and tactics."[73] The Yenan Period represented for Mao a time when revolutionary fervor was at its height and education was characterized by egalitarian principles organized around dedication to the cause and a great deal of self-sacrificing hard work. However, it was clear that almost twenty years of socialist education had not completely eliminated socially negative ideas among some sectors of the Chinese people. The educational system of the early 1960s provided adequate proof. Mao sought an explanation for this phenomonon in his understanding of Marxism and his previously stated theory of knowledge. He again attacked a mechanical Marxist explanation of knowledge and ideas and asserted that:

> Although the social and economic systems have changed [since 1949], yet the vestiges of reactionary ideas left behind from the old era are still found in the minds of quite a sizable section of poeple. This means ideas of the bourgeoisie and the upper echelons of the petty bourgeoisie will not change overnight. The change will take time—a very long time. This is the class struggle in society.[74]

In short, Mao was attempting to communicate again a set of educational principles consistent with his previous work in this area; principles he felt had been abandoned following the Great Leap Forward.

What were the specific goals and aims which Mao felt the educational system should strive to achieve? Schools were to provide the means whereby students could acquire academic expertise while at the same time learning a variety of technical and semitechnical skills. The educational setting should also provide a forum for the criticism of non-Marxist pedagogical ideas; a forum, in short, for the criticism of the bourgeoisie.[75] Educational goals and aims articulated by Mao during the Yenan Period were reprinted in the official press during the GPCR. Mao's exhortation that political input was a fundamental aim in the educative process was repeated in 1966: "All work in schools is for the purpose of transforming the students ideologically. Political education is a link of the center, and it is undesirable to teach too many subjects. Class education, Party education and work must be strengthened."[76] Thus, a reiteration of Mao's educational goals and aims during the 1930s and 1940s provided the guidelines for the sixties. Both periods were characterized by social and political crisis and the consequent belief by Mao and his supporters that the future of the revolution was directly threatened with extinction.

In line with Mao's restatement of the goals and aims of education came a series of policy directives, issued by Mao, to provide specific directions as to the shape of the new education. As reforms began to be implemented, Mao criticized the previous policy of having work-teams from the central Party and government organs provide leadership and instead suggested that the reform process rely only upon the "revolutionary teachers and students at the schools."[77] A decentralized decision-making structure aided Mao in his political struggle and at the same time provided the framework for future management of the schools. The primary and secondary schooling cycle also came under attack by Mao who suggested a more practical policy which included a reduction of the school term:

> It takes a total of sixteen, seventeen or twenty years for one to reach the university from primary school, and in this period one never has a chance to look at the five kinds of cereals, to look at how the workers do their work, how peasants till their fields, and how traders do business. In the meantime, one's health is also ruined. Such an educational system is very harmful indeed.[78]

This guideline was eventually implemented to take the form of a nine-year unified primary and secondary cycle interrupted by a two-year work moratorium before one could apply for higher education. As for higher education itself, Mao indicated that sweeping reforms were necessary to fully achieve the goals and aims he felt constituted a genuine socialist education:

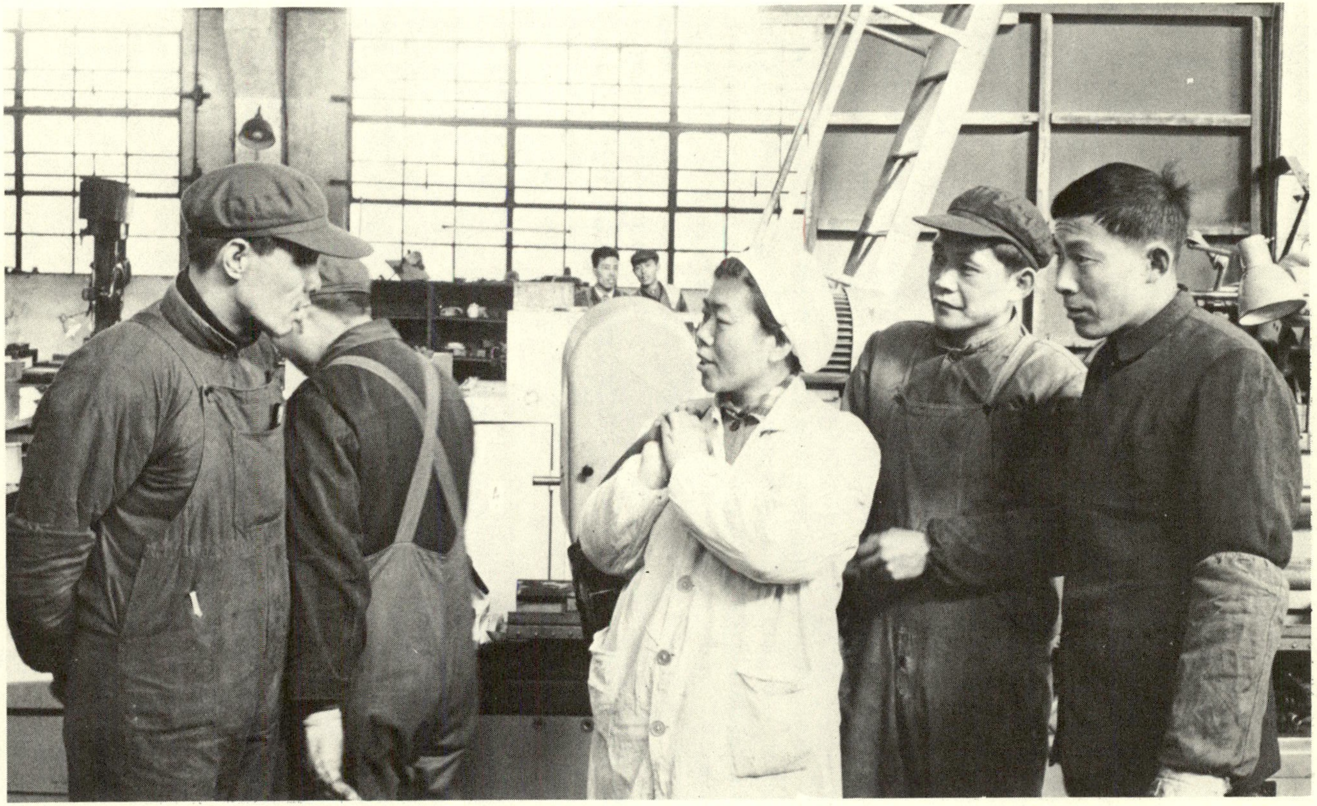

Fig. 11. Workers and students exchange views in a factory.

> We must still run physics and engineering colleges, but the period of schooling ought to be shortened, the education [curriulum] revolutionized, proletarian politics put in command, and the way of training personnel from the ranks of the workers advocated by the Shanghai Machine-Tool Factory adopted. Students must be selected from workers and peasants with practical experience, and after their study at school for several years they should return to practical production.[79]

This statement concisely expresses many of Mao Tse-tung's earlier, more involved writings and concepts on the nature of socialist educational goals, aims, and basic principles. The value of practical activities as a vehicle to knowledge is observable throughout Mao's directives from the shortening of the schooling cycle to the eventual return of graduates to "practical production." In short, the ultimate goal of education was to create a new socialist man; one who possessed a high level of political conciousness and dedication as well as a variety of academic and technical skills. In the post-Cultural Revolution period many of Mao Tse-tung's beliefs and convictions regarding education were realized on a mass scale for the first time. He has continued to give high priority to a politicized, universal educational system which will eventually create the kind of society he has envisioned for over four decades.[80]

Fig. 12. Students and teachers hold a mass rally in Tienenmen Square in Peking.

5 MAO TSE-TUNG ON EDUCATIONAL ADMINISTRATION

The running of education also depends on the cadres. Whether or not a school is well run is determined by the political level of its principal and Party committees. The principal and teaching staff of a school should serve the students, not vice versa—Mao Tse-tung. ["Talk with the Guinean Educational Delegation (August 8, 1965)," *CB*, No. 888 (August 22, 1969), p. 15.]

THE DEVELOPMENT OF MAO TSE-TUNG's concept of educational administration is related to his understanding of political and cultural leadership as a whole. Nowhere, perhaps, in the field of education have the Chinese Communists and Mao proved themselves more adaptable. This flexibility is almost certainly the result of the humble beginnings of the CCP and the even more difficult road which lay before them following the destruction of the Party apparatus in 1972. It is a truism that administration also grows more complicated and difficult as the organization of which it is a part grows. The problems of the Kiangsi Soviet period (1927-1934) were certainly of a different order than those of the Yenan period (1935-1949); neither period could in any way compare with that following the establishment of the People's Republic of China. Yet, fundamental patterns of administration were established during the early stages of Chinese communist growth. Concepts of management and administration produced by trial and error as well as ideological (Marxist) and traditional concepts found their way into the Chinese Communists' administrative approach. Mao's role in administrative organization, especially in the area of education, was of course preeminent. The net result was an educational administrative pattern which was experimental and unique and eventually instituted on a nationwide scale in the 1970s.

Kiangsi Soviet: 1927-1934

The period of the Kiangsi Soviet covered a time span of only seven years; yet it was at this time that the Chinese Communist Party began to learn the sophisticated techniques of rural organization and administration. In April, 1927, the CCP structure was attacked in its urban base, Shanghai, and many members either were killed or were forced to flee to other cities. By July the previous cooperation between the CCP and the KMT had disintegrated and the center of Party authority shifted to the rural areas. Mao's first guerilla base was established in the Chingkang Mountains in south China and gradually other Communist leaders found their way to the only area temporarily secure from KMT attack. While Mao was criticized by certain elements of the CCP for following a "peasant line," it soon became apparent that this course of action was the only way for the CCP to remain an active force in Chinese politics.[1]

In December, 1931, Mao became chairman of the National Soviet Government with its capital in Juichin, Kiangsi. This new base of power, though small, afforded the CCP with its first opportunity to administer a government, formulate public policy, and make decisions affecting a sizable proportion of people. An administrative structure for land reform was established along with various ministries and committees including a central authority for the development of an educational system.[2] These early attempts at governmental organization and administration were not well developed and were later criticized for being excessively vertical with lack of Party control.[3] Indeed, it appears that prior to 1934 much of the organizational impetus was informal and spontaneous coming from the natural revolutionary fervor of the peasants. This quickly changed as the power and stability of the Soviet began to decline in 1934. At that time the direction of administrative authority and the origin of policy was distinctly from the top down, and it has been suggested that this sort of administrative excess was a factor in the eventual capture of the Soviets by the KMT in 1934.[4]

Mao Tse-tung as a student had demonstrated his dislike of administrative procedure and excessive management particularly with regard to education. In 1923 Mao had initiated the Hunan Self-Study University which combined what he considered to be the best elements of the traditional Chinese academy or college (*shu-yuan*) with the more modern, Western schools (*hsueh-hsiao*). Mao felt that the traditional school was superior to the modern school in at least one important respect: teachers were allowed more freedom; there was no ". . . management of instruction . . . ."[5] Mao preferred the relaxed atmosphere of the traditional school combined with the modern content of the Western schools. Mao also came to recognize the importance of local control and organization of education. During his investigation of the peasant movement in Hunan Mao noted that on their own initiative the peasants were establishing evening classes which they considered to be "peasant schools":

> . . . the peasants are very enthusiastic about these schools and regard them, and only them as their own. The funds for the evening schools come from the "public revenue from superstition," from ancestral temple funds, and from other idle public funds or property. The county educational boards wanted to use this money to establish primary schools, that is, "foreign-style schools" not suited to the needs of the peasants, while the latter wanted to use it for peasant schools, and the outcome of the dispute was that both got some of the money, though there are places where the peasants got it all.[6]

Mao carried these early ideas to the guerilla base areas and the Kiangsi Soviet, but soon found that spontaneous organization and local control had to be tempered with a certain level of formal organization and administration.

The village soviets in the Kiangsi region had organizations at many levels including various youth and student groups. The new Soviet government led by Mao laid down a general requirement that every village attempt to appoint a teacher at the primary level to be salaried at a minimum level and to teach school at night. Students were to be admitted at any age and coeducation was encouraged.[7] A "Central Educational People's Committee" was established and a series of investigations carried out to determine the success in establishing the "people's schools." The educational committee was closely tied with the Party organization and cadres were primarily in charge of the investigations.[8] The results of these investigations indicated that roughly one primary school per 500 people had been established, one night school per 100 people and that the majority of sixteen-year-olds had passed through literacy classes.[9] The new Soviet government had therefore established the rudiments of an education ministry capable of carrying out intensive investigations, communicating decisions, engaging in planning efforts, and executing policy; in short, all the operations common to most educational administrative organizations.[10]

While a central authority had been established to generally oversee educational matters, local school management maintained a fair amount of autonomy. Mao's early predilection for informal management and flexible policy at the local level is evident in administrative policy in the first three years of the Kiangsi Soviet (1930-1933). Youth groups and student groups were actively encouraged to participate in the management of the schools providing they had already attended one of the "people's schools" and were literate.[11] The principals of the schools were to be chosen from the local region or village and were not required to be literate. The primary requirement was that they possessed "enthusiastic leadership ability" and the ability to work well with people and manage what administrative details might arise. They too were required to attend classes if they had not already been through the primary cycle.[12] Leadership and management in the schools thus came to resemble a human relations approach with much more in the way of horizontal relations than line and staff.[13] The net result was a system composed of a vertically organized Party and governmental structure providing loose leadership over educational affairs and a locally controlled school system managed by local "leaders" in a more horizontal and informal fashion. As the Soviet government came under attack from the KMT in 1934, the Party was forced to tighten up its organizational structure and this affected the administration of education as well. Mao began to criticize the lack of direction and control over education and

FIG. 13. Peasants operate a school in rural China.

suggested that a special branch of education be established with more control over local affairs.[14] However, scarcely had the work of reorganizing the educational apparatus begun than the Soviet government and the Red Army were forced to abandon the Kiangsi region and begin their historic "Long March" which would finally take them to Northwest China. The Kiangsi period was clearly one of experimentation and Mao learned that a delicate balance exists between the kind of spontaneous, local administration and control on which he placed a high value and the need to provide for central planning in order to realize concrete collective goals.

The Yenan Period: 1935-1949

The Yenan period is crucial to understanding the theory and practice of Chinese Communist organization and administration. Instead of being excessively concerned with territorial expansion the CCP now turned its attention inward in an attempt to develop the kind of administrative techniques necessary to penetrate to the village level and gain the support and respect of the peasantry. The perennial problem of balancing village loyalties with a larger cause provided the CCP with its greatest challenge yet. Quite simply, it was the difficulty of replacing existing village social relations based on kinship and friendship with loyalty to the Party and broader social goals. Unlike the Kiangsi period when administrative structure had been excessively vertical, a more complex system evolved composed of many horizontal, staff, and line relationships. The administration of the border regions as a whole resembled an interlocking system including the Party organization, the military, the government, and the mass organizations. There was extensive communication among all levels as well as autonomy of decision-making (although this eventually declined in the military structure) yet the Party began to exercise increased leadership functions and was represented at most levels in both the governmental organizations and mass organizations. Responsibility for the administration of education fell within the government's domain, and one of the eight departments at the regional level was the department of education. A Party cadre was assigned to the department of education as well as to the mass organizations involved in educational affairs (e.g., youth groups, student groups, etc.). While the Party provided leadership and direction, by 1944 a viable system had been established which linked the village to the higher administrative levels, and local participation and decision-making was genuinely practiced. In short, it appeared as if the administrative mix Mao desired between enthusiastic local participation and higher level planning and goal-achievement was finally becoming a reality.[15]

In general, Mao Tse-tung's program for education centered on the political and military policy of resisting Japan and he suggested in 1937 that the existing educational system be reformed to so coincide.[16] Mao also later came to be disillusioned with the conventional organization of education and criticized the lockstep process whereby students moved straight through the schooling cycle with little or no practical knowledge:

> Now let us take a look at certain students, those brought up in schools that are completely cut off from the practical activities of society. What about them? A person goes from a primary school of this kind all the way through to a university of the same kind, graduates and is reckoned to have a stock of learning. But all he has is book-learning; he has not taken part in any practical activities or applied what he has learned to any field of life. Can such a person be regarded as a completely developed intellectual? Hardly so, in my opinion because his knowledge is still incomplete.[17]

This statement of course reflects Mao's understanding of epistemology and was present in the administrative structure of the Yenan school system.

The ideal model for Mao of school administration at this time was "self-sufficiency." This extended to all areas of school organization including financing. Mao praised those schools which did not have to depend upon government funds for financial support and who managed to erect educational and productive facilities and fund their own projects. To depend on the government for financing meant that the peasantry would have to be taxed and taxation was never popular in rural China. Mao encouraged schools to engage in their own productive enterprises which would in the end contribute to their financial viability.[18]

Apart from financial self-sufficiency Mao's Border Region educational authorities encouraged the combination of popular management of the schools (*min-ban*) with public support and direction. They criticized past policies of government-controlled education and suggested that the masses be given much more responsibility with regard to educational administration:

> We only know how to have the government come in and op-

FIG. 14. Teachers and peasants discuss political issues.

> erate the schools; we do not understand how to apply correctly the force of the masses, how to have schools run by the people themselves in accordance with their own ambitions; therefore both the form and content of education is decided by the people . . . we must take the majority or perhaps all of the primary schools and turn them over to the local masses to run by themselves; the government will then give material assistance and will offer guidance in matters of policy.[19]

The system of interlocking administration and Party influence in the local popularly controlled schools continued to be emphasized:

> The policy of popular management cannot be divorced from that of government assistance. Popular-management schools cannot be allowed to run their own course; it is incorrect to think that we will lighten our responsibilities through popular-management; in fact, the reverse is true; we must strengthen our leadership.[20]

It was suggested that the responsibility for direct leadership in the schools must eventually fall to the local leaders with higher level cadres providing guidance and regulation where necessary.

The vehicle for school management and administration involved the concept of "leading groups" (*ling-tao ku-kan*) which were considered an improvement over a one-man management approach:

> A school of a hundred people certainly cannot be run well if it does not have a leadership of several people, or a dozen or more, which is formed in accordance with the actual circumstances (and not thrown together artificially) and is composed of the most active, upright, and alert of the teachers, the other staff, and the students.[21]

Management thus was to be spread widely including as many local elements as possible (e.g., students) who were all to have genuine authority in such areas as teacher selection, salaries, class size, selection of school sites, curricula, and texts. In all these areas the government and Party would not interfere unless problems arose. In most cases, official interference in school affairs took the form of general policy guidelines and aid in solving problems when asked.[22] Leading groups were chosen according to four criteria: devotion to the cause of socialism and resisting Japan, good relations with the local population, ability to innovate and act independently, and ability to practice self-discipline.[23] Leaders and administrators were to be in close contact with the people in their organizations and develop the ability to transform local desires into specific policy which the people concerned would then accept as their own. This concept of the "mass-line" has remained an integral part of the Chinese Communists' leadership patterns.[24]

In late 1948 on the eve of victory in the civil war Mao became come much more complex. Administration of the numerous urban schools throughout China presented a different problem than the administration of the few small schools in Yenan. Administrative procedures were tightened up and Mao urged the Party to quickly organize and train all possible elements of the intelligentsia to aid in the administration of education in the large cities and also aid in the reopening of schools which had been closed due to war conditions.[25] In addition to enlisting the support of the intellectuals Mao suggested that the army (PLA) contained a natural leadership corps and encouraged leading PLA cadres to gain as much experience as possible in the management of schools and other educational facilities. The practice of the army performing civilian functions thus entered at this stage:

> The army is a school. Our field armies of 2,100,000 are equivalent to several thousand universities and secondary schools. We have to rely chiefly on the army to supply our working cadres.[26]

The committee system and leading groups likewise received more organizational instructions, and Mao listed eleven points that all Party committees were to follow in solving the enormous administrative tasks now facing the Chinese Communist Party as potential leader of the state: (1) all problems were to be investigated as thoroughly as possible utilizing investigation squads of from ten to twenty people; (2) all issues were to be brought into the open for discussion; (3) information between committees and squads was to be exchanged and shared to ensure lateral communication; (4) leaders were to learn from subordinates and cadres were urged not to be afraid to ask advice about things of which they were unsure; (5) committees were to coordinate efforts where possible; (6) committees were to be aware of the quantitative aspect of various problems and keep accurate statistics; (7) the public was to be involved at all levels by issuing notices of mass meetings in advance; (8) administrative committees were to be trimmed to a workable size; (9) cadres were urged to continue to work with and listen to those whose ideas were different or opposed to the general line; (10) cadres were urged to adopt a humble attitude and avoid arrogance in dealing with non-Party personnel; (11) cadres were to distinguish between programs that served the revolution and those that would hinder it.[27] It was clear administration of all types including education was entering a new phase. The establishment of the People's Republic in October, 1949, placed the CCP and Mao in charge of reorganizing education throughout China proper, and they were to find that although the Yenan experience had been limited many important patterns had developed; trial and error had produced both success and failure and administrative procedure from that point on would clearly bear the imprint of earlier policies and practices.

For his part, Mao Tse-tung became the architect of an educational administration which exhibited characteristics of both local control and central planning. Leadership committees at the local level operated fairly flexibly, informally, and democratically. Many of the practical problems of schooling were decided at this level and the *min-ban* (popular-management) concept was a genuine reality. Mao also realized the necessity of a strict staff and line administrative structure. The Party and government provided educational leadership at this level. Central planning with local control became the curious mix developed by Mao with the cadre providing the link between the two. This system became more complex in the years following the establishment of the People's Republic and particularly was attacked during the 1960s but it remained a basic component of Mao Tse-tung's thought.

The People's Republic of China: 1949-1973

Administrative problems of all types faced the Chinese Communists and Mao Tse-tung when they entered Peking in 1949. The Yenan Border Region government and earlier efforts to organize the peasantry had undoubtedly provided both Mao and the Party with valuable experience in administration. Yenan had a well organized government apparatus, schools, medical program, tax system, and other civil organizations all of which required some level of management and administration. Yet it was all on a small scale compared with the immense tasks facing the new government in 1949. With the establishment of the People's Republic of China large numbers of administrators had to be recruited to staff the numerous governmental and public positions throughout China, managers had to be found to fill administrative posts in the industrial sector, and a network has to be organized to efficiently administer a widespread educational system. The result in the long-run was that administration became more complex, requiring the services of a bureaucracy and presenting to Mao and the Party the spectre of bureaucratic excesses and red tape, a condition they had scrupulously sought to avoid while in the caves of Yenan. Mao could no longer, of course, exercise the degree of direct influence over administrative matters that he had while acting as leader of the Border Region government. These responsibilities proliferated to countless committees, governmental, and Party organs.[28] For this period accordingly it is not surprising that Mao's statements are difficult to locate on a specific a subject such as educational administration. Two major periods stand out as representing stages revealing Mao's continued concern with this question. The first is associated with the Great Leap Forward in 1958 and the second with the Great Proletarian Cultural Revolution beginning in 1966. During both of these movements Mao attempted to assert what he considered to be a series of revolutionary reforms designed to rectify counter-revolutionary tendencies in Chinese society. In both cases, opposition to his policies was strong and the movements became identified with larger political struggles. Nevertheless, Mao's vision of educational administration emerged most clearly during these campaigns, and educational administration in the 1970s in China more closely approximates his ideals than at any time since the 1940s.

Educational Administration and The Great Leap Forward: 1949-1958

Of the numerous governmental ministries established in 1949 at least four were directly related to education (Ministries of Culture, Education, Higher Education, and Health). Below the higher level ministries several committees and commissions existed complete with staff and line relationships and standard bureaucratic organization.[29] The first period of policy-making at all levels witnessed a carry-over from the Yenan period and consisted of a political-military administrative network.[30] Mao had been moving in this direction during the civil war. The military (PLA) had been viewed as a "school" both to train administrative cadres as well as provide personnel to staff new positions as they developed. This situation changed in the mid-fifties when a more formal bureaucratic structure developed and the role of the military shifted to professionally trained administrators. Although the CCP and Mao experimented with varied approaches to upper-level administration, the basic formula included a dual governmental and Party structure at the top with proliferating committees involving mass organizations at the lower levels.[31] The administrative mix which Mao had achieved in Yenan understandably underwent change now that the territory included the entire mainland of China.

It is possible that Mao Tse-tung found himself faced with the same question writ large; that is, how to balance local control of the schools with centralized planning. In general, he asserted that it was necessary to have both. He indicated that overall planning in education was necessary, and that short-range solutions involving only a segment of society were undesirable. On the other hand, he continued to stress the need to be cognizant of local needs and especially of local mass organizations. Decision making should be widespread and participatory but in the last analysis planned.[32] As the Great Leap Forward began to develop into a full-blown political movement Mao began to level a more harsh form of criticism at those responsible for educational planning of the "overall" variety. It appeared to him that perhaps planning was overcentralized and administration of local schools unnecessarily rigid.[33]

In typical fashion Mao shifted his attention during the Great Leap Forward to the rural areas which he felt provided the key to the eventual economic and political development of China. Rural China had always lacked educational facilities; although the situation improved in the first decade of the People's Republic, shortages in teaching staff and facilities continued to plague educational planners in Peking. The administrative organization had inhibited a more widespread educational network because of lack of trained cadres and officials. Formal schooling simply could not be provided to all areas with the low level of resources available. Mao criticized this dependence on official bodies to establish and staff schools and instead urged local communes and brigades to establish and operate their own schools according to their own local needs. Furthermore, he approved of shortening the schooling term to a seven or eight-year unified cycle.[34] He encouraged Party members to investigate local conditions and discuss problems with those concerned before making decisions affecting the operation and administration of schools in the villages and towns in rural China.[35] In the administrative structure of the schools themselves the Party committee and the mass organizations involved were to cooperate jointly in the administrative process.[36] In short, a move toward decentralization of educational decision-making took place during the Great Leap Forward which encouraged much more in the way of local participation and involvement.

Educational administration was also encouraged to broaden its base to include and cooperate with the economic sector of society as was true during both the Kiangsi and Yenan periods. Mao Tse-tung ascribed importance to those educational institutions which had achieved a high degree of financial and administrative self-sufficiency, and this had implications for decentralized administrative control as well.[37] At the height of the Great Leap Forward Mao advanced the slogan that, "From now on, schools should run factories and factories should run schools. . . ."[38] By implication the ideal was to include in the administration of the schools other sectors of society. In this way, students and teachers while participating in the management of the schools could also involve themselves in learning a variety of technical skills. Pedagogical goals would thus be realized while at the same time the schools would be provided with additional financial stability; "As far as circumstances permit, all secondary vocational schools and skilled workers' schools should tentatively run factories or farms for carrying out production so as to become self-supporting or semi-supporting."[39] Industrial and agricultural colleges were also encouraged to establish factories or laboratories, or both for productive purposes including signing contractural agreements with local firms.[40]

The Great Leap Forward revealed Mao Tse-tung's continued suspicion of bureaucratic decision-making structures. His fascination with understanding local conditions and involving in the decision-making process all groups concerned finds expression in Great Leap policy statements. The Party and government continued to be organized vertically, including those ministries and committees influencing the development of education, but the balance between centralization and local control (organized in a horizontal fashion) appears again briefly during this campaign.

With the setbacks of the Great Leap Forward and the eventual abandonment of many of Mao's policies, the bureaucracy and other power groups in China became far less compliant with the kinds of administrative experiments of 1958.[41]

Educational Administration and the GPCR: 1964-1973

The Cultural Revolution so radically transformed educational administration in China that what eventually emerged bore little resemblence to previous structures. For a period of two years (1966-1968) most schools in China were closed and formal educational administration did not exist at any level (the Ministry of Education was abolished in 1966 and only started to emerge again in a new form in 1972). It was at this time that Mao Tse-tung outlined what he considered to be the most workable and revolutionary educational administrative structure.

During the early 1960s schools in China again fell under the fairly rigid control of the ministries in Peking and the committees at the provincial and county (*hsien*) levels (the Ministry of Education was subdivided in 1964 into a Ministry of Higher Education and Ministry of Education to ensure more efficient control).[42] As the larger political struggle began to take shape Mao began to criticize the inflexible approach taken to educational administration in general. When floods destroyed many educational facilities in Hopei province (1964), educational authorities in the area were understandably upset. Mao, however, noted that because of the disaster ad hoc schools were established and operated by the local people and the net result was that primary and secondary education became more accessible than before. This was proof to Mao that the organization, establishment, and administration of schools were not dogmatically dependent on conventional administrative structures.[43]

It was not long before more specific criticism was leveled at educational administrators. Mao charged that schools were being solely run by "bourgeois intellectuals" and professional pedagogues and that this one-sided management should cease.[44] The basic criterion to determine how well a school was administered was suggested by Mao in 1965: "Whether or not a school is well run is determined by the political level of its principal and Party committees. The principal and teaching staff of a school should serve the students, not vice versa."[45] Students shortly began to take matters into their own hands and the summer of 1966 was characterized by student and faculty strikes and the mass cessation of formal education. Mao encouraged the new level of participation of students and faculty in education and blamed the professionals for lacking the insight to change administrative organs before trouble broke out: "The revolution has been imposed on you people [in the Central Committee] because you did not carry out the revolution yourselves."[46] While the students provided the driving force controlling local educational institutions, very early in the struggle Mao encouraged them to recruit "revolutionary teaching staff and workers" to balance out the new administrative staffs.[47] This, however, did not happen immediately and a period of prolonged struggle took place before conditions finally stabilized and a new administrative model emerged.

Early in the Cultural Revolution it was clearly apparent that the military (PLA) would play a role in any future administrative system which developed. In a statement remarkably similar to one made in 1949 (see, Mao Tse-tung, "Turn the Army into a Working Force" [February, 1949], *SW*, IV, 338-339) Mao suggested that the PLA consider itself a form of school for training personnel in a variety of skills.[48] Finally, Mao issued a call for the reopening of all levels of education from primary to university and encouraged students and teachers to return to the schools to begin a concrete reform program.[49] The specific administrative structure Mao envisioned took the form of "three-in-one" committees whose task it would be to carry out "struggle-criticism-transformation" or in other words, to continue the political struggle within the schools while at the same time reforming the educational and administrative systems concerned.[50] The PLA was encouraged to play a central role in the reforms especially in terms of reopening the schools, establishing the "three-in-one" committees, and mediating between hostile factions of students and teachers.[51] By 1968 order had been restored, most of the schools were back in session, and the final administrative pattern had emerged. The future organization and administration of education encompassed, according to Mao, a more complete form of working-class leadership, decentralized to the level of the schools themselves. The "three-in-one" combination included PLA personnel (gradually to be replaced by Party committees), students and teachers, and activists among local industrial workers, or in rural schools peasants of the poor or lower-middle category.[52] This system eventually prevailed throughout China and is the basic administrative unit of the schools at this time (1973).[53]

The "Yenan model" of educational administration which combined a degree of centralized planning with a significant degree of local control and management (*min-pan*) appears to have remained an important ingredient in the make-up of Mao Tse-tung's educational thought. When a crisis occurred between central leadership and local demands, Mao invariably threw his support behind the latter. He has attempted to flatten the organization structure since the Cultural Revolution by reducing the number of administrative levels between the highest and the lowest.[54] In Mao's view, staff and line structures still exist, but formal paths are not always followed nor should they be.[55] Leadership in the schools themselves is closer to the *min-pan* concept than ever before with the added ingredient of the "three-in-one" committees. The ideal leader emerges as one who recognizes the importance of the institution and the need for some comformity of role behavior but who also is concerned with individual and local problems.[56] In short, Mao has again searched for and found the administrative mix he feels will guide China along the path of development while at the same time remaining in touch with and satisfying regional and local needs.

6 MAO TSE-TUNG ON CURRICULUM

At present there are too many courses of study in the schools, and the pressure is too great for the students—subjects are also not properly taught. The method of examination deals with the students as enemies and launches surprise attacks against them. This is disadvantageous to the development, with initiative and in a lively manner of the young people, morally, intellectually and physically—Mao Tse-tung. ["Comment on Courses of Study and Examination (March, 1964)," *CB*, No. 891 (October 8, 1969), p. 45.]

ONE OF THE MOST IMPORTANT pedagogical questions which has faced the CCP and Mao from 1927 to the present concerned the nature of the curricula for their developing school system. The period before the establishment of the People's Republic (1927—1949) was characterized by special problems owing to the nature of the guerilla bases. Cut off from the urban centers of education and adhering to fundamentally different educational goals the CCP and Mao Tse-tung were forced to consider curricular revision as a major priority. The curriculum of the Communist-controlled portions of China during this entire period were quite distinctive in relation to their counterpart in the Nationalist (KMT) sections of the country. Following the victory of the CCP in 1949 and the capture of major cities the Party and Mao were faced with problems of a different magnitude. Both periods, however, provided Mao and the CCP with an opportunity to experiment and discover through trial and error the answers to three of the most important questions concerning curriculum: (1) who controls curricular revision and development; (2) what should be taught; (3) how should the material be presented?[1] In answering all of these questions Mao drew both upon his professional experiences as a student and teacher in Ch'iangsha as well as upon his long years of practical political and ideological education. Indeed one of the most unusual features of contemporary Chinese education is the organization, content, and development of the curriculum.

The Early Years—The Kiangsi Soviet: 1917-1934

Mao Tse-tung's experiences as a student in both the traditional Chinese school and the "modern" teacher's training school in Ch'angsha established his dislike for a heavy curriculum and the overemphasis on study for the sake of study. In 1917 he was able to write with spirit of a student protester:

> In the educational system of our country, required courses are as thick as the hairs on a cow . . . . Speculating on the intentions of the educators, one is led to wonder whether they did not design such an unwieldy curriculum in order to exhaust the students, to trample on their bodies and ruin their lives . . . . How stupid![2]

In addition, Mao was dissatisfied with the content of the texts, especially those on the Chinese language. Chinese language lessons were unnecessarily long and complicated according to Mao. He suggested that the number of lessons be cut and the material presented utilize the common language of the average citizen (*pai-hua*) rather than the difficult literary language of the scholars (*wen-yen*).[3] In this respect, Mao was in agreement with reformers who were urging the adoption of the vernacular in literature and education. He was also within the current cultural renaissance later termed the May Fourth Movement.[4]

Mao found fault with both the traditional Chinese curriculum

(". . . the content of study in the [traditional] colleges was simply, 'the eight-legged essay' etc. These are only a kind of plaything."[5]) and that of the modern Western oriented schools. As for Western learning he noted that while the content was basically positive the delivery system was weak. Because of the excessive numbers of required courses, class hours were too long, creativity was stifled, and the students eventually became passive.[6] These features when combined with the rigid, inflexible nature of the new modern schools moved Mao to establish his Self-Study University (1921) and construct his own curriculum. Because students were to study on their own, course selection was optional. Basically, Mao followed the curriculum of the modern schools and offered a wide variety of courses: Chinese literature, foreign literature, English language, logic, psychology, ethics, pedagogy, sociology, history, geography, journalism, philosophy, political science, economics, etc. Mao's experience with the Self-Study University did not exhibit a real advance in curricular revision since he followed the established model of the modern schools. It did demonstrate his dissatisfaction with existing curricular structures which finally expressed itself in a total curricular revision in the ensuing decade.[7]

When Mao moved in 1925 to organize the Hunan peasantry, he learned that the educational needs of the rural farmers differed considerably from those of urban workers and intellectuals. The curriculum he had established in the Self-Study University in Ch'angsha found little enthusiastic response among students of peasant background. The existing primary schools in the rural areas of Hunan used texts similar to those utilized by Mao in the Self-Study University and according to Mao were ". . . entirely about urban things and unsuited to rural needs. . . . Hence, the peasants preferred the old-style schools [Chinese academies—*shu-yuan*] to the modern schools [those teaching modern subject matter—*hsueh-hsiao*]."[8] Another problem related to teaching workers and peasants concerned teaching method. Mao, at this time an active revolutionary, was convinced that instructional material should be meaningful to the social class to which it was presented. With the workers and peasants lectures and texts should be politically instructive quite apart from simply transmitting the desired academic information. Thus, when teaching Chinese to illiterate workers and peasants in Hunan, Mao on one occasion began by writing the characters for "hand" and "foot." He then asked the students to ponder over the fact that although all wealth and power in the world are created with the hands of the workers and peasants they do not receive the wealth they create. Although both rich and poor have legs to walk with, when the rich go out they are carried by workers and peasants in sedan chairs or rickshaws.[9] This approach infused political concepts into the curriculum in a form digestible and understandable to workers and peasants and became more developed during the Kiangsi and Yenan periods.

From 1930 to 1934 the soviet areas in south China grew in size and importance as did Mao's position as leader of these guerilla-base areas. It was at this time that genuine curricular revision took place as Mao and the CCP were forced to devise materials related to the needs of the rural peasantry while still attempting to cope with the major pedagogical problem of this period—illiteracy. Earlier Mao had acquired some experience in this respect in the educational program of the Red Army which was composed primarily of illiterate peasants. Because of the mobile nature of the soldier-students in the literacy classes of the Red Army, Mao suggested that the political department of the Party be given an entirely free hand to compile whatever texts they felt would best serve the needs of teaching the soldiers the fundamentals of the Chinese language. These could consist of commercial texts, the more traditional "thousand character" books, or any materials thought suitable for class use.[10] This attempt to revise on an ad hoc basis continued following the establishment of the Kiangsi Soviet in 1931.

The new educational administrative apparatus and the diverse school system in the soviet areas (consisting of evening schools, part-time schools, and regular day-time schools) presented a fundamentally changed environment for the CCP and Mao. In light of these circumstances and with little previous experience in educational matters, curricular revision was carried out in a singularly unorganized manner. In recognizing that the primary educational goal was to raise literacy levels Mao suggested that the standard curriculum of both the traditional Chinese school and the modern school be abandoned and that in their place teachers and educational authorities adopt whatever materials would best serve the needs of eliminating illiteracy. For this purpose, newspapers, posters, youth books, children's books, and books compiled by the students themselves were all to be used if the peasants found them interesting.[11] One of the primary goals for Mao in compiling textual literature was that they be simple in format and concise in content.[12] The Kiangsi period failed in many respects to carry out a sustained program of curricular revision, but Mao's basic approach to problems related to curricular reform and revision date from this time.[13] Following the move to Yenan in 1934—1935 Mao devoted more attention to this question and the beginnings of what could truly be called a curricular development program emerged.

The Yenan Period: 1935-1949

The more complete educational system in Northwest China (cf. Chapter Five) demanded a more serious approach in coming to terms with the three curricular questions mentioned above. Mao Tse-tung provided the theoretical guidelines in this endeavor, but the merging of theory with practice was not always smooth.

The question as to who should control the development of the curriculum was related to the general mass-line concept in governmental administration: from the masses and to the masses. Yet, with regard to educational materials very often the educational organs acted without consulting local needs. This approach was criticized by educational authorities under Mao, and it was suggested that it produced an anti-educational bias on the part of the peasantry. Since they lacked control over curriculum and felt that the materials did not have any practical benefit, they did not encourage their children to attend the schools. However, by actively involving the local people in the formation of policy and materials it was felt that they would then take a more positive interest in the development and growth of education in the border regions: "Regarding the system, content, etc. of education in the popular-management primary schools, the opinions of the masses should be respected. . . . Course curricula may be accommodated to the desires of the people, and those courses that for the time being are not urgently required may be abolished."[14] The government further suggested that it was not necessary nor desirable to have a uniform curriculum and that this question should be decided by the local regions. If the peasants wanted to use older, traditional texts (i.e., *Miscellaneous Character Book*, *Hundred Names Book*, etc.), then those group engaged in textbook revision should utilize old forms but with a revised contemporary content.[15]

The practical question, of course, concerned actual course offerings. What did Mao consider to be an adequate curriculum

Fig. 15. Peasants, teachers, and students discuss textbook compilation.

during this period? His general policy for education centered around the overall task of resisting the Japanese invasion and this meant that the Party and government: "Change the existing education system and curriculum and put into effect a new system and curriculum aimed at resisting Japan and serving the nation."[16] The other dimension of this general policy related to the Second United Front formed with the Nationalist government in late 1936. Mao stressed that the educational policy, including the curriculum, be formulated in a fundamentally different manner than during the stage of the agrarian revolution (Kiangsi period). Mao termed as "ultra-leftist" those cadre who insisted that the main content of education be designed to promote communism.[17] However, curriculum development was strongly related to Mao's Marxist ideology; he viewed the entire realm of knowledge in class terms:

> Ever since class society came into being the world has had only two kinds of knowledge, knowledge of the struggle for production and knowledge of the class struggle. Natural science and social science are the crystalization of these two kinds of knowledge, and philosophy is the generalization and summation of the knowledge of nature and the knowledge of society.[18]

Having thus categorized subject matter in these terms Mao next suggested that two additional inputs into the curriculum included learning political theory and combining academic instruction with practical, manual labor:

> In ancient times the youth of China who studied under a sage neither learned revolutionary theory nor took part in labor. Today there is little revolutionary theory taught and there are no such things as production movements in the schools over vast regions of our country. It is only here in Yenan and in the anti-Japanese base areas behind the enemy lines that the young people are fundamentally different.[19]

As for the major emphasis of the curriculum Mao continued to view literacy-training as a fundamental task of the school system. He had moved beyond his earlier concern of replacing the literary language with *pai-hua* and now questioned whether the system of Chinese characters could survive: "Sooner or later, we believe, we will have to abandon the Chinese character altogether if we are to create a new social order in which the masses fully participate."[20]

Nevertheless, Mao suggested that from one-quarter to one-third of total school time be devoted to literacy, reading, and composition. The remaining work was to be in the fields mentioned above of the natural and social sciences including philosophy.[21]

Equally important to Mao was curriculum design and the format in which the material was finally presented to the student. Mao himself had contributed to the writing of a textbook on the history of the Chinese revolution and the growth of the CCP. The style employed by Mao in one of the chapters written entirely by him can be taken as a model of the style he preferred for text writing in general. The chapter was written in a simple style, employing uncomplicated sentence structure (unlike some of Mao's other writings), limited vocabulary, and clear concise organization of data.[22] In preparation of texts and other written material Mao was cognizant of the educational and cultural level of the people to whom it was presented. Although literacy levels had greatly increased in the Border Regions due to the extensive educational efforts of the Border Region government and the CCP, many of the peasants had a minimum level of literacy in comparison with the intellectuals who were writing most of the educational materials. Mao criticized those cadres and intellectuals who continued to write in a style which was overly long, complicated, and full of empty rhetoric. He realized that if education and political understanding were to be grasped by the peasantry (and eventually the equally illiterate urban working-class) writing styles had to be concise, clear, and to the point.[23]

Apart from writing style one of the major problems Mao noted in the presentation of course materials concerned the tendency of both writers and teachers to concentrate more on theoretical presentation rather than on practical application. His experience in Hunan province and later in the Kiangsi Soviet had convinced him that the peasantry did not accept education readily unless it could be related to their immediate needs. Furthermore, Mao felt that it was pedagogically undesirable to produce students who had only learned theories without learning the techniques of utilizing theory in practice.[24] Teachers in Yenan quite often were especially guilty of separating theory from practice:

> In the schools . . . teachers of philosophy do not guide students to study the logic of the Chinese revolution; teachers of economics do not guide them to study the characteristics of the Chinese economy; teachers of political science do not guide them to study the tactics of the Chinese revolution. . . .

> Thus a perverse mentality has been created among many students; instead of showing an interest in China's problems and taking the Party's directives seriously, they give all their hearts to the supposedly eternal and immutable dogmas learned from their teachers.[25]

Mao's approach to preparation and presentation of teaching materials was directly related to his perception of the needs of the students to whom such materials were directed; political implications were also a major consideration.

Nowhere did Mao make more clear these two major concerns (intended audience and political orientation of textual materials) than during the course of a forum on literature and art held in Yenan in May, 1942.[26] Mao suggested that literature and art, like all subject matter, have specific functions which must be understood by those individuals engaged in producing such materials. The first important factor concerned the question of social class—who is the material intended for? Mao's answer is consistent with his Marxist ideology—the proletariat and peasant masses. Artists and writers therefore were inveighed to learn "the language of the masses" and work with them in order to understand how to write and create for them.[27] Intellectual workers were also to study and attempt to understand the theories of Marxism—Leninism so that their work would contain the correct "world-view" and political orientation. Finally, artists and intellectuals faced the task of coming to terms with the academic level of their works. Should priority be given to raising standards or to popularization? Mao indicated that there should definitely be an emphasis on popularization so that workers and peasants would relate to the materials produced. On the other hand, there should be a continual attempt to raise standards from the existing level of the workers and peasants to one which would complement the goals of creating a new socialist man. Art and literature, as well as other intellectual endeavors, should not seek to become the bastions of a new elite but rather should draw their inspiration from the masses and be produced by and for the masses.[28] Mao summed up his views on the relation of politics to culture and art (including education) as follows: "In the world today all culture, all literature and art belong to definite classes and are geared to definite political lines. There is in fact no such thing as art for art's sake, art that stands above classes or that which is detached from or independent of politics."[29] In short, practical needs were to be satisfied against the background of socialist ideology. Mao's answers to the three curricular questions posed at the beginning of this chapter could be summarized as follows: The mass-line concept of "from the masses, to the masses" ought to be the guiding principle in determining who controlled curriculum development. As for content, the primary thrust of the curriculum ought to focus on literacy education and labor education with substantial offerings in the natural and social sciences. In preparing and presenting course materials those in charge ought to adopt a simple and concise style emphasizing the unity of theory and practice.

What form did the curriculum of the Yenan school system take? As late as 1944 it was officially reported that serious problems remained precisely in this area. A report issued at this time criticized the failure of the school authorities to come to terms with the needs of the masses and their failure to solve the problems (discussed by Mao in the *Yenan Forum on Literature and Art*) of whom to educate and control of the curriculum. The report also decried the uncritical imitation of Western curricular forms; especially those of the United States.[30] The report echoed Mao's flexible approach in determining the nature of curricula by declaring that it ". . . must be decided in the light of conditions in the various base areas, the composition of the student body, and the nature and format of the schools; a fixed course schedule is of no value."[31] Other suggestions included trimming the curriculum by eliminating unnecessary courses and shortening others, adding new courses of a practical nature and organizing the entire curriculum around a core of reading, writing, and accounting (arithmetic).[32]

The actual curriculum that eventually emerged was in fact very close to that suggested by Mao and the official report. It was determined fairly democratically with mass organizations participating and students taking an active role. The basic emphasis was on literacy and mathematics as well as such practical subjects as "border region construction" and first aid. Four special characteristics were listed which related to the new curriculum: (1) the practical nature of it—courses were cut from a previous high of ten and twenty to a total of eight; (2) the simplicity and streamlined nature of course offerings; (3) the concentration of subject matter to provide for more detailed study; (4) the integration of subject matter and course presentation so that they fit together in a meaningful pattern.[33] A similar situation prevailed in the organization of higher education curriculum.[34]

Mao Tse-tung's concept of curricular development thus developed over a forty-year period from a vocal dissatisfaction with traditional Chinese education and the turn-of-the-century attempts to modernize the curriculum (resulting in an unwieldy imitation of the West), to a form of curricular revision during the Yenan period. The latter stage clearly showed a sustained effort on the part of the CCP and Mao to consistently improve (in their own terms) the teaching-learning process. Mao began to move in a direction (which became more developed following the establishment of the People's Republic in 1949) of placing more emphasis on the meaning of information than on the acquisition or transmission of data. Part of the reason for this orientation was related to the deprived conditions of the Border Region and the constant need to innovate and create in the area of curriculum and instruction. The inevitable conflict between those who favored technological hardware in the learning process and those concerned with method was to come in the next two decades.

The People's Republic of China: 1949-1973

With the establishment of the People's Republic in 1949 the question of curricular development assumed new proportions. A variety of textbooks had to be provided for all levels of education and the new political stance of the government had to replace that of the previous regime in the curriculum. The flexibility of the Yenan Period which allowed diversity in the writing of texts and curricular units largely disappeared in the early years of the People's Republic. The position of Mao Tse-tung on this question appears clearly only during the Great Leap Forward (1958) and the Cultural Revolution (1966). From his statements during these two critical periods it seems likely that he maintained earlier (pre-1949) views on curricular development. The three questions posed above concerning the control, content, and format of curricular development are again considered by Mao but in less detail. In any case, it is possible to see the continuation of the conflict between professional, centralized curricular development and Mao's inclination to favor programs which involved decentralization and practicality.

Curriculum and the Great Leap Forward

The uncomplicated, practical, and flexible primary school curriculum developed during the Yenan period (emphasizing literacy, mathematics, and science) continued during the 1950s. A major difference, however, was the inclusion of Soviet materials

FIG. 16. A high school lecture in modern Chinese history.

and textbooks, some of which were directly translated without revision into Chinese. Secondary education, on the other hand, developed into a very heavy curriculum involving over thirty class periods (fifty minutes) per week and including such subjects as plane, solid, and analytical geometry; trigonometry; geography; and foreign languages..[35] Examinations were difficult at this level (including an entrance exam) and the result was a dual-track system whereby only the academic elite entered the regular secondary school. The majority of students who could enter school were forced to seek post-primary training in one of the numerous varieties of vocational-technical schools. This of course represented a clear departure from the universal, polytechnical dimension of education discussed by both Marx and Mao. The exact content and nature of the curriculum especially at the secondary level was determined by the Ministry of Education in Peking and communicated to the provincial and county educational authorities.[36] Thus, decision-making with regard to curricular development was highly centralized with strong controls exerted by professional pedagogues and administrators.

As with other areas of educational administration it is likely that Mao was unhappy with the degree of centralization that had taken place with respect to curricular development. Decision-making in Peking, translations from Soviet texts, and a heavy secondary curriculum were all at odds with Mao's experiences prior to 1949. In the year immediately prior to the Great Leap Forward (1957) Mao traveled to various cities in China and saw the state of education firsthand. He was dissatisfied with the fact that textbooks were uniformly compiled in Peking and suggested that (specifically referring to agricultural texts) the individual provinces take charge of textbook compilation.[37] Mao was again fearful that education was becoming divorced from the practical needs of local regions and that this was true in the content of academic texts as well: "Material of instruction should bear a local character and some more local or indigenous teaching material should be used. . . . Some indigenous literature should be taught and this also applies to natural science."[38]

Mao also recognized several problems in the political orientation of instructional materials:

> Recently there has been a falling off in ideological and political work among sutdent and intellectuals, and some unhealthy tendencies have appeared. . . . It seems as if Marxism was once all the rage but is currently not so much in fashion. To counter these tendencies we must strengthen

> our ideological and political work. Both students and intellectuals should study hard. But in addition to the study of their specialized subjects, they must make progress both ideologically and politically which means they should study Marxism, current events, and political problems. Not to have a correct political point of view is like having no soul.[39]

The relationship between politics, theory, and practice, and mental and manual labor was extremely important to Mao who saw the ideal combination realized in some form of polytechnical education. It is not surprising then that immediately before and during the Great Leap Forward he urged both rural and urban primary and secondary schools to revise their curriculum to provide for a more politically oriented polytechnical education. Students in the rural areas were encouraged to work with the agricultural cooperatives and take part in production at least part of the day. Urban students were either to set up their own factories or work in existing factories in order to complement conventional academic subjects with skill-training. This was to be universal for all schools and posed a direct threat to the existing dual-track system.[40] Universities and colleges were to do likewise and those with extra land were to set up farms where students and teachers could take part in agriculturally related labor.[41] In short, at all levels Mao stressed the need to revise the curriculum to provide for "the integration of education with productive labor."[42] The result of these reforms would have produced a more decentralized method of textbook compilation, a revolutionized content and format designed for practical needs, and the integration of theory with practice. As with Mao's other reforms, his suggestions for the curriculum were largely ignored following the setbacks of the Great Leap Forward. By 1960 the dual-track once again emerged complete with the kind of curriculum characteristic of the pre-Great Leap period. It was necessary, it seemed, to have another revolution to bring about the kind of educational program Mao desired.

Curriculum and The Cultural Revolution

By 1964 Mao Tse-tung was unequivocally critical of the status of curriculum development. On the eve of a renewed effort by the PLA to encourage the study of the "thoughts of Mao Tse-tung" (during which the famous "little red book" of quotations from

Mao Tse-tung was published) Mao leveled his strongest criticism yet of the curricula at every level of the schooling cycle:

> There are too many courses of study at present. They are harmful to people and cause the students of middle and primary schools and universities to lead a strained life every day. Myopia has been on the increase every day because of poor equipment and lighting. Half of the courses of study may be dropped away. Confucius taught only the six arts-propriety, music, archery, charioteering, poetry, and writing—but his teaching brought forth four great men of virtue—Yen, Tseng, Tzu and Meng. It won't do for students to go without cultural recreation, swimming and sports. . . . One cannot read too many books, Marxist books should be studied but we also cannot read too many of them. . . . Should one read too many of them, one would proceed to the negative side and become a bookworm or a revisionist.[43]

The points raised above are surprisingly similar to those Mao identified in 1917 as being the weaknesses of the school system he attended. This kind of general criticism continued throughout 1964 and 1965. Mao concentrated on several themes—examinations, lack of physical exercise in the curriculum, and number of hours spent in class (Mao suggested that one-third of all activities be cut from the curriculum).[44]

In November, 1965, the historian and Vice—Mayor of Peking, Wu Han, came under attack and the first salvos of the Cultural Revolution were heard in China. As political tensions increased, Mao stepped up the level of criticism of the educational system especially with regard to curriculum. Mao concurred with a student who suggested that liberal arts students go to work either in the rural areas or in industry and indicated that spending some time engaged in agricultural production might be the most important measure that could be taken to broaden and make more practical the scope of the curriculum.

> We must contact reality gradually, and work in the countryside for a few years in order to learn something about agriculture, botany, soil, fertilizer, science, bacteriology, forestry, water conservation, etc. It is not necessary to learn too much of these subjects; a little knowledge of them will do us good.[45]

The colleges of arts were specific targets for reform, and Mao specified that especially in this area students should "go to the lower levels to work in industry, agriculture, and commerce."[46] The polytechnical schools were, according to Mao, in less need of such reform because of the intrinsically practical nature of their curriculum. However, they were encouraged to have their own workshops and laboratories "where they can rest and put what they have learned to practice."[47]

One specific feature of the organization of course work that irritated Mao was the examination system both in the secondary and post-secondary levels of schooling. In a pungently critical manner, Mao attacked the very basis of the examination system:

> Examinations at present are like tackling enemies, not people. They are surprise attacks, full of catch questions. They are nothing but a method of testing official stereotyped writing. I disapprove of them and advocate wholesale transformation.[48]

Specifically, Mao felt that examinations that were designed simply to test the student's ability to parrot back to his instructor the latter's own ideas or some official position did not test the student's overall abilities. Instead, greater importance should be attached to the student's ability to grasp and solve practical problems. Or, in other words, "One should not just walk after one's teachers without developing one's own initiative."[49] As during his Yenan days Mao saw little utility in following rigid, stereotyped practices in writing style, curriculum, or instruction.

What guidelines should be followed then to effect a genuine curricular reform program? In the first place, Mao felt that all written instructional material ought to be written in a "practical" style in order to attract the largest audience, rather than a "textbook" style which would only be read by those in specific fields.[120] Secondly, Mao suggested that all teaching materials undergo extensive editing to abridge and simplify the content. The desired result was to cut the bulk of the curriculum by one-third to one-half by simply eliminating "teaching material which is erroneous or repetitious. . . ."[51] In many instances, this directive meant that textbooks which had been uncritically translated from either Russian or Western texts directly into Chinese be reedited to provide a closer fit with actual conditions in China.[52] Another way to cut down on the content of textbooks was to eliminate those topics that could be learned in a practical manner either by

Fig. 17. High school students display their English language papers.

experimentation or during field trips. This process was easier for the technical schools to realize and Mao suggested that they establish workshops to this end. As for the social sciences Mao indicated that it would be difficult to set up specific workshops for this purpose and instead suggested that students of literature, history, economics, etc. "take the whole of society as [a] workshop."[53] Students were encouraged to get involved in community affairs, concentrate on current sociological and historical problems, and learn as much as possible from their own experiences.[54]

One final dimension of curricular reform concerned the relationship of subject matter to politics and political struggle. Mao had discussed this at length in Yenan but felt a need to reaffirm his basic position on this subject. He encouraged students to participate in the political struggles currently underway (specifically the Socialist Education Movement in 1964 and the Cultural Revolution in 1966): "The class struggle is a principal subject for you. Your college should go to the countryside to carry out the four cleanups campaign [*ssu-ch'ing* or Socialist Education Movement] and to the factories to carry out the five-anti campaign. . . . [if] you know nothing about the class struggle, how can you be considered as university graduates?"[55]

An official directive of the Central Committee in 1966 sanctioned most of the curricular reform proposals advanced by Mao both before and during the GPCR and the task of reconstructing the school system began.[56] Since 1968, when schools finally reopened, the individual schools have been experimenting with new programs designed to more closely approximate those advocated by Mao. The schooling cycle of both primary and secondary education has been shortened and the curriculum trimmed and simplified. Politics has assumed a more important role, and control of the curriculum is locally based. The university cycle has also been reduced and significant curricular reform is underway. Books are being rewritten by the schools themselves and productive labor has been introduced into the curriculum at all levels. Examinations either have been eliminated or fundamentally altered.[57] In short, curricular reform and development are being pursued simultaneously in China along the lines laid down by Mao Tse-tung both before and after the establishment of the People's Republic of China in 1949.

The organization of the curriculum in China has been a major feature in both the successes and failures of the Chinese educational system since 1949. The degree to which it can provide an adequate training program for China's developmental and political needs will in a significant way determine the future course of China's educational revolution.

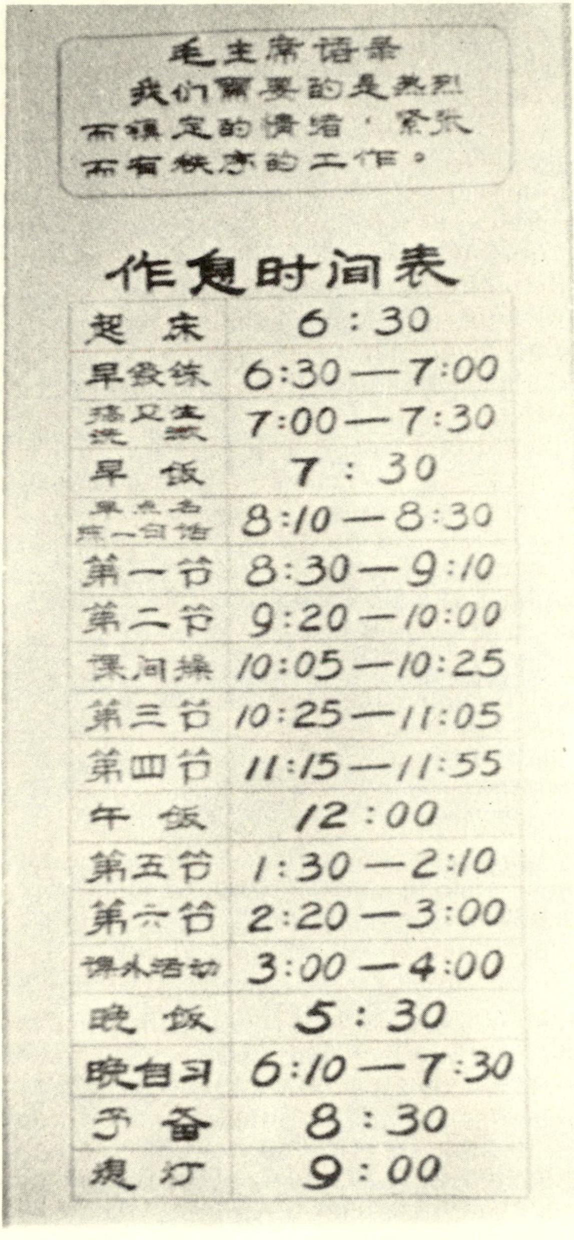

FIG. 18. Daily class schedule for deaf-mute school in Peking.

7 MAO TSE-TUNG ON TEACHERS, STUDENTS AND INTELLECTUALS

Hand in hand with companions we used to come; vivid yet
Those salient months and years;
Young then we were, school mates,
At life's full flowering, filled
With the scholar's enthusiasms,
Criticising without let:
Advice on national affairs,
Exhortation or exposure with the written word:
Truly as dung those mighty warlords in our eyes;
Remember still
How we, venturing midstream, struck the waves
And impeded the swift sails?—Mao Tse-tung
["Ch'angsha [1925]," trans. in *Poems of Mao Tse-tung* (Hong Kong: Eastern Horizon Press, 1966), pp. 2-4.]

MAO TSE-TUNG HAS ALWAYS felt a great affinity for both students and teachers; his own student days were memorable and he served for one year as director of a teacher's college in 1920. Yet, it is precisely the students and intellectuals who have received some of the most severe criticism from Mao. Mao's vision of a socialist China recognized the need for an educated citizenry with the necessary social and technical skills to bring about a

Fig. 19. Mao chats informally with students.

society built upon the principles of Marxism—Leninism. However, in the early period of the CCP the intellectuals and students were primarily products of either traditional Chinese education or the new "modern" Western schools, which in Mao's view left them tainted with bourgeois tendencies. Mao needed them to serve as the corps to aid in building a new educational system (which would eventually produce a new socialist-intellectual) but distrusted the schools because of their obvious ideological shortcomings. These two sentiments of recognizing the worth and need of students and intellectuals while at the same time criticizing their world outlook and mentality characterize Mao's approach to this problem during the years prior to and following the establishment of the People's Republic of China.

The Early Years—The Kiangsi Soviet: 1917-1934

As a young student Mao was caught up in the vigorous activities of the time and naturally identified with the student protests occurring in many parts of China. That he was still influenced by traditional student-teacher relations is evident from a letter he and a classmate wrote in 1917 to a Japanese supporter of Sun Yat-sen considered by Mao to be a revolutionary (Miyazaki Toten).[1] However, Mao was very much in the mainstream of student politics and as such extremely critical of teacher-student conditions. Not yet a Marxist, most of Mao's criticism concerned existing educational realities and the lack of articulate organization to rectify the situation. In an article in 1919 Mao urged many sectors of Chinese society to form "unions" (*lien-ho*) in order to further their ends, and this held true for students and teachers as well. The plight of students was especially critical according to Mao. They were humiliated at the hands of arrogant professors, they were forced to study within the confines of poor facilities ("The windows in our classroom are so tiny that the light does not reach the blackboard, so that we become nearsighted. The desks are extremely ill-adapted and if we sit in them for very long we get 'curvature of the spine.' "[2]) and were forced to study meaningless materials. Mao's contempt for the overemphasis on classical studies shows clearly when he suggested that the writings of Confucius are nothing more than: ". . . a lot of stinking, corpse-like dead writings . . . ."[3] Mao concluded that the students could solve their dilemma by forming a union and engaging in "self-instruction."[4] Mao himself, of course, was a primary school teacher and was particularly aware of the problems facing this educational group. Again, the major emphasis was on the poor conditions and facilities available to teachers in the Ch'angsha area. The teachers had neither study facilities nor organizations to help them upgrade their knowledge nor were there places for them to relax in their spare time. The curriculum was set in such a way that the teachers could not innovate or create new methods of transmitting knowledge. Instead, according to Mao, teachers simply". . . turn into phonographs, doing nothing all day long but putting on a performance of the lectures correctly transmitted which the teachers of former days taught to us."[5] Finally, salaries were low and corruption rife in the educational administrative structure. This situation forced teachers to live separately from their families and thus deprived their students of models of social behavior.[6]

An important consideration for educators has always been the social status of teachers and the relationship between teachers and politics. Mao first came to terms with this problem shortly following his adoption of Marxism as a guiding ideology. In his analysis of classes in the Hunan countryside Mao classified intellectuals, students, primary and secondary teachers as members of the petty bourgeoisie; a class which vacillates with regard to revolutionary demands and therefore can not totally be relied upon.[7] While this analysis categorized them generally, in specific terms Mao realized that trustworthy or not they were necessary for the construction of a new educational system and for the struggle against illiteracy in the new Soviet government in Kiangsi. Mao encouraged the Party and government to provide for the livelihood of the teachers both in terms of food and lodging.[8] Part of the Soviet cultural policy articulated by Mao entreated the cadres to work with intellectuals: "In order to educate worker-peasant intellectuals and in order to develop culture and education we must utilize the landlord-bourgeois intellectuals who serve the Soviet—this is also a Soviet cultural policy that can not be ignored."[9] Thus, intellectuals and teachers formed a social class not totally trusted by the Party and new Soviet government but, nevertheless, a class able to play a constructive role in the revolution.

The relationship between teachers and students also involves the teaching methods of the teachers on the one hand and the study habits of students on the other. Mao has always had strong ideas on curriculum and presentation of materials (see Chapter Six) and as a student-teacher in 1917 (teaching in the worker

FIG. 20. Students form study groups in Peking.

evening school he established) he became more explicit in this regard based on his own teaching experience: "Lecture notes should contain a few simple sentences and should not be distributed at once. Just make known the spirit of the lectures, and it will be sufficient to read over the lecture notes once in the end. I feel that the teaching of current history with this method is much more lively."[10] A simple, down-to-earth teaching style was always favored by Mao and thought to be the best method to aid students in grasping the material. He carried these ideas to the Kiangsi Soviet region and in 1929 expanded on them by listing ten points that all teachers were to follow in their educational work:

1. Resort to the method of enlightenment (abolish inculcations);
2. Proceed from the short-range to the long-range;
3. Proceed from the superficial to the deep;
4. Speak in popular language;
5. Be explicit;
6. Make what you say interesting;
7. Aid speech with gesticulation;
8. Review concepts taught last time;
9. Utilize an outline;
10. Utilize discussion groups.[11]

This check-list would serve as a good general guide for any teacher, and although many of the points raised by Mao appear to be common sense, seldom are they practiced even today.

For all his criticism of Chinese classical education Mao did respect one aspect of this tradition; the closeness of teachers and students. The advent of the modern school sullied the relationship between students and teachers to the point that ". . . teachers and students do not have any affection for each other. The teachers cherish only money, the students only the diploma; to trade one for the other, to give and receive instruction is merely like a market place!"[12] This criticism sounds surprisingly modern. Mao realized that teaching method and the study habits of the students were closely related. If the teacher was cast in the role of being a cold, authority figure, student disaffection and alienation would certainly result. An attempt to avoid this problem was experimented within the Kiangsi Soviet where students were put in charge of discipline problems (such as truancy) thus removing the teachers and other educational authorities from performing this unpopular task.[13]

In short, the ideal teacher and student became one who could relate to the needs of the peasantry and serve the cause of the revo-ution.[14] These factors weighed heavily for Mao in determining whether or not a teacher or educated student could be trusted within the revolutionary ranks. One practical method of demonstrating enthusiasm for the revolution was the degree to which the intellectuals were willing to engage in productive, manual labor.[15] This requirement has continued up to the present to be a main ingredient in assessing the revolutionary potential of teachers and students. The move to Yenan, however, and subsequent political developments required of Mao a shift in emphasis with regard to the treatment and utilization of teachers and students.

The Yenan Period: 1935-1949

Mao Tse-tung's earlier assessment of intellectuals and students and their role in the Chinese revolution was not sufficient to meet the needs of the larger, more complex base area in Yenan, as well as the increasingly complicated political situation within China. Mao gave serious thought to the position of intellectuals in Chinese society and expressed his conclusions in two articles written in 1939. The general term "intellectual" (*chih-shih-fen-tzu*) came to mean anyone who had received either a middle school or university education (secondary or university teachers, various professionals, secondary and university students).[16] In terms of social class, intellectuals and students were not considered by Mao to occupy a special category. Rather, they belonged to the broad category of the petty bourgeoisie. The implications of this categorization were several. First, their position in society was considered unstable: ". . . most intellectuals and students are oppressed by imperialism, feudalism, and the big bourgeosie, and live in fear of unemployment or of having to discontinue their studies."[17] Second, Mao felt that because of the insecurity of their lives and because of their high level of education (albeit bourgeois education) intellectuals were able to grasp radical ideas and play a leadership role in the Chinese revolution: "[Intellectuals] . . . often play a vanguard role or serve as a link with the masses in the present stage of the revolution . . . . In China it was among the intellectuals and young students that

Marxist—Leninist ideology was first widely disseminated and accepted."[18] Mao's political training recognized the necessary relationship between intellectuals and the masses of people in successfully carrying out a political and social revolution. At the same time he realized the weaknesses of the intelligentsia and their tendency to waver and vacillate politically:

> But the intellectuals often tend to be subjective and individualistic, impractical in their thinking and irresolute in action until they have thrown themselves heart and soul into mass revolutionary struggles, or made up their minds to serve the interests of the masses and become one with them . . . not all of them will remain revolutionaries to the end. Some will drop out of the revolutionary ranks at critical moments and become passive, while a few may even become enemies of the revolution. The intellectuals can overcome their shortcomings only in mass struggles over a long period.[19]

Mao's approach to teachers and students was framed within the general approach to intellectuals outlined above.

Socio-Political Role

As the struggle with the Japanese became more critical Mao and the CCP began to consider more seriously the feasibility of forming a second United Front with the KMT government of Chiang Kai-shek. As events moved in this direction, Mao's emphasis on the political role of teachers and students followed a parallel course. Mao noted the urban protests by teachers and students who were encouraging the government (KMT) to oppose Japanese aggression. He suggested that the CCP unite with progressive students and teachers and criticized those cadres who according to Mao were mechanically applying Marxism—Leninism to exclude intellectuals from the revolutionary movement.[20] Following the Sian Incident in 1936 the second United Front was formed with the KMT and Mao increasingly encouraged intellectuals and students to join in the struggle while at the same time urging the various CCP organs to actively recruite intellectuals and to soften their attitude toward the weaknesses Mao had earlier discussed with regard to students and teachers.[21] Special mention was also made of the progressive leadership role educated women could and should play in the revolution.[22] The Party policy toward students and teachers thus followed the overall political policy of the United Front.

Intellectuals and students were actively involved during the rectification campaign (1942-1944). Mao attempted to clarify further the relationship between this social group, the Party, and the revolution.[23] This was a period of intensive education in the fundamentals of Marxism—Leninism and Mao's thought; many teachers and students were exposed to these ideas for the first time. In attempting to utilize class analysis Mao encountered resistance on the part of students and teachers who tended to express themselves in absolutes. In response to inquiries regarding such concepts as "human nature" Mao replied:

> Is there such a thing as human nature? Of course there is. But there is only human nature in the concrete, no human nature in the abstract. In class society, there is only human nature of a class character; there is no human nature above classes. We uphold the human nature of the proletariat and of the masses of the people, while the landlord and bourgeois classes uphold the human nature of their own classes, only they do not say so but make it out to be the only human nature in existence.[24]

In this manner Mao hoped to move intellectuals in the direction of thinking in social class terms rather than in the general terms they were accustomed to. Part of the difficulty arising out of the rectification campaign was the inevitable anti-intellectualism it inspired in the peasants, workers, and soldiers who criticized the intellectuals with great relish. To counteract this tendency Mao continued to stress the importance of the intelligentsia and indicated that while they had many bad points they could be rectified by engaging in productive labor.[25] In practical terms, CCP policy toward the intellectuals remained fairly relaxed as local communities retained the authority to hire, fire, and provide for the welfare of their own teachers.[26]

The advent of civil war in 1946 suggested to Mao a parallel with the anti-KMT outburst among urban-based Chinese students and teachers. Mao viewed this as a positive indication that CCP policies and actions were favored by a large and important sector of the population.[27] He continued to stress the importance of winning teachers and students to the side of the revolution and criticized as excessively "left" the policy held by some CCP members excluding intellectuals regardless of their political position:[28]

> We must avoid adopting any adventurist policies towards students, teachers, professors, scientific workers, and ordinary intellectuals. The experience of China's student movement and revolutionary struggles has proved that the overwhelming majority of these people can take part in the revolution or remain neutral; the die-hard counter-revolutionaries are a tiny minority. Our Party should, therefore, adopt a careful attitude towards students, teachers, professors, scientific workers, art workers, and ordinary intellectuals. We should unite with them, educate them and give them posts according to the merits of each case, and only a tiny number of die-hard counter-revolutionaries among them will have to be appropriately dealt with through the mass line.[29]

Furthermore, intellectuals were to be recruited into the various governmental and administrative organs of the Border Region government and represented in the numerous policy-making conferences which were taking place.[30] Intellectuals who came from former landowning families or rich peasant families were to be allowed to aid in governmental work in the base areas, however, they were to be reeducated and not allowed to work in their local districts for fear that they would reestablish themselves, displacing middle-level and poor peasants mass organizations.[31] As victory neared, Party policy and Mao's position with regard to teachers and students continued to be one of acceptance with qualifications. Mao's final warning to the intellectuals during this period was that they should struggle with their individualistic tendencies and break free from their uncritical admiration of foreign governments and their political systems especially those of the United States.[32]

Having thus formulated Party policy toward teachers and students Mao also outlined the specific activities teachers and students could engage in to win the respect of Party members, worker, and peasants. In other words, what distinguished a revolutionary intellectual from a nonrevolutionary intellectual? "Whether or not the intellectuals are willing to form one or are actually integrated with the worker-peasant masses is the dividing line to tell whether they are revolutionary, non-revolutionary, or counter-revolutionary."[33] For Mao knowledge of the revolutionary theories of Marxism—Leninism was not sufficient to classify one as a revolutionary; practical activities received higher priority. Mao especially singled out for criticism students who came to the base areas full of enthusiasm but ignorant of the harsh realities of a peasant revolution. He encouraged students to join with the workers and peasants in their various struggles. Too often, Mao suggested, students talked about revolution but failed to make an active contribution.[34] The emphasis on intellectuals linking up with the masses of Chinese working people (and thereby being reeducated) had to do with Mao's belief that significant knowledge is acquired through practical studies: "[Intellectuals] . . . ought to be aware of the truth that actually many so-called intellectuals are, relatively speaking, most ignorant and the workers and peasants sometimes know more than they do . . . ."[35] Mao was not expressing another form of anti-intellectualism here but rather speaking of a real problem in the Chinese intellectual tradition. Many teachers and students in China even as late as 1940 still carried with them a distaste for any manual labor even if it would further develop their knowledge in a particular field. Mao related how even he as a student thought that " . . . intellectuals were the only clean people in the world, while in comparison workers and peasants were dirty."[36] He gradually came to realize, however, that ". . . the unremoulded intellectuals were not clean and that, in the last analysis, the workers and peasants were the cleanest people, and even though their hands were soiled and their feet smeared with cow-dung, they were really cleaner than the bourgeois and petty-bourgeois intellectuals."[37] This attempt to educate intellectuals to overcome traditional elitist tendencies eventually bore fruit and was a factor in the steps toward modernization taken by the Chinese Communists since 1949.

Those intellectuals who seriously attempted to serve the needs of the revolution, who integrated with workers and peasants and who sought to reform their view of themselves were accorded various benefits from Mao and the CCP. Part of Mao's "Ten-Point National Salvation Program" submitted to the KMT in 1937 included the clause that the government should attempt to improve the working conditions of teachers and students.[38] The same policy held true within the Border Region where the CCP and the government sought to provide school for those students forced to drop out, and work for those teachers who were unemployed.[39] Furthermore, in the course of the land reform movement teachers and students were specifically excluded from having their land confiscated, although many of them came from families in the landlord or rich peasant category.[40] Finally, the practice of allowing diverse opinions to be expressed was upheld by Mao who suggested that ". . . ideas can never be suppressed by force of arms."[41]

Teachers, Students, and the Masses

One theme runs so consistently through Mao Tse-tung's writings on students and teachers that it deserves special mention. Mao's dualistic attitude toward intellectuals (recognizing the need for them while remaining cautious with regard to their ideological makeup) found a form of resolution through Mao's faith in the creative and transformational nature of the masses of workers and peasants. All the shortcomings of intellectuals could be overcome by their integration with the laboring people and by their taking part in productive labor. The intellectuals most in need of such reeducation at the hands of the proletariat (including peasantry) were those who were products of a Western—type education (especially those educated in Europe, America, and Japan) and who in Mao's view did not understand the new culture which, under the leadership of Mao and the CCP, the workers and peasants were creating.[42] Mao did not exclude himself and other communists from the need to learn from the working people, and this attitude, described by some as populist, or voluntarism, has been a fundamental part of Mao's understanding of the concepts—teacher and student: "It has to be understood that the masses are the real heroes, while we ourselves are often childish and ignorant, and without this understanding it is impossible to acquire even the most rudimentary knowledge. . . . It is my wish to go on being a pupil, learning from the masses, together with all other Party comrades."[43] The masses then prove to be among the most significant, effective, and practical teachers for the entire country.

Traditional academic expertise was of course still considered important but only if put to practical use or enriched by practical experience: "How can those who have only book-learning be turned into intellectuals in the true sense? The only way is to get them to take part in practical work and become practical workers, to get those engaged in theoretical work to study important practical problems."[44] The importance of combining theory with practice extended to students as well and Mao criticized those students, recently arrived in Yenan, who concentrated on theoretical knowledge while failing to conduct practical experiments and research.[45] Included in this category were those students who considered themselves revolutionaries and Marxists and whom Mao described derisively as, "seventeen- and eighteen-year-old babies [who were] taught to gnaw on *Capital* and *Anti-Duhring*."[46] Ability to eloquently quote from the Marxist classics did not qualify one as a revolutionary in Yenan; ability to solve practical problems out of a Marxist framework did.

The New Intellectual Worker

It was hoped that a new kind of "intellectual-worker" would result from this struggle between the teachers, students, and masses. Mao Tse-tung, both for practical and ideological reasons, wanted the old intellectuals (meaning those trained in non-Communist schools) to reform their world-view, develop new methods of teaching and research, and above all merge with the social classes they had traditionally avoided—the workers and peasants. All of these desires were consistent with the pedagogical basis of Marxism—combining theory with practice, mental with manual labor (concept of polytechnism), and recognizing the transformational nature of the educative process and the masses.

In attempting to communicate these ideals to the students and teachers Mao made use of individuals who could serve as models for others to emulate. In a significant letter to a former teacher Mao outlined the qualities he felt a good teacher should possess:

> You were my teacher twenty years ago. You are still my teacher and you surely will still be my teacher in the future. When the revolution failed [1927] many Communists left the Communist Party and some went over to the enemy side. But you joined the Communist Party in the fall of 1927 and adopted an extremely positive attitude. During the protracted hard and bitter struggle from that time up to now, you have been more energetic than many young and able-bodied people in the matter of defying difficulties and humbly learning new things . . . . You know much, but you think at all times that you do not have enough knowledge. . . . You say and carry out what you have in mind. . . . You are with the masses at all times. . . . . You play everywhere the role of the model in observing the discipline of the Party and the revolution. . . . You give first consideration to the revolution, work and other people. . . . You always choose

FIG. 21. Secondary students learn politics and history.

> the difficult things for yourself and never shun your responsibility. . . . I admire you for all this, and am willing to go on learning from you. I also wish that comrades of the whole Party will learn from you. . . . May you be the model of all revolutionary Party members and the whole people.[47]

For the students, Mao put forth as a model the writer Lu Hsun (see note 44 in Chapter Four). Mao urged the students of the North Shensi Public School to learn from Lu Hsun in being able to put up with difficult material conditions while at the same time acquiring revolutionary theory and academic knowledge. Students should be oriented to and be prepared to sacrifice for the cause of the revolution.[48] The ideal student would be one who was forthright, honest, well-disciplined, humble, and hardworking.[49] Thus, both students and teachers were to follow basically the same set of behaviorial guidelines; guidelines which in the future would create the new intellectual worker.

Toward the end of the Yenan period Mao's view of intellectuals focused on two primary problems which he had considered for almost twenty years. First he knew the intellectuals would play an important role in any final settlement of the impending civil war. As such, they were extremely valuable and were to be treated with respect by the CCP, government officials, and the masses. Second, no matter how skilled or educated an intellectual or student might be he could not avoid the political realities of the time. In Mao's view they would have to "get involved" in some way in order to be truly useful. The apparent dichotomy between political motivation and understanding and academic expertise continued to be a source of friction between Mao and the intellectuals and continued into the post-1949 period.[50]

The People's Republic of China: 1949-1973

In 1949 both Mao Tse-tung and the CCP had to rely initially on whatever educated and skilled personnel was available. As during the Yenan period Mao had to devote considerable attention to maintaining good relations with educated students and intellectuals while at the same time attempting to modify their world outlook and general behavior. With regard to the latter task one of the first actions taken by the Party and government was the launching in 1951 of a "thought reform" movement (*ssu-hsiang kai-tsao*) to communicate to the intellectuals the fundamentals of Marxism—Leninism while at the same time identifying their lack of ideological understanding. Even those intellectuals who considered themselves Marxists fell under fire because of their excessively theoretical approach to Marxism—Leninism and inability to analyze and solve practical problems.[51] As for students and youth in general Mao was much more sympathetic and naturally held higher hopes for their academic and political development:

> Let me say a few words to the young people:
> 1. May they enjoy good health;
> 2. May they learn well;
> 3. May they work well.
>
> New China must care for her youth and show concern for the growth of the younger generation. Young people have to study and work, but they are at the age of physical growth. Therefore, full attention must be paid both to their work and study, and to their recreation, sports, and rest. The young workers and peasants, the educated youth, and the young people in the armed forces are heroic and energetic and well disciplined. Without them the cause of revolution and construction cannot be successful.[52]

In this initial statement Mao's earlier views and attachments to students in particular again found expression. He saw in them the hope of building a new China.[53] Whereas it was necessary to utilize the vacillating older intellectuals, the educated youth of China provided an energetic and active group, many of whom were sympathetic to and had supported the CCP during its struggle in Yenan. As the new government began to organize itself and consolidate its political base, the relationship among all three groups (students, intellectuals, and Party-government) grew in complexity. It was during the two critical periods of the Great Leap Forward and the Great Proletarian Cultural Revolution that Mao's basic views on teachers and students were expressed most clearly. In both periods the two groups played significant roles and Mao's thoughts on teachers and students even became known outside China as rebellious European and American students began quoting "Chairman Mao" as an authority in their own attempts to reform education.

Teachers, Students, Intellectuals and the Great Leap Forward

The early years of the People's Republic were characterized by a series of campaigns (thought reform, three antis, five-antis)[54] all designed to reshape the orientation of the educated groups in China toward socialism and the new government. The "Hundred Flowers" movement of 1957 and the "anti-rightist" campaign which immediately followed both served to reinforce the Party's position vis-a-vis the intellectuals.

On the eve of the Hundred Flowers movement Mao outlined the current state of affairs with regard to the intellectuals. Of the over five million intellectuals Mao estimated that only three percent were completely opposed to Marxism—Leninism and a socialist form of economy and government. Another ten percent were totally in favor of the new government. The remaining majority, according to Mao were either unsure or were adopting a wait-and-see attitude. They agreed with certain policies but disagreed with others. Yet, Mao indicated they should not be stifled in their criticism of the new government:

> There will be people of this sort for a long time to come, and we should allow them to disagree. Take some of the idealists for example. They may support the political and economic system of socialism but disagree with the Marxist world outlook. The same holds true for the patriotic people in religious circles. They are theists and we are atheists. We cannot force them to accept the Marxist world outlook.[55]

In short, Mao identified three kinds of intellectuals: "resolute, wavering, and antagonistic."[56] He concluded that this kind of situation would remain a part of the Chinese social milieu for some time and that eventually the wavering elements would accept Marxism through intensive reeducation efforts. Mao's faith in the power of education reappears at this time, and it is likely that the Hundred Flowers movement was supported by Mao for precisely these reasons.[57]

During the anti-rightist campaign (in which many intellectuals were severely criticized) in June, 1957, Mao further attempted to clarify the Party's policy toward intellectuals and students. He criticized the Party and bureaucracy for performing in an unnecessarily rigid manner and ignoring the needs and demands of the masses. Intellectuals and students, on the other hand, were primarily guilty of individualism. Both groups, Mao suggested, must strive to reeducate themselves to avoid future mistakes. The general policy expressed by Mao at this time consisted basically of praise for the positive contributions of intellectuals and students and at the same time criticism for whatever political and social shortcomings they exhibited at any given time. Specific guidelines tended to concentrate on the social and political role expected of teachers and students and on the relationship between the educated, professional sector of society and the mass organizations.

Socio-political role

What exactly did Mao expect of the students and teachers as they studied and performed other professional duties? Mao has always viewed education in a broad sense and the activities of intellectuals fell within this category. Regardless of the occupation an educated person might hold he was first and foremost an educator: ". . . writers, artists, scientists and technicians, professors and teachers are all educating students, educating the people. Being educators and teachers they themselves must first be educated."[58] Mao's dictum for a good teacher was formulated at this time and continues up to the present: "To be a good teacher, one must first be a good pupil."[59] Because education was singularly important and because teachers and intellectuals occupied such powerful positions in this respect, Mao recognized the need to continually attempt to "educate the educators."

As for students it was expected that they would be diligent in their studies, positive in political orientation, and be willing to return to their native regions to apply their skills upon graduation.[60] During the Great Leap Forward students were introduced to the concept of combining their studies with productive labor. Mao urged all students and teachers at the primary and secondary level to combine theory and practice and mental and manual labor by working either in factories and communes or by establishing their own school-operated workshops.[61] University and college level students were also encouraged to undertake these kinds of activities.[62]

Politically, teachers and other intellectuals were expected to consistently increase their knowledge of Marxism—Leninism and actively engage in political affairs. Mao continued to criticize their lack of understanding of socialism and class dictatorship. Even intellectuals and teachers in the Communist Party were chastised for their weak ideological understanding of Marxism:

FIG. 22. Rural primary students.

> Our Party has a large number of new members who are intellectuals (there are even more such members in the Youth League) and some of them actually possess rather grave revisionist ideology . . . . They appreciate bourgeois liberalism and are opposed to the leadership of the Party. They endorse democracy but are opposed to centralism.[63]

It would seem that many of the problems associated with intellectuals and discussed by Mao during the Yenan period continued to be present during the first decade of the People's Republic. It was clear that further struggles were forthcoming. As for the students, Mao conceded that some political problems were present. There were clearly certain "rightist" tendencies among some students but for the most part Mao suggested that students represented a positive force in Chinese society and that even the rightists should be allowed to continue their studies.[64]

Teachers, students, intellectuals and the masses

Mao Tse-tung's faith in the educational potential of the masses remained part of his program for reeducating intellectuals and the latter were encouraged to ". . . go among the masses, to [the] factories and villages."[65] It was Mao's belief that contact with laboring people (industrial workers and those engaged in agriculture) would serve to educate and broaden the outlook of the professionals who quite often were out of touch with the work-a-day life of people in China. Mao suggested that intellectuals could simply plan to make periodic visits to factories and farms or they could settle down for more sustained periods of time to conduct on-the-spot investigations or in some other way increase their knowledge of Chinese society. He sought to recreate conditions which had existed in the "old days": "We should create an atmosphere in which 'getting close to the workers and peasants' virtually becomes a habit. . . . In the old days when we were in Yenan, the intellectuals were enabled to make direct contact with the workers and peasants."[66]

The differences, of course, between the Yenan period and the People's Republic were considerable. It is possible that others in the Party and government felt Mao to be excessively romantic in his conviction that somehow the relatively uncomplicated conditions of the 1940s could be fashioned again in the 1950s.[67] Yet, Mao continued to stress values he had inherited from an earlier time and the enthusiasm created by the Great Leap Forward strengthened this tendency. Encouraging intellectuals to engage in productive labor or "contact the masses" was a method of de-sanctifying them in the eyes of the ordinary Chinese citizen. It was also a way for intellectuals to prove their support for the ideals of socialism and Mao's thought. To the average Chinese citizen he offered this advice:

> A celebrated person, like a fat pig, is in danger. The celebrities are most backward, most timid, and least creative. Why? Because they have made a name for themselves . . . . Don't be cowed by celebrities and men of great learning. You must dare to think, to speak, and to act. . . .[68]

The Great Leap Forward provided Mao with his first real opportunity to apply values and concepts of the Yenan period to the entire nation of China. His faith in the masses reached new heights and his belief that ". . . the lowly are the most intelligent while the elite are most ignorant . . ." found new forms of expression.[69]

Integrating with the masses was not limited to the higher intellectuals. Students and teachers were also directed to merge theory with practice and make contact with the masses. The students were encouraged to learn from industrial workers how to construct school-run factories and how to combine mental with manual labor. Teachers were to reform the teaching process by bringing into the schools people from the community in order to "concentrate the wisdom of the masses in a number of ways."[70] The result was a broader participation of intellectuals, students, teachers, and mass organizations in the education system of China. The rollback of the policies of the Great Leap Forward temporarily curtailed Mao's program and created the conditions for a future conflict involving students and teachers on an even larger scale.

Teachers, Students, Intellectuals and the GPCR

Mao Tse-tung has recently (1971) stated that he would most like to be remembered simply as a teacher.[71] However, at other times he has stated his desire to ". . . continue to be a schoolboy."[72] Certainly during the Cultural Revolution he sympathized with, and drew support from, the student struggle which broke out in August, 1966. Mao became the teacher par excellence as millions of students went on strike, engaged in more active forms of political struggle, and trooped to Peking to be reviewed by the "Great Teacher, Great Leader, Great Supreme Commander, and Great Helmsman."[73] His decision to mobilize and take sides with rebellious students (and later teachers) was hinted at in 1965 when Mao suggested that there were still too many intellectuals in China who were anti-Marxist and were passing these beliefs on to their children. The vision of apathetic and possibly cynical students was not welcomed by Mao who placed great hopes on the progressive enthusiasm of young people to keep the revolution alive.[74]

Just as Mao had criticized the heavy curriculum, excessive academic pressure, and the examination system, he now leveled equally severe criticism at teaching methods in general.[75] To a group of educators Mao gave the following advice:

> The students should be allowed to doze off when lessons are taught by teachers. Since you are unable to teach well, rather than to require others to listen to your tasteless lectures, it is better for them to doze off and take a rest. The students refuse to listen to you when you just make a lot of noise.[76]

This kind of admonishment was probably not well received by most professional educators, particularly at the university level. Yet, what Mao was suggesting is surprisingly contemporary. Instead of daily lectures Mao urged university professors to have their lecture notes printed and distributed before the class to allow class time for discussion and further clarification. The role of the teacher was to organize and prepare materials on a given subject and to allow students to learn more at their own pace. He noted how "even bourgeois educators had opposed the inculcation method of teaching back in the May Fourth Movement [1919]."[77] While this method differs from "continuous progress learning," it did represent a break from previous instructional practices in China.

Socio-political role

As the political struggle increased in intensity, Mao slowly shifted from proposing reform measures to sanctioning outright rebellion on the part of the students. On the eve of the Cultural Revolution Mao was still encouraging students and teachers to get involved productively in society whether that be in a factory, commercial enterprise, or commune.[78] Graduates of secondary

FIG. 23. A student Red Guard pins an armband on Mao during the Great Proletarian Cultural Revolution.

school were especially urged to work for a few years before considering entering higher education. College students with a few years of study but lacking a degree were also encouraged to "go to the lower levels" to continue their education in productive labor.[79]

With the closing of the schools in the summer of 1966 and the publication of Mao's "big character poster" (*ta-tzu-pao*) *Bombard the Headquarters,* reform efforts gave way to revolution. From the start Mao supported the student strikes and demonstrations but also urged that the students ally with all possible factions within the schools. Even those people who had made "grave mistakes" were to be criticized and then "given a way out."[80] His position with regard to the rebelling students and teachers reinvolved around support and caution. It was not an outright endorsement for an overall changing of the existing order even when Mao criticized members of his own Party and Central Committee for opposing the students.[81] When other sectors of Chinese society resisted the activities of the student Red Guards, Mao continued in his support and issued directives indicating that the student movement should be allowed to run its course.[82] The enthusiasm of the Red Guards at times exceeded Mao's expectations and later erupted into full-scale violence. However, the popularly held view that Mao later put down the students after first supporting them ignores that he always stressed the need for a broad united front against the "handful" of enemies at the top. Some segments of the Red Guards clearly failed to follow Mao's directives and guidelines in this regard.[83]

Toward the end of 1967 the situation had deteriorated into factionalism and it was clear that the movement was in need of change. With the Party in disarray Mao called upon the most disciplined and loyal organization remaining, the army. He indicated that they should take a leading role in reforming education in general and the students and teachers in particular. The PLA was to instruct the students precisely in those areas they were weakest: ideological work, discipline, humility, and hard work.[87] By 1968 most schools had reopened and students were back in attendance. The factionalism had been curtailed and the administrative pattern of three-in-one committees was being put into effect. The next major problem for teachers and students concerned reeducation for those who had failed to follow Chairman Mao's instructions correctly and had consequently led others astray in the GPCR. Characteristically, Mao turned to the "masses" to perform this latter task.

Teachers, students, intellectuals and the masses

Going to the masses as an educational experience assumed new proportions during the GPCR. In 1964 while speaking to a group of Nepalese educators Mao assigned greater importance than ever before to the need for teachers and students to learn from the common people of China:

> Strength comes from the masses. Without reflecting the demands of the masses nobody is equal to his job. One should learn knowledge from the masses, lay down policies and after that go back to educate the masses. Therefore, in order to be a teacher, one should first be a pupil. No teacher is not a pupil first. Furthermore, after becoming a teacher, one also must learn from the masses in order to understand how he stands in his own studies. That is why there are two branch of science—psychology and education—in the science of education. Those who have no knowledge of reality will be unable to apply what they have learned.[85]

The combining of theory with practice and mental and manual labor is reflected in this statement but always in relation to the interaction between the highly skilled and the laborers. This would seem to be the formula for the complete education of students and teachers. Pedagogy then consists of changing one's view of reality by interacting with the masses (psychology) and acquiring the more conventional academic tools (education). The essential ingredient, however, continued to be the "masses" who were now encouraged to "handle their own affairs" without relying "merely on the leaders alone"[86]

As students and teachers began to return to the schools in 1968, the call went out for those students and intellectuals who had already received the majority of their education in the "old-style" (pre-Cultural Revolution) schools to begin to integrate themselves with the workers and peasants.[87] Obviously, this action reflected a desire to break up the in-fighting which had been taking place among Red Guard factions within the large, urban universities. The other and more important reason was to reverse the tendency of students to remain in the cities upon graduation even though their skills were desperately needed in the rural areas. The rural-urban dichotomy which plagues so many developing countries was present in China as well in the 1960s and it was Mao Tse-Tung's desire to achieve a reasonable balance in this area. Finally, at the end of 1968 the directive became official and Mao initiated his program to reform the schools and transfer educated personnel to the communes to apply their skills and be reeducated:

> It is absolutely necessary for educated young people to go to the countryside to be reeducated by the poor and lower middle peasants. Cadres and other city people should be persuaded to send their sons and daughters who have finished junior or senior middle school, college or university to the countryside. Let us mobolize. Comrades throughout the countryside should welcome them.[88]

The movement of educated youth to the rural areas appears to be the key element in realizing Mao's goal of creating the "new intellectual worker." Previous attempts had failed to sufficiently impress upon students, teachers, and intellectuals the importance of combining education with productive labor, theory with practice, and the other pedagogical goals expressed by Mao Tse-tung. The professionally skilled sector of Chinese society continued to remain aloof from the industrial working-class and the peasantry and was unable to emulate the models put forth by Mao during the Yenan period. The requirements of industrialization and the shift after 1949 from the rural areas to the cities all adversely affected the relationship between teachers, students and intellectuals, and the masses. The current attempt is to establish a new balance between a rural based, educated corps and the traditional urban intelligentsia.

In a sense, Mao seems to be recreating "the Yenan Way" at least for a significant portion of China's educated youth. The hoped for result would be a new type of intellectual who has mastered the skills of his field, integrated with the laboring people, achieved a high degree of political consciousness and dedication, and acquired the ability to adapt creatively to new conditions. The entire process is meant to represent a major step on the way to the eventual elimination of the conventional division of labor and roles that results in occupational groups such as teachers, students, intellectuals, and workers. Man in short, would be on the way to reaching the ideal expressed by Marx in which his roles could be diversified sufficiently to enable him to "do one thing today and another tomorrow, to hunt in the morning, fish in the afternoon, rear cattle in the evening, criticize after dinner . . . without ever *becoming* hunter, fisherman, shepherd, or critic."[89]

8 MAO TSE-TUNG ON SPECIAL FORMS OF EDUCATION

". . . in our education we must have not only regular primary and secondary schools but also scattered irregular village schools, newspaper-reading groups and literacy classes. Not only must we have schools of the modern type but we must also utilize and transform the old style village schools."—Mao Tse-tung. ["The United Front in Cultural Work (October 30, 1944)," *SW*, III, 235.]

THE GREATER BULK of Mao Tse-tung's pronouncements on education is related to conventional educational forms of a formal nature. Nevertheless, since 1927 both Mao and the CCP have shown considerable interest in the educational potential of society in general and have sought to institute informal educational structures to solve pedagogical problems falling outside the regular school system. These attempts have taken the form of extracurricular schools for adult and continuing education, army education, minority education, and education for members of the Chinese Communist Party. Party and governmental efforts have

FIG. 24. Students, intellectuals, and cadres take part in productive labor.

been considerable in this regard. In the years both before and after the establishment of the People's Republic, Mao's writings on this subject unfortunately are few. There is sufficient information, however, to determine Mao's general orientation to this question, and it is clear that his ideas contributed to final policy formation. Mao's understanding of Marxism—Leninism was a basic factor in his approach to informal education, particularly in such areas as mental and manual labor, school and society, and polytechnical education.

The Kiangsi and Yenan Periods: 1927-1949

Mao's first experience with informal education came after he had become a Communist but before the establishment of the Kiangsi Soviet in 1927. The "Self-Study University" founded by Mao in 1923, and the peasant-operated evening schools Mao observed in 1927, convinced him of the efficacy of certain types of informal education. The "Self-Study University" was to take the form of the traditional Chinese college (*shu-yuan*) combined with the curricular content of the modern, Western-style schools (*hsueh-hsiao*). The distinctive feature, however, was that the students were not compelled to attend class at a special hour or even to take a predefined core of course work. The motto of the school as declared by Mao was, ". . . read by oneself, ponder by oneself, mutually discuss and mutually study."[1] The other feature of this type of school that was very important for Mao (and became an issue forty years later in 1966) was its policy of admitting students without examination or fee. This meant that regardless of social status or previous cultural experience students could enter the school and begin their studies at points parallel to their own educational level.

When Mao toured Hunan province four years later in 1927 he noted the natural dislike expressed by the peasantry toward formal education and their preference for evening schools more related to their own life-style and social and economic needs. Moreover, these schools were to be operated and managed by the peasant associations. Mao's assessment of this rural phenomonon sums up his attitude toward locally operated adult education:

> The development of the peasant movement [to set up peasant evening schools] has resulted in a rapid rise in their cultural level. Before long tens of thousands of schools will have sprung up in the villages throughout the province;

> this is quite different from the empty talk about "universal education" which the intelligentsia and the so-called "educationalists" have been bandying back and forth and which after all this time remains an empty phrase.[2]

Mao expressed little doubt as to his support of informal educational movements organized and operated by the groups involved. He noted their potential for success and the lack of results obtained by total reliance on the more conventional educational establishment.

The consolidation of the base areas in Kiangsi and the growth of Mao's peasant army necessitated another form of educational effort. A peasant army in China was by definition an illiterate army and remained so under the leadership of KMT commanders and other regional commanders. Mao, on the other hand, was convinced of the importance of an educated military and very early set about to establish the pedagogical framework necessary to attack illiteracy within the Red Army. The army was already highly organized and the major responsibility for internal army education lay with the political departments within the PLA. Mao directed that it was their responsibility to compile literacy texts from the scarce materials available. These texts varied in form and sometimes were edited versions of commercial texts, "thousand character" books, or whatever best related to the educational needs of the peasant-soldiers. Each troop unit was to establish a youth-soldier school, divided into three or four classes with no more that twenty-five students per class. The leaders of the political units were to serve as principals and each class was to elect one leading teacher. Funding for these schools was to be provided by the Party and government in order to purchase supplies for the students.[3] It is not known how successful army education was, but various foreign observers commented on the relative high level of literacy of soldiers in the People's Liberation Army in Yenan and outlying rural regions.[4] In any event, it is clear that Mao's desire to spread literacy and general education to broad sectors of the population included rank and file military personnel.

The establishment of schools for the children of peasants from 1927 on was a major step in Chinese Communist educational history. However, the problem remained of massive adult illiteracy which carried with it peasant suspicion of education in general. Mao came to grips with this difficulty by encouraging and supporting a variety of adult education enterprises. The basic unit in this attempt at adult education was the night school where peasants could attend literacy classes following the day's work. The students in these schools were primarily working adults who were either totally illiterate or were only able to recognize a few Chinese characters. Each school had one educated teacher who shouldered the primary teaching responsibility and one principal who was not necessarily literate but possessed superior leadership abilities; he or she (many principals were women) attended classes along with the students. Because of the scarcity of materials the students were to supply their own reading materials. These materials consisted of whatever was most available and included newspapers, children's books, and other easy-to-read forms of literature. In addition to literacy training, techniques of calculation were taught for the purpose of enabling peasants eventually to keep their own village records and statements of financial affairs.[5] Despite the availibility of evening schools there were peasant families who for various reasons could not attend at night. This was a special problem for women who may have had to stay home to watch the children while the husband attended the school or who lived too far from the school. For these peasants Mao suggested and encouraged the establishment of spare-time schools which could be set up any place, at any time, and could have any number of students attend. The students in these classes were told to keep personal notebooks in which they would trace the Chinese characters. They were assisted by a teacher from one of the evening schools. At ten-day intervals the notebooks were turned over to the principal of the evening school who had them checked by a trained teacher and then returned them to the students. Students were expected to learn from 450 to 750 characters in this manner.[6] This approach to the adult population and their peculiar educational needs became a basic part of the Chinese Communist's educational strategy following the establishment of the People's Republic in 1949. Spare-time and part-time education have enormously expanded literacy rates in China, and even during this period of guerrilla activity had a dramatic impact on the centuries-old pattern of rural illiteracy.[7]

An interesting form of extracurricular study that merged the regular school students with the adult community was the club [*chu-le-pu*]. Clubs engaged in a variety of cultural and educational activities such as physical education and writing village newspapers. Mao noted the usefulness of such clubs in raising the cultural level of a village especially through the medium of the wall newspaper, normally put on display in the village primary school and was a joint student-community effort.[8]

Probably the most difficult educational problem the Chinese Communists and Mao had to face concerned the numerous minority groups located in widely separated regions throughout China. While the CCP and Mao had experienced only peripheral contact with these groups, particularly on the "Long March," by the time they had reached Yenan they were aware of the magnitude of the minority question and realized that a rational policy had to be formulated. In China roughly ninety-five percent of the population fall under the category of Han Chinese. The remaining five percent are represented by about fifty groups of minorities. These minorities are based on linguistic rather than racial divisions and in addition differ in various cultural respects (dress, social organization, eating habits, etc.).[9] Although they are numerically small they nevertheless occupy strategically important positions, primarily on China's borders and frontiers. Chinese history is replete with examples of Han-minority antagonisms, and as a result the minorities had generally viewed with suspicion Han efforts to make contact. During the "Long March" the Chinese Communists also experienced the hostility that had characterized these relations for centuries. The "Long March" carried the Chinese Communists and Mao through many minority regions, and the CCP and Mao were able to form some alliances with the various groups because they were being mutually harassed by the same enemy, the Kuomintang.[10] Although Mao's attention had been focused primarily on the educational problems facing the Han Chinese, he was aware that in the future the question of minority education would become increasingly important. Instead of adopting a simplistic approach that would either ignore the minorities or attempt to absorb them into the Han culture Mao suggested a policy revealing his sensitivities to this complex question. He stipulated that the cultural practices and divergent religions of the minorities be respected and preserved. In the field of education he further suggested that the minorities be allowed to receive instruction in their own language rather than the national language (the Peking dialect spoken by most Han Chinese) and that their spoken literature and oral traditions be preserved.[11] This represented a sophisticated and intelligent approach to minority education and ultimately formed the basis for the national program which developed in the 1950s.

Finally, and probably most significantly, Mao stressed the necessity of instituting a vigorous program of internal Party education. The focal point of this educational effort was the Party cadre (*kan-pu*). A Party cadre was anyone who held a responsible position within the Party and as such made decisions affecting others.[12] He was the backbone of the Party and therefore required a special form of educational training. In general, Mao formulated this educational training on two levels: theoretical and practical.[13] Once a cadre achieved literacy, the main purpose of his study was to gain a theoretical and working knowledge of the basic principles of Marxism—Leninism. In addition, courses were given in the Party schools on Chinese history and current affairs. Mao then urged the Party members to utilize their knowledge to help educate those with low levels of schooling or no education at all. He continued to insist that education in general and the study of Marxism—Leninism in particular were of no use if they did not aid the cadre in social change efforts of a practical nature.[14] The cadre's duty and responsibility in this regard were dual: "Complacency is the enemy of study. We cannot really learn anything until we rid ourselves of complacency. Our attitude toward ourselves should be 'to be insatiable in learning' and towards others 'to be tireless in teaching.' "[15] Mao expected of the cadre the highest level of political and practical understanding and saw the need for an ongoing internal education uniting the special skills of the Party-trained official with the basic needs of the local community.[16]

Mao Tse-tung thus recognized a wide range of educational possibilities apart from the formal school system, and while the difficulties of government were tremendous in the Border Region (and thereby limited informal educational attempts) special forms of education were available for many sectors of society. The very lack of facilities forced Mao and the CCP to rely on less conventional means of raising cultural and literacy levels, and this experience contributed greatly to the widespread programs of this nature which followed the installation of a new government in 1949.

The People's Republic of China: 1949-1973

Mao Tse-tung made even fewer references to informal education following the establishment of the People's Republic in 1949 than during the period prior to the seizure of power. This fact unfortunately obscures the considerable importance of these educational forms in providing experimental models which ultimately influenced the more formal educational structure. Much of the

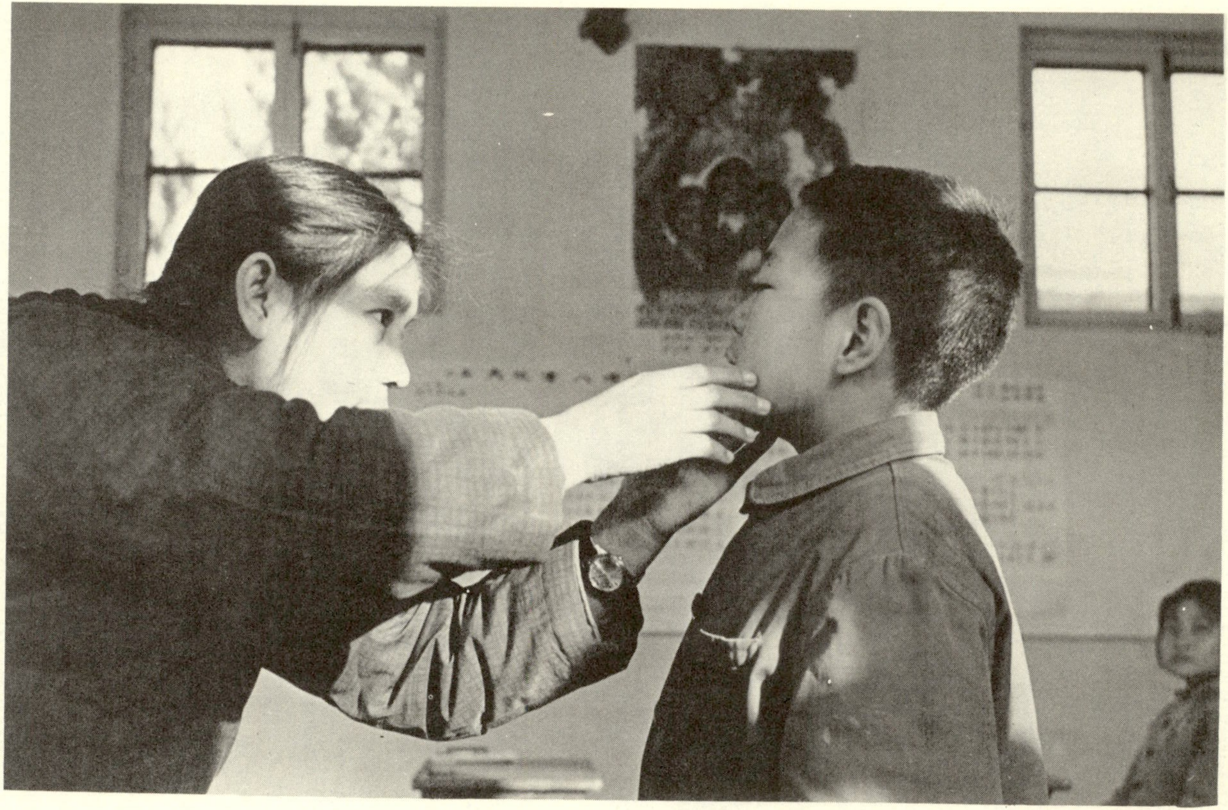

Fig. 25. A linguist aids a mute student to speak.

pattern of schooling existing in China today is based upon earlier innovations in literacy education, worker education and the half-work, half-study schools. All of these attempts sought to broaden the network of learning in China beyond the conventional institutionalized forms of education, and many of them were carried over from the Kiangsi and Yenan periods.

Early in the 1950's Mao decried the lack of educational facilities for the vast territory now controlled by the new government. The major pedagogical problem remaining was the elimination of illiteracy, particularly among the rural peasantry. This problem involved not only the increased numbers of school-aged children but illiterate adults as well. Mao recognized the need for peasants to organize their own *ad hoc* educational facilities of whatever form they desired and encouraged them to prepare their own texts and other materials.[17] To aid in the establishment of such facilities Mao suggested that students who had already passed through the primary-secondary cycle play a large role. They were to help prepare materials and generally contribute to the development of village-based literacy and technical schools:

> At the present time [1956] most of our villages, at least, should establish this kind of evening technical school. Youth corps organizations on various levels should take charge of this program. The youth corps should provide the overall supervision in integrating technical training for peasants and the elimination of illiteracy. Teachers of evening technical schools may be appointed locally, and they should be encouraged to learn while they teach.[18]

The relationship between literacy education and the future training of technical personnel was very close in Mao's mind. It was necessary to find the correct balance between agriculture and light, medium, and heavy industry. The eventual training of skilled labor for the various economic sectors depended heavily on informal and adult educational programs. Mao recognized the limited number of standard polytechnical colleges and universities and suggested that the training of skilled technicians could be achieved in a more informal setting. Mao urged individual industries to establish their own technical training programs and recruit students from among their own work force.[19] Technicians did not have to be trained in the "orthodox" [*k'o-pan ch'u-shen*] way.[20] However, in reality the major educational effort to train technicians before 1958 continued to rest with the standard higher educational institutions. It is not likely that Mao Tse-tung's program for worker education received much official support in the 1950's.[21]

Although initially the spare-time schools and half-work, half-study schools were designed to promote literacy and up-grade workers' skills, by 1958 (on the eve of the Great Leap Forward), Mao was suggesting that virtually all schools, both formal and informal, develop some program of part-work, part-study. The integration of mental with manual labor and education with productivity became the hallmark of this period. The result would have been the elimination of discrepancies between rural and urban education and the standard schools and less formal institutions.[22] The setbacks of the Great Leap Forward also inhibited the informal experiments in education. The rural half-work, half-study schools and red and expert colleges almost disappeared in their original form and were replaced by a highly modified program which broke up the integration of labor with education.[23] As the second decade of Chinese education approached, the conflict between Mao's vision of school and society and the official program began to emerge more clearly.

By extolling already existing models Mao was able in the 1960s to communicate to others in the Party and government his ideas on the importance of combining mental and manual labor in both an informal and formal educational context. He encouraged other provinces to follow the lead of the Kiangsi Communist Labor University and to establish work-study arrangements in their own provincial universities as well as in primary and middle schools. Mao further suggested that virtually all sectors of society including Party, government, and mass organizations (workers, women, youth, etc.) experiment with such programs. On a nationwide scale this endeavor would have resulted in a more universal educational system predicated on certain Marxist assumptions concerning the integration of theory and practice, polytechnical education, and local (worker) control.[24] In fact, through the 1960s down to 1966 the school system continued with a conventional two-track program which ignored most of the principles stated above. The reorganization of education following the Cultural Revolution opened the way for the first time for Mao Tse-tung to implement on a mass scale a system of education which in the past had existed only in an experimental and informal sense.

The Cultural Revolution also saw the emergence of one of the most unique forms of continuing education in the People's Republic of China. These institutions became known as the May Seventh Cadre Schools and their significance is such that a detailed explanation of this educational form is necessary. In the long-run this special form of education may have more impact on Chinese society than those discussed above. Directly inspired by Mao these schools are charged with the ideological education and reeducation of Party, governmental, and army cadres—in short, the bureaucracy. The continuing education of this element of Chinese society has been a major pedagogical problem since the founding of the new government in 1949.[25]

Of the many ills associated with modernization and industrialization, the phenomenon of rising complex organizations and bureaucratic indifference on the part of the ruling officialdom is often considered one of the most disconcerting. Many sociologists, particularly those influenced by Max Weber, associate modern society with an expanding and alien bureaucracy staffed by stony-faced and usually arrogant bureaucrats. While many socialists and Marxists felt that socialism would solve some of the problems created by the irrational and unplanned character of capitalist development, Weber simply saw socialism as the "extension of bureaucratic authority to the entire society, resulting in a 'dictatorship of the bureaucrats rather than of the proletariat."[26] His vision seems correct with regard to the first socialist country, the Soviet Union, where bureaucracy and all the ills associated with it seem very much in evidence. In such a society officials are more inclined to serve themselves and the organization than the people they supposedly represent.

Chinese society, with perhaps one of the oldest traditions and cultures in history, has had extensive experience with bureaucratic structures and the attendant problems. It is quite likely that the Chinese invented governmental bureaucracy, having utilized a civil service system dating back 100 years B.C. The establishment of socialism in China and the organizational structure of a Leninist Communist party proved in its early days at least to exhibit many of the same characteristics associated with bureaucracy. The influence of the Soviet Union was very profound in the 1950s and was expressed by the character of the official and non-Party cadres. The tendencies toward bureaucratization and the separation of the officials from the public slowly became evident in the first decade of the People's Republic, and campaigns were periodically launched by the Party in hopes of checking some of the less desirable aspects of bureaucracy.[27] In all these movements certain characteristics of cadres and the bureaucracy were attacked: sectarianism or separation from the masses, elitism, arrogance, dishonesty, "stronghold mentality" or being unresponsive to change, and so on. Admittedly, the Chinese have had the experience of the Soviet Union to give them a negative example of the ills of bureaucratic operation; yet, credit must be given to the way in which they have persistently (although by no means unified internally on the purpose and methods) attempted to curb the undesirable aspects of bureaucracy.

As the Party was being rebuilt in 1966 and 1967, it became clear that the old methods of cadre rectification (which generally had been considered punishment by the cadres themselves) were inadequate to prevent the kinds of bureaucratic tendencies which had been developing. During and following the GPCR the primary source of direction for Party affairs came from Mao Tse-tung. In a series of directives and instructions he sought to provide the general guidelines for governmental cadres as to their future role and action in society. In a letter dated May 7, 1966, Mao instructed the army to become a "great school."[28] He specified that the purpose of this "school" would be to reestablish close ties with the masses, learn from the masses, and also engage in various forms of agricultural and industrial production. Further in the letter, he stipulated that these kinds of activities should also be adopted by students and Party and governmental cadres. It is from this directive and the resultant changes in government, military affairs, and education that the May Seventh Cadre Schools take their name and inspiration.

Essentially the purpose of the schools is to bring the cadre-officials back into closer contact with the masses of people they were to represent. Old cadres as well as the new and inexperienced cadres are required to attend the schools. While the main task of the students is to grow crops and establish limited types of rural industry, the combination of theory and practice is always followed. During the busy season one to three hours of ideological study each day is attempted, and during the slack season the rule is half-work, half-study. The ideal of living a plain life and learning from the poor and lower-middle peasants is followed. There are no permanent teachers and each class elects its own discussion leaders.

It is, of course, unclear how successful this program will be in combating some of the more obvious defects of bureaucratic management. The Chinese admit that many problems have arisen and still remain. Yet, this movement is unlike past attempts in that it is considered permanent and relates to all cadres, young and old, good or bad, high or low. It is not to be considered punishment but something which officials should welcome to promote Mao's ideals of "serving the people" and being a "student of the masses." At the very least, it will serve to maintain closer ties between urban based decision-makers and the masses of rural people who are daily affected by the decisions.

Throughout the period under discussion it appears as if Mao Tse-tung's experimental educational programs had a larger purpose in mind. The literacy classes of the 1930s and 1940s, the part-work, part-study schools of the 1950s and 1960s and the variety of other unconventional educational enterprises (evening technical schools, spare-time education for workers and peasants, adult literacy, May Seventh Cadre schools, etc.) all eventually have been integrated with the formal educational pattern. The school system today resembles these models more closely than before, including such technical programs as medical training (barefoot doctors).[29] By breaking down traditional barriers between school and society Mao Tse-tung has succeeded in creating a "learning" society whereby education becomes the task of virtually all institutions instead of being restricted to the more formal educational institutions.

9 MAO TSE-TUNG'S EDUCATIONAL THOUGHT AND THE FUTURE DEVELOPMENT OF CHINA

NOW THAT MAO TSE-TUNG's educational thought has been put into practice on a scale never before realized what are the long-range implications both in social and economic terms? Part of the answer lies in an analysis of China's past economic performance during the period 1949 to 1966.[1] During this period, while the educational system did not fully accord with Mao's program, significant portions of it were in practice providing a glimpse of what a total Mao educational approach might mean to social and economic development. There is no doubt that in quantitative terms economic development in China has proceeded at a respectable pace. The Chinese gross national product has grown at an annual rate of five to seven percent and per capita income has continued to rise from 1950 to 1966 at a rate of five percent.[2] Industrial production, employment, labor productivity, and other indices of economic growth have all experienced a steady rise (given short periods of crises) since 1949.[3] Social services such as health care, education, and housing have made impressive advances, and when compared with a country like India or other nations at similar levels of development the Chinese appear to be far in the lead. How much of this development can be attributed to the fit between China's educational system and manpower needs, and specifically what was the relationship between this development and Mao's educational program?

As we have seen, Mao was not always successful in implementing his pedagogical ideas, and serious constraints were imposed on him at selected times. During the 1950s economic development and consolidation had priority, and many of Mao's ideas regarding the decentralization of administration, curriculum, and the integration of mental and manual labor were ignored. With the Great Leap Forward (1958) the educational system began to approach that envisioned by Mao, only to be abandoned following the economic retreat in 1959. A mixed educational system evolved during the 1960s as Mao and his supporters struggled with more conservative elements in the Ministry of Education—a struggle finally erupting into full-scale revolution in 1966. Since 1968 China has experimented with an educational program which draws heavily on the goals and aims expressed by Mao over the past forty years. It is not surprising that the twists and turns in educational policy and practice have been paralleled by a similar development in the economic sphere.[4] The difficulty arises in attempting to isolate the elements of the educational system contributing positively to economic development.

Mao at various times has criticized as nonsocialist an undue emphasis on development for the sake of development. His vision has tended to concentrate on the total social, political and economic development of society and not only that portion measured in productivity and capital accumulation. He does not seem impressed with large, elaborate cities, massive automobile production or a proliferation of nonessential consumer goods. Some cities in China are large and basic consumer goods are widely available and in good supply but the balance between rural and urban development has always been one of the goals

Mao has encouraged, even at the cost of a more rapid pace of industrial growth.

It appears that some of the problems in the 1960s which finally led to the Great Proletarian Cultural Revolution were closely related to a fundamental difference of approach between Mao and his opponents to the questions of economic development and education. China's educational system was producing a sufficient quantity of skilled personnel to supply the rapidly expanding industrial sector and to contribute to further growth. Problems existed particularly with regard to overspecialization of tertiary level technical graduates, but generally the 1960s were a period of very satisfactory economic growth. It soon became apparent, however, that while most levels of industry were growing (light, medium, and heavy) the dual-track educational system was not providing the middle-level technicians necessary to maintain the new industries and to consolidate the growing industrial base.[5] Furthermore, rural development suffered as investment and growth began to concentrate in the cities as did other social services such as hospitals, regular primary and secondary schools, and the institutions of higher learning. Material incentives were introduced both in the factories and on the communes and worker-management morale declined.[6] Mao feared that the revolutionary elan which he had always hoped would remain alive both in education and society at large was about to be abandoned. In its place a centralized, unresponsive bureaucracy was emerging which while having success in developing the economy was ignoring both the needs and participation of the masses of Chinese people. The commune ideal, whereby each unit was self-sufficient to the degree possible and locally controlled, was threatened and with it the future of China. His answer to this whole set of problems was to encourage another revolution.

The post-GPCR era has seen the transformation of the educational system in accordance with Mao's long-stated program, continued economic growth (although possibly more slowly in certain sectors), proliferation of service industries to the vast rural areas, renewed efforts at birth control, and a totally new foreign policy stance which finds China taking her place again as an equal among the nations of the world. The regearing of the educational system now places emphasis on the overall intellectual, physical, and political-moral development of the student and concentrates on preparing him for a technically oriented workforce. Higher level technicians are recruited from the workforce and trained in institutions actively engaged in production. The generalists lacking in the 1960s are now being produced in significantly larger numbers. The program announced by Mao to send educated youth to the rural areas could have the important effect of speeding up the rate of rural development as industries are constructed and relocated within the commune structure of rural China. This attempt to balance the pace of economic development so that eventually the entire society will become a great "commune" as well as a great "school" is perhaps one of the most ambitious national development programs currently underway. Whether these ideals will ever be fully realized is a question unanswerable at the present time. It is enough to say that the potential for achieving some of the goals outlined by Mao is very great. However the educational system fares in the years to come, the experiments and policies of Mao Tse-tung have left their impact on the largest single concentration of people in the world and have contributed to one of the most remarkable stories of social and economic construction in the twentieth century.

Appendixes

Abbreviations

CB	*Current Background*. Hong Kong: U.S. Consulate General.
CCP	Chinese Communist Party.
CPSU	Communist Party of the Soviet Union.
GPCR	Great Proletarian Cultural Revolution.
KMT	Kuomintang (Nationalist Party).
MC	*Mao Tse-tung chi*. Edited by Takeuchi Minoru. Tokyo: Hokubosha, 1970.
MP	*Mao Papers: An Anthology with Bibliography*. Edited by Jerome Ch'en. New York: Oxford University Press, 1970.
PLA	People's Liberation Army.
PRC	People's Republic of China.
SW	*Selected Works of Mao Tse-tung*. Peking: Foreign Languages Press, 1965.

Glossary of Educational Terms Used by Mao Tse-Tung

Academic freedom	students and teachers should be allowed and encouraged to debate and criticize official policy within the boundaries of building socialism
Bourgeois intellectuals	primarily intellectuals who had been educated abroad and did not work out of a Marxist-Leninist framework or who exhibited characteristics similar to intellectuals educated in non-Marxist schools
Culture and education	almost synonomous in meaning these terms describe any process or activity which contributes to the moral, intellectual and physical development of the individual
Evening technical schools	encouraged by Mao in 1956 to augment the existing village educational system and provide middle level technical training for adults

Half-work, half-study	an informal educational attempt to raise the cultural and technical level of the rural peasantry
Higher education	following the Great Proletarian Cultural Revolution this term represented higher level technical training for workers and peasants in formal and informal institutions and higher level social science education in colleges and universities and in community work
Inculcation method of teaching	opposed by Mao as representing a mechanical approach to teaching characterized by rote learning
Integrate mental and manual labor	this term was used by Mao to describe the ideal form of education whereby the student would achieve a respect for manual labor while at the same time acquiring expertise in conventional academic knowledge
Intellectual [chih-shih fen-tzu]	a general term to describe anyone with a middle school or higher education
Knowledge [cognition]	that which results from engaging in social practice ("material production") but containing within it several qualitatively different stages
Leading groups [ling-tao ku-kan]	the primary unit of school administration during the Yenan period consisting of community representatives, students, teachers, and Party personnel
Literacy classes	in a broad sense any educational program designed to eliminate illiteracy but specifically during the Kiangsi and Yenan periods these classes were conducted during the day for peasants and soldiers
May Seventh Cadre Schools	designed to reeducate Party and governmental cadres and reestablish ties between them and the average Chinese citizen

Night schools	schools established for the purpose of providing literacy training for working adults
Peasant schools	schools in the 1920s and 1930s which were peasant-operated enterprises
People's schools	schools operated and managed by local districts in the Kiangsi Soviet
Petty bourgeoisie	the class to which intellectuals, students, and primary and secondary teachers belong
Political education	the primary link between academic subjects and the acquisition of knowledge; consists of the study of the works of Marx, Lenin, Stalin, and Mao
Popular management of schools [min-pan]	schools which are managed and administered by the members of a locality but which also receive public support and direction; developed during the Yenan period
Primary and secondary education	following the Great Proletarian Cultural Revolution this term described a unified nine-year schooling cycle
Red and expert	describes the contradiction between political consciousness and academic expertise; a contradiction thought by Mao to be resolvable
Self-sufficient education	an educational structure in which the individual schools are able to finance their own operations without relying on the state or Party
Spare-time education	an informal attempt to raise the cultural and technical level of the urban working-class
Struggle-criticism-transformation	a process whereby students and teachers mutually criticize each other in order to "transform" their world outlook

Theory and practice	two interrelated concepts; the former is derived from the latter and provides a guide to action
Thought reform [ssu-hsiang kai-tsao]	a process designed to change the general outlook and behavior of an individual; used especially in reference to intellectuals
Three-in-one committees	the basic administrative unit which emerged during the Great Proletarian Cultural Revolution; it includes—army-Party representatives, students and teachers, and workers and peasants
Universal education [p'u-ch'i chiao-yu]	basic education for the broadest possible portion of society but especially for workers and peasants; the term does not assume compulsory education
Worker-peasant intellectuals	intellectuals drawn from these two social classes who are able to combine the two concepts, "red" and "expert"; the long-term goal of Mao's educational system
Youth clubs [er-t'ung chu-le-pu]	formed during the Yenan period these organizations provided a link between the students and the adult community; they engaged in a variety of cultural and educational enterprises

Mao Tse-Tung: A Chronology

1893	December 26	Mao born in the village of Shaoshan, Hunan Province
1898		Mao tutored in reading and writing
1906		Mao begins working full-time on his father's farm
1907		Mao married for the first time (arranged)
1910		Mao enrolled in the Tungshan Primary School in Hsianghsiang, Hunan
1911	Summer	Mao enrolls in the Hsianghsiang Middle School in Ch'angsha, Hunan
	Fall	Mao joins up with the anti-imperial army in support of Sun Yat-sen's Republican Revolution
1912	February	Mao demobilized from the Republican Army
		Mao briefly enrolled in a school of commerce and then into the Hunan First Middle School
	December	Mao introduced to books by European scholars
1913		Mao enrolls in the Fourth Teachers' Training School which combines in the Fall with the First Teachers' Training School in Ch'angsha
1914		Mao reads further in European literature including F. Paulsen's, *A System of Ethics*; he becomes increasingly radical

1915		Mao becomes active in student politics and is elected secretary of the Student's Society
1916		Mao distributes literature critical of Yuan Shih-kai's attempt to restore the monarchy
1917	Spring	Mao elected Chairman of the Student's Society
	Summer	Mao meets Li Li-san who later became influential in the Chinese Communist Party
	Autumn	Mao's first major article, "A Study of Physical Culture," is published in the influential journal, *Hsin ch'ing-nien*
1918	April	Mao organizes an evening school for workers and graduates from the First Teachers' Training School in Ch'angsha
	September	Mao travels to Peking; works in the Library of Peking University and is introduced to Marxist and anarchist ideas
1919	February	Mao leaves Peking and visits Shanghai
	March	Mao publically lectures in Ch'angsha on the subject of Marxism and assumes a position as teacher at the Hsiu-yeh Primary School
	June	Mao helps organize a student union to protest Japanese policy toward China and support the May Fourth Movement in Peking
	July-August	Mao becomes editor of the *Hsiang River Review* and *New Hunan*
	December	Mao again visits Peking and perhaps reads for the first time *The Communist Manifesto*
1920	January	Mao reads more Marxist literature in Peking
	April	Mao visits Shanghai and meets the Marxist Ch'en Tu-hsiu; he now considers himself a Marxist
	July-September	Mao returns to Ch'angsha and is appointed Director of the Primary School section of the First Teacher's Training School; he establishes the first Communist study group in his native village Shaoshan and in Ch'angsha; a socialist youth corps is founded in Ch'angsha
1921	July	Mao participates in the founding of the Chinese Communist Party in Shanghai

	August	Mao establishes the Self-Study University in Ch'angsha; he becomes active in the trade union movement in Ch'angsha and Anyuan
	October	Mao becomes first secretary of the Hunan branch of the CCP
1922	May	Mao continues to work with the Anyuan miners
	July	Mao is not present at the Second Congress of the CCP
	November	Mao becomes chairman of the Hunan Association of Trade Unions and gives up his post as Director of the Primary School Section of the First Teacher's Training School
1923	April	Mao's arrest is ordered in Ch'angsha and he leaves for Shanghai where he continues his work with the CCP
	June	Mao goes to Canton and takes part in the Third Congress of the CCP; he is elected to the Central Committee
	July	Mao works in Shanghai coordinating policy between the CCP and KMT
	December	Mao travels to Canton to attend the First Congress of the KMT
1924	January	Mao elected an alternate member of the Central Executive Committee of the KMT
	Autumn	Mao criticized by the CCP, takes ill and returns to his native village
1925	January	Mao fails to attend the Fourth Congress of the CCP and is not reelected to the Central Committee
	May-June	Mao works with peasant organizations in Hunan
	August	Mao works with the Peasant Bureau of the KMT
	October	Mao moves to Shanghai and works with the newly created peasant department of the CCP
1926	January	Mao attends the Second Congress of the KMT and is reelected an alternate member of the Central Committee
	March-October	Mao sails to Shanghai and heads up the Peasant Department of the CCP; returns to Hunan to organize peasants

1927	January	Mao investigates the peasant movement in Hunan
	April	Mao attends the Fifth Congress of the CCP
	May	Mao elected chairman of the All China Peasants' Union
	July-August	Mao takes part in the Autumn Harvest peasant uprising and the CCP-KMT alliance breaks down
	October	Mao establishes his first revolutionary base in the Chingkang Mountains
1928	January-December	Mao consolidates his position in the Chingkang Mountains, in the CCP and with other military units; he regains his position on the Central Committee of the CCP and Special Committee of the CCP
1929	January-November	Mao's troops invade and harass several southern provincial regions (Kiangsi, Fukien, Chekiang)
	November-December	Mao struggles within the Party for leadership
1930	January September	Mao writes several political tracts and discusses the formation of a more formal Soviet-type government
	October	Mao forms the Kiangsi Provincial Soviet Government
1931	January-September	Mao attempts to consolidate the Soviet areas while resisting the encirclement campaigns of Chiang Kai-shek
	November-December	Mao chosen as Chairman of the Kiangsi Soviet Government
1932		Mao continues his struggle against the KMT encirclement campaigns
1933	February	Mao's position in the Party comes under attack
	June-August	Mao begins a land investigation campaign and is involved in educational affairs including the establishment of a Soviet University
1934	February	Mao elected the Chairman of the Soviet Government at the Second National Congress held in Juichin
	July	Mao begins preparations for the Long March

	October	Mao begins the Long March
1935	January	Mao elected Chairman of the Politburo at the Tsunyi Conference
1936	July	Mao grants an interview with Edgar Snow
	Winter	Mao writes several important articles on military affairs and other subjects
1937	Spring-Summer	Mao attempts to gain support in the Party for his United Front Policy
	October	Mao grants an interview with James Bertram
1938		Mao writes a series of articles on military strategy and provides a theoretical justification for the Second United Front
1939	October	Mao stresses theoretical and ideological education and establishes a new Party organ, *The Communist*
1940		Mao writes, *On New Democracy* and other significant articles; CCP and KMT relations begin to deteriorate
1941		Mao initiates a Party rectification movement involving further study of Marxism-Leninism
1942		Mao's thought becomes an essential ingredient in the Party rectification movement
1943		The study of "Mao Tse-tung's Thought" reaches a high pitch
1944	November	Mao meets U.S. Ambassador Patrick Hurley in Yenan
	December	Mao's *Selected Works* (first edition) are published
1945		Mao enters into extensive negotiations with American representatives and those of the KMT including Chiang Kai-shek; Mao and Chiang sign an agreement on the cessation of hostilities; Mao's thoughts are proclaimed as one of the guiding ideologies
1946	Summer	Mao criticizes American aid to Chiang Kai-shek; writes a series of political articles; meets two American journalists
	Winter	Mao's thoughts are printed extensively in the *Liberation Daily*; the Civil War begins between CCP and KMT

1947	March	Mao and the CCP are forced out of Yenan by KMT troops
	June	Mao's arrest is ordered by the Nationalist Government
	October	Mao formulates a new land law
	December	Mao's *Selected Works* (second edition) are published
1948	March	Mao moves to Shansi
	May	Mao calls for a political consultative conference
	November	Mao predicts the imminent victory of the PLA
1949	January	Mao declines Chiang Kai-shek's peace plan and announces his own
	June-July	Mao speaks to the Political Consultative Conference and makes a statement explaining the policy of the "people's democratic dictatorship"
	August	Mao criticizes the U.S. *White Paper*
	October	Mao proclaims the founding of the People's Republic of China in Peking
1950	January-February June	Mao visits the Soviet Union and signs a Treaty of Friendship, Alliance and Mutual Assistance; Mao-study is promoted on a mass-scale
	October	Mao's *Selected Works* are revised and edited for a new edition; Korean War begins
1951		Mao launches a "thought reform" movement for intellectuals and a campaign against counter-revolutionaries
1952		Mao's *Selected Works* (three volumes) are published
1953		Mao takes part in an intra-Party struggle during which two major Party officials are purged
1954		Mao presides over the opening meeting of the National People's Congress
1955		Mao initiates and launches the agricultural cooperativization movement in the countryside
1956	April	Mao discusses "de-Stalinization" in a *Jenmin jih-pao* editorial

	Summer-Fall	Mao becomes more politically active and presides over the Eighth Congress of the CCP
1957	February	Mao speaks on "The Correct Handling of Contradictions Among the People"
	November	Mao visits Moscow for the second time
1958	January-March	Mao visits several provinces in China
	May	Mao's Great Leap Forward Plan is adopted
	August-December	Mao travels widely in China and announces his policy of rural communes
1959	July-August	Mao heavily criticized at the Lushan Conference for the failures of the Great Leap Forward
	September	Sino-Soviet relations begin to deteriorate
1960	April	Soviet technicians are withdrawn from China
	June	Volume Four of Mao's *Selected Works* is published
1961		Mao meets foreign guests from Asia and Africa
1962	September	Mao launches the Socialist Education Movement in the countryside and stresses the need to consolidate the communes
1963	May	Mao criticizes "revisionism" and calls for the Chinese to engage in the "three great revolutionary movements": class struggle, struggle for production and scientific experiment
	June-October	The CCP and Mao declare that the center of world revolution has shifted from Europe (specifically Moscow) to the "third world" countries
1964	February	Mao criticized by the Soviet Union and in turn blames Russia for the rift
	March	Mao-study launched within the PLA
	May	*Quotations from Mao Tse-tung* (the "little red book") published
	August	Mao begins to concentrate on the problem of revisionism in China and maintaining revolutionary enthusiasm among the young

1965	January	Mao intensifies his participation in the Socialist Education Movement
	November	Wu Han criticized signalling the beginning of the Cultural Revolution and Mao-study carried out at a higher level in the PLA
1966	May-July	Mao swims in the Yangtze River and refers to revisionists at the top levels of the CCP
	August	Mao supports the rebellious student Red Guards and writes his own "big character poster" entitled, "Bombard the Headquarters"
	September-November	Mao reviews millions of Red Guards who have traveled from all parts of China to Peking
1967	January	Mao announces that revolutionary "three-in-one" committees should seize power from the Party and other governmental organs
	May-October	Mao actively present at major national celebrations while other top Party leaders are not (i.e., Liu Shao-ch'i); he calls for reopening of schools, and tours China
	November-December	Mao's thought declared absolute and his works published on a mass scale
1968	January-February	Mao meets with members of the People's Liberation Army
	May-June	Mao attends the May Day celebrations in Peking; he meets with PLA soldiers who are engaged in the study of Marxism-Leninism and Mao Tse-tung's thought
	July	Mao meets with major Red Guard student leaders to urge them to end the factionalism and fighting and reopen the schools
	August	Mao receives more PLA study classes
	October	Mao attends the National Day celebrations in Peking
	December	Mao issues his directive on sending educated young poeple to the countryside
1969	January	Mao receives 40,000 "revolutionary fighters" in Peking
	February	Mao meets with a Guinean government delegation

	April	Mao presides over the Ninth Congress of the Chinese Communist Party
	Summer	Mao issues several short new directives on re-educating cadres
	October	Mao attends the National Day celebrations in Peking
1970		Mao's views on rebuilding the Party are widely quoted in the Chinese press
	May	Mao attends the May Day celebrations in Peking
	Summer-Fall	Mao receives numerous foreign guests
	October	Mao attends the National Day celebrations in Peking
	Winter	All people are urged to study the works and philosophy of Chairman Mao
1971	March	Mao sends a note of congratulations and encouragement to the guerilla fighters in Laos, Cambodia, and Vietnam
	April	United States table tennis team invited to visit China
	May	Mao attends the May Day celebrations in Peking
	October	The People's Republic of China admitted into the United Nations
1972	January	Mao attends the funeral of Foreign Minister Ch'en Yi
	February	Mao meets with President Bhutto of Pakistan
		Mao meets with President Richard M. Nixon
	April	Mao sends a message of congratulations to Premier Kim Il Sung on his 60th birthday
	July	Mao meets with Prime Minister Sirimavo Bandaranaike of Sri Lanka
		Mao meets with French Foreign Minister Maurice Schumann
	September	Mao meets with Prime Minister Kakuei Tanaka of Japan
	November	Mao meets with Prime Minister Bista of Nepal

1973 January	Mao meets with Minister of Foreign Affairs Nguyen Thi Binh of the Provisional Revolutionary Government of south Vietnam
	Mao meets with President Mobuto of the Republic of Zaire

*Compiled from the following sources: Jerome Ch'en, ed., *Mao* (New Jersey: Prentice-Hall, 1969); Jerome Ch'en, *Mao and the Chinese Revolution* (New York: Oxford University Press, 1967); Stuart Schram, *Mao Tse-tung* (London: Penguin Press, 1966); Huang Yu-ch'uan, ed., *Mao Tse-tung sheng-p'ing tzu-liao chian-pian* (Hong Kong: Union Research Institute, 1970). Other material regarding Mao's life was obtained from various accounts in the Chinese press.

Notes

Notes

Notes to Introduction

1. Edgar Snow, "A Conversation with Mao Tse-tung," *Life* (April 30, 1971), pp. 46-48.

Notes to Chapter 1

1. Edgar Snow, *Red Star Over China* 2nd. ed; (New York: Grove Press, 1968), p. 154.

2. Much of the following discussion of Marxist epistemology is from the author's *Educational Theory in the People's Republic of China: The Report of Ch'ien Chun-jui,* Asian Studies in Hawaii, No. 6 (Honolulu: University of Hawaii Press, 1971), pp. 3-7.

3. Karl Marx, *Capital,* Vol. I. (New York: International Publishers, 1967), p. 19.

4. V. I. Lenin, *Collected Works,* Vol. XIV (Moscow: Foreign Languages Publishing House, 1962), pp. 260-261.

5. Max Wingo, *The Philosophy of American Education* (Lexington, Mass. D.C. Heath and Company, 1965), p. 24.

6. Lenin, *Collected Works,* Vol. XIV, p. 142.

7. Lenin, *Collected Works,* Vol. XXXVIII, p. 195.

8. Lenin, *Collected Works,* Vol. XXXVIII, p. 171.

9. Karl Marx, *Critique of Political Economy* (Chicago: Charles H. Kerr & Co., 1904), pp. 11-12

10. Karl Marx, *Critique of the Gotha Programme* (New York: International Publishers, 1938), pp. 20-21.

11. Quoted in Wingo, *The Philosophy of American Education,* p. 362.

12. George S. Counts, *The Challenge of Soviet Education* (New York: McGraw-Hill, 1957), p. 47.

13. Counts, *The Challenge of Soviet Education*, p. 47.

14. V.I. Lenin, *On Socialist Ideology and Culture* (Moscow: Foreign Languages Publishing House, n.d. [taken from excerpt dated October 8, 1920]), pp. 78-79.

15. Karl Marx and Frederick Engels, *The Communist Manifesto* (New York: International Publishers, 1948), p. 31.

16. Marx, *Capital*, Vol. I, pp. 482-484.

17. Marx, *Capital*, Vol. I, p. 488.

18. Loyd D. Easton and Kurt H. Guddat, (eds.), *Writings of the Young Marx on Philosophy and Society* (New York: Doubleday and Company), pp. 401 and 394.

19. Easton, *Writings of the Young Marx*, p. 120.

20. Maurice Shore, *Soviet Education: Its Psychology and Philosophy* (New York: Philosophical Library, 1947), p. 112.

21. John T. Zepper, "Recent and Contemporary Soviet Educational Thought," *School and Society*, 100, No. 2338 (January, 1972), 41-42. The five stage scheme is as follows: (1) radical transformation: 1917-1920; (2) struggle for establishment of socialist school and Marxist-Leninist pedagogy: 1921-1930; (3) realization of universal primary and secondary education, struggle for pedagogy's recovery of rights: 1931-1940; (4) the war years and post-war years of restoring public education and introduction of the ten year school: 1941-1956; (5) new system of educational reconstruction of polytechnical education, combining teaching with productive labor: 1957-1972.

22. Ruth Widmayer, "A Historical Survey of Soviet Education," in *Soviet Society: A Book of Readings*, ed. by Alex Inkeles and Kent Geiger (Boston: Houghton Mifflin Company, 1954), p. 430.

23. Widmayer, "A Historical Survey of Soviet Education," p. 430.

24. Shore, *Soviet Education*, pp. 128-130. Lenin's program in brief included the following points: (1) free education; (2) separation of school from church control; (3) free compulsory, general and polytechnical education for both sexes to age 16—linking instruction to actual productive labor; (4) free food, clothing and school equipment; (5) local control and self-government of schools; (6) prohibition of child labor; (7) daycare centers in all enterprises.

25. James Bowen, *Soviet Education: Anton Makarenko and the Years of Experiment* (Madison: University of Wisconsin Press, 1962), pp. 30-34.

26. Shore, *Soviet Education*, pp. 187-188.

27. Shore, *Soviet Education*, p. 140.

28. Raymond Bauer, *The New Man in Soviet Psychology* (Cambridge: Harvard University Press, 1959), p. 44.

29. Widmayer, "A Historical Survey of Soviet Education," p. 430.

30. Widmayer, "A Historical Survey of Soviet Education," p. 433.

31. Widmayer, "A Historical Survey of Soviet Education," p. 433.

32. Albert Pinkevitch, *The New Education in the Soviet Republic* (New York: The John Day Company, 1929), p. 152.

33. Pinkevitch, *The New Education*, p. 155.

34. Bowen, *Soviet Education*, pp. 17-18.

35. Bowen, *Soviet Education*, pp. 143-144.

36. Bauer, *The New Man*, pp. 19-22.

37. Widmayer, "A Historical Survey of Soviet Education," p. 435.

38. Bauer, *The New Man*, p. 32.

39. Widmayer, "A Historical Survey of Soviet Education," p. 435.

40. Shore, *Soviet Education*, pp. 155 and 160; also see, Bauer, *The New Man*, p. 45.

41. Mikhail Ivanovitch Kalinin, *On Communist Education: Selected Speeches and Articles* (Moscow: Foreign Languages Pubishing House, 1950), pp. 15, 18, 21, 134 and 139. Note the elitist nature of his discussion of the rank system in the military on page 374.

42. Bowen, *Soviet Education*, pp. 147-148. For a discussion of pedology see, Bauer, *The New Man*, p. 123.

43. Shore, *Soviet Education*, pp. 193-195. Another argument stated that Soviet technical and developmental needs had surpassed levels which the school-run factories and factory-run schools could operate on.

44. Widmayer, "A Historical Survey of Soviet Education," p. 436.

45. Zepper, "Recent and Contemporary Soviet Educational Thought," p. 32.

46. Zepper, "Recent and Contemporary Soviet Educational Thought," p. 33.

47. Shore, *Soviet Education*, pp. 235-239.

48. Zepper, "Recent and Contemporary Soviet Educational Thought," p. 33.

49. Ina Schlesinger, "Soviet Educational Change," *School and Society*, 100, No. 2338 (January 1972), 43-44.

50. Raymond A. Bauer, Alex Inkeles and Clyde Kluckholn, *How the Soviet System Works: Cultural Psychological and Social Themes* (Cambridge: Harvard University Press, 1956), pp. 106-107. The Harvard Project of 1950-1951 obtained this data through refugee interviews.

51. For a discussion of this interesting period of the Khrushchev reforms (which in some ways parallel those of the post-Cultural Revolution period in China) see, Schlesinger, "Soviet Educational Change," pp. 44-45, and Zepper, "Recent and Contemporary," p. 36.

52. Schlesinger, "Soviet Educational Change," p. 46 and Zepper, "Recent and Contemporary," p. 37.

53. For a statistical breakdown and detailed discussion of the Soviet method of programmed learning see, Zepper, "Recent and Contemporary Soviet Educational Thought." pp. 38-39.

54. Li Yu-ning, *The Introduction of Socialism into China* (New York: Columbia University Press, 1971), p. 4.

55. Li, *The Introduction of Socialism into China*, p. 7. For a discussion of the 1898 reforms see, Meribeth H. Cameron, *The Reform Movement in China: 1898-1912* (New York: Octagon Books, Inc., 1963). The reforms proposed by K'ang Yu-wei, Liang Ch'i-chao and others deals with everything from education to commerce and military affairs.

56. Li, *The Introduction of Socialism into China*, p. 13.

57. Li, *The Introduction of Socialism into China*, p. 22.

58. Helen Carrere d'Encausse and Stuart R. Schram, *Marxism and Asia: An Introduction with Readings* (Baltimore: Penguin Press, 1969), p. 23. This study is the most complete discussion available on the movement of Marxism to China.

59. d'Encausse, *Marxism and Asia*, p. 26.

60. Benjamin I. Schwartz, *Chinese Communism and the Rise of Mao* (Cambridge: Harvard University Press, 1964), p. 16.

61. Schwartz, *Chinese Communism*, p. 16.

62. Jerome Ch'en, *Mao and the Chinese Revolution* (New York: Oxford University Press, 1967), p. 77.

63. Ch'en, *Mao and the Chinese Revolution*, p. 77.

64. d'Encausse, *Marxism and Asia*, p. 52. In 1927 the shaky alliance between the CCP and KMT fell to pieces and the urban, industrial sector of the CCP was virtually destroyed. A useful reference on this period is Harold R. Issacs', *The Tragedy of the Chinese Revolution* (Stanford: Stanford University Press, 1961), pp. 175-185.

Notes to Chapter 2

1. Joseph R. Levenson, *Modern China and its Confucian Past* (New York: Doubleday Anchor Book, 1964), pp. 210-211.

2. Richard H. Soloman, "Educational Themes in China's Changing Culture," in *Education in Comparative and International Perspective*, ed. by Kalil I. Gezi (New York: Holt, Rinehart and Winston Inc., 1971), pp. 158-179. In this article the author utilizes the interesting technique of comparing pre-communist school texts to communist school texts to determine through content analysis the expressed value of education.

3. T.I. Dow, "Neo-Confucian Philosophical Systems and Mao's Theory of Multiple Contradictions" (unpublished report to the 10th Annual Southwestern Regional Conference of the Association of Asian Studies held at Rock Hill, South Carolina, January, 1971), pp. 1-14. In this paper the author argues persuasively that many elements in Chinese neo-Confucian thought are not unlike those found in the writings of Marx, Engels, and Lenin particularly in the area of dialectics and the concept of internal and external contradictions. He concludes that because of China's philosophical past the Chinese had less difficulty accepting Marxist materialism and dialectics than other cultures.

4. Frederick W. Mote, *Intellectual Foundations of China* (New York: Alfred A. Knopf, 1971), pp. 10-11.

5. This point was originally developed by Ho Ping-ti, "Salient Aspects of China's Heritage," in *China in Crisis: China's Heritage and the Communist Political Tradition*, ed. by Ho Ping-ti and Tang Tsou (Chicago: University of Chicago Press, 1968), pp. 10-15.

6. M. Kusumoto, "Educational Thought of the People of China," *Yearbook of Education, 1957* (New York: World Book Co., 1957), pp. 115-116.

7. Ho, "Salient Aspects of China's Heritage," p. 30.

8. William Theodore deBary, Wing-tsit Chan, and Burton Watson, eds., Vol. I of *Sources of Chinese Tradition* (New York: Columbia University Press, 1960), p. 147.

9. Ho, "Salient Aspects of China's Heritage," p. 27. The phrase, *yu chiao wu lei* was more theoretical than real. It is questionable as to whether *lei* should be subscribed the same meaning as the modern sociological term, "class." As Derke Bodde comments in the same source (p. 55) Ho perhaps overidealized the Confucian ideal of social equity with regard to education. Education was never seriously intended to reach a significantly broad section of the population.

10. Kusumoto, "Educational Thought of the People of China," p. 122.

11. Idealism is considered here to mean broadly that the fundamental interpretive principle for the Chinese was ideal or of preeminent value; pragmatism refers to the general principle that in order to consider the truth of any statement one must ascertain the practical consequences of the statement.

12. Kusumoto, "Educational Thought of the People of China," p. 113.

13. Benjamin Schwartz, "Some Polarities in Confucian Thought," in *Confucianism and Chinese Civilization*, ed. by Arthur F. Wright (New York: Atheneum, 1964), pp. 3-15. The Chinese Communists perhaps represent a coalescing of these two traditions in that they express a deterministic view of consciousness (c.f. Legalism) but appear to give great attention to the "inner" realm as evidenced by the continual attempts at rectification and thought reform.

14. deBary, *Sources of Chinese Tradition*, p. 24. The quote is from the *Analects*, a book which served as a basic text for Chinese students for 800 years.

15. Ping-wen Kuo, *The Chinese System of Public Education* (New York: Teachers College, Columbia University Press, 1915), p. 21.

16. Kuo, *The Chinese System of Public Education*, p. 22. This kind of problem solving was not technical but philosophical in nature and content.

17. See, deBary, *Sources of Chinese Tradition*, p. 148 and Michael Loewe, *Imperial China: The Historical Background to the Modern Age* (New York: Praeger, 1965), p. 77.

18. deBary, *Sources of Chinese Tradition*, p. 481.

19. Dow, "Neo-Confucian Philosophical Systems," p. 2.

20. deBary, *Sources of Chinese Tradition*, p. 481. Also see Dow, "Neo-Confucian Philosophical," p. 5 for a discussion of Chu Hsi's conception of knowledge.

21. Dow, "Neo-Confucian Philosophical Systems," p. 6.

22. deBary, *Sources of Chinese Tradition*, pp. 393-394.

23. Levenson, *Modern China and its Confucian Past*, p. 64.

24. Cyrus H. Peake, *Nationalism and Education in Modern China* (New York: Columbia University Press, 1932), pp. 1-18. For an in-depth discussion of the early reform attempts see William Ayers, *Chang Chih-tung and Educational Reform in China* (Cambridge: Harvard University Press, 1971) and Knight Biggerstaff, *The Earliest Modern Government Schools in China* (Ithaca, New York: Cornell University Press, 1961).

25. Peake, *Nationalism and Education*, pp. 50-51 and Y.C. Wang, *Chinese Intellectuals and the West: 1872-1949* (Chapel Hill: The University of North Carolina Press, 1966), pp. 362-363.

26. Peake, *Nationalism and Education*, pp. 78-79.

27. See, Peake, *Nationalism and Education*, pp. 80-90 and Wang, *Chinese Intellectuals*, pp. 99-104. It is important to remember that most of the new educational innovations during this entire period (1911-1949) took place only narrowly at the urban level and did not constitute a public, nation-wide educational program.

28. Henry McAleavy, *The Modern History of China* (New York: Praeger Publishers, 1967), p. 238.

29.Peake, *Nationalism and Education*, pp. 90-91.

30. Wang, *Chinese Intellectuals*, pp. 123-124.

31. Wang, *Chinese Intellectuals*, pp. 123-124.

32. Wang, *Chinese Intellectuals*, pp. 121-126.

33. Wang, *Chinese Intellectuals*, p. 362.

34. Wang, *Chinese Intellectuals*, p. 373.

35. Wang, *Chinese Intellectuals*, pp. 370-377

36. Wang, *Chinese Intellectuals*, pp. 169-170.

37. Solomon, "Changing Themes," p. 168.

Notes to Chapter 3

1. This chapter briefly summarizes major events in the life of Mao Tse-tung abstracted from the three most complete and useful biographies. For the period of his early life and down to the 1930s there is still no substitute for Edgar Snow's *Red Star Over China,* 2nd ed. (New York: Grove Press, 1968). An analysis of Mao and his role in the Chinese revolution is found in Jerome Ch'en's *Mao and the Chinese Revolution,* (New York: Oxford University Press, 1967); this brings Mao's activities down to the establishment of the People's Republic of China in 1949. The most complete study remains Stuart Schram's *Mao Tse-tung* (London: Penguin Press, 1966) which brings Mao's life down to the outbreak of the Great Proletarian Cultural Revolution. It should be understood that the bulk of the information in this chapter is derived from these three texts. Footnote references are therefore limited to identifying major events that may be of interest to the reader.

2. Snow, *Red Star Over China,* p. 133; Schram, *Mao Tse-tung,* p. 21; Ch'en, *Mao and the Chinese Revolution,* p. 20.

3. Snow, *Red Star over China,* pp. 40-41; Schram, *Mao Tse-tung,* p. 36; Ch'en, *Mao and the Chinese Revolution,* p. 32.

4. Snow, *Red Star over China,* pp. 150-152; Schram, *Mao Tse-tung,* pp. 48-49; Ch'en, *Mao and the Chinese Revolution,* pp. 52-53.

5. A translation of this article by Stuart Schram appears in, "The Great Union of the Popular Masses," *The China Quarterly,* No. 49 (January-March 1972), pp. 76-87. The original document can be found in: *Mao Tse-tung chi,* edited by Takeuchi Minoru, Vol. I. (Tokyo: Hokubosha, 1970), 57-60.

6. Snow, *Red Star Over China,* p. 155; Schram, *Mao Tse-tung,* p. 57; Ch'en, *Mao and the Chinese Revolution,* pp. 70-71.

7. Snow, *Red Star Over China,* p. 157; Schram, *Mao Tse-tung,* pp. 64-66; Ch'en, *Mao and the Chinese Revolution,* pp. 77-81.

8. Snow, *Red Star Over China,* p. 159; Schram, *Mao Tse-tung,* pp. 68-70; Ch'en, *Mao and the Chinese Revolution,* pp. 81-87.

9. Snow, *Red Star Over China,* pp. 190-193; Schram, *Mao Tse-tung,* pp. 146-177; Ch'en, *Mao and the Chinese Revolution,* pp. 175-184.

10. Snow, *Red Star Over China,* pp. 190-209; Schram, *Mao Tse-tung,* pp. 177-211.

11. Schram, *Mao Tse-tung,* pp. 240-245; Ch'en, *Mao and the Chinese Revolution,* pp. 277-312.

12. Schram, *Mao Tse-tung,* pp. 261-263.

13. Schram, *Mao Tse-tung,* pp. 266-269.

14. Schram, *Mao Tse-tung,* pp. 278-284.

15. Schram, *Mao Tse-tung,* pp. 287-290.

16. Schram, *Mao Tse-tung,* pp. 297-298.

17. Richard Baum and Fredrick C. Teiwes, *Ssu-Ch'ing: The Socialist Education Movement of 1962-1966* (Berkeley: Center for Chinese Studies, 1968), pp. 1-48.

18. For a discussion of Mao's role during the Great Proletarian Cultural Revolution and subsequent events see: Edward E. Rice, *Mao's Way* (Berkeley: University of California Press, 1972).

Notes to Chapter 4

1. For a discussion of other reformers and reform attempts in China see, William Ayers, *Chang Chih-tung and Educational Reform in China* (Cambridge: Harvard University Press, 1971) and Y.C. Wang, *Chinese Intellectuals and the West: 1872-1949* (Chapel Hill: The University of North Carolina Press, 1966). A translation of Mao's article appears in Mao Tse-tung, "A Study of Physical Education," in *The Political Thought of Mao Tse-tung*, ed. and trans. by Stuart R. Schram, 2nd ed. (New York: Praeger Press, 1970), pp. 152-160. The article originally appeared in Mao Tse-tung, "T'i-yu chih yen-chiu." *Hsin ch'ing-nien*, III, No. 2 (April 1, 1917).

2. Mao, "A Study of Physical Education," p. 153.

3. Mao Tse-tung, "Communism and Dictatorship," in *The Political Thought of Mao Tse-tung*, ed. and trans. by Stuart R. Schram, 2nd ed. (New York: Praeger Press, 1970), pp. 296-298. Originally published in Mao Tse-tung, *Hunan li-shih tzu-liao*, No. 9 (1959), pp. 83-84. [Two letters to Tsai Ho-sen].

4. Mao Tse-tung, "Report on an Investigation of the Peasant Movement in Hunan" [1927], in *The Selected Works of Mao Tse-tung* [hereafter cited as *SW*], I (Peking: Foreign Languages Press, 1965), 23-59.

5. Mao, "Report on an Investigation," p. 53.

6. Mao, "Report on an Investigation," p. 54.

7. Mao Tse-tung, "Fen-sui wu-ts'e wei chiao-yu ssu-wei-ai chiang-chi chien-she jen-wu" [October 3, 1933], *Mao Tse-tung chi* [hereafter cited as *MC*], ed. by Takeuchi Minoru, III (Tokyo: Hokubosha, 1970), 337.

8. Mao Tse-tung, "Kuan-yu chiao-yu kung-tso" [September 15, 1933], *MC*, IV, 29-31.

9. Mao Tse-tung, "Chung-hua ssu-wei-ai kung-ho-kuo lin-shih chung-yang cheng-fu ch'eng-li liang chou-nien tui ch'uan t'i hsuan-min ti kung-tso pao-kao shu" [October 24, 1933]. *MC*, IV, 107-108.

10. Mao Tse-tung, "Talk at the Second National Soviet Conference of the Central Executive Committee of the Soviet Republic of China" [January, 1934], *Current Background* [hereafter-CB], No. 891 (October 8, 1969), p. 2; also see Mao Tse-tung, "Be Concerned with the Well-Being of the Masses, Pay Attention to Methods of Work" [January 27, 1934], *SW*, I, 149.

11. Mao Tse-tung, "Problems of Strategy in China's Revolutionary War" [December 1936], *SW*, I, 189-190. In this classic military document Mao stresses the importance of "learning by doing": "Reading is learning, but applying is also learning and the more important kind of learning at that. Our chief method is to learn warfare through warfare. A person who has had no opportunity to go to school can also learn warfare—he can learn through fighting war." p. 189-190.

12. Mao Tse-tung, "On Practice: On the Relation Between Knowledge and Practice, Between Knowing and Doing" [July 1937], *SW*, I, 295.

13. Mao, "On Practice," pp. 296-297. This orientation is illustrated by the following statement: "In class society, everyone lives as a member of a particular class and every kind of thinking, without exception, is stamped with the brand of a class . . . . The Marxist philosophy of dialectical materialism has two outstanding characteristics. One is its class nature . . . the other is its practicality: it emphasizes practice and in turn serves practice." pp. 296-297.

14. Mao, "On Practice," p. 303.

15. Mao, "On Practice," p. 304.

16. Mao, "On Practice," p. 306.

17. Mao, "On Practice," p. 307.

18. Mao, "On Practice," p. 308.

19. Mao Tse-tung, "On Contradiction" [August, 1937], *SW*, I, 311-347.

20. Mao, "On Contradiction," p. 319.

21. Mao, "On Contradiction," pp. 320-321.

22. Mao, "On Contradiction," pp. 322-335.

23. Mao, "On Contradiction," p. 336.

24. See below, Part I, Chapter 2; also see T.I. Dow, "Neo-Confucian Philosophical Systems and Mao's Theory of Multiple Contradictions (paper presented at the 10th Annual Southwestern Regional Conference of the Association of Asian Studies held at Winthrop College, Rock Hill, South Carolina, January 29-30, 1971), pp. 1-14; S. Dai, "Mao Tse-tung and Confucianism" (unpublished Ph.D. dissertation, University of Pennsylvania, 1952).

25. The two most important articles in this respect are Mao Tse-tung, "On Protracted War," [May, 1938], *SW*, II, 151; and Mao Tse-tung, "Reform Our Study" [May, 1941], *SW*, III, 17-25.

26. Mao, "Reform Our Study," p. 12; also see Mao Tse-tung, "Rectify the Party's Style of Work" [February, 1942], *SW*, III, 35-52.

27. There is considerable controversy over Mao's third significant theoretical document of this period entitled, "Dialectical Materialism—Notes and Lectures" (Pien-cheng-fa wei-wu-lun—chiang-shou t'i-kang) [1938]. The controversy centers primarily on the dating of the articles (estimates ranging over a period from 1936-1940) and the level of sophistication of Mao's analysis in con-

trast to "On Contradiction." The most complete text (*MC, VI, 265-303*) reveals that this article is indeed a simplified exposition of Marxist dialectics, the kind of presentation that might well be utilized in a course to introduce the subject to recently literate CCP cadres. The fact that "On Contradiction" is a more developed and polished presentation does not seem particularly important. For various discussions of this document wee Stuart R. Schram, *The Political Thought of Mao Tse-tung,* 2nd ed. (New York: Praeger Press, 1969), p. 85; Arthur A. Cohen, *The Communism of Mao Tse-tung* (Chicago: University of Chicago Press, 1964), pp. 7-28, 139-146; K.A. Wittfogel and C.R. Chao, "Some Remarks on Mao's Handling of Concepts and Problems of Dialectics," *Studies in Soviet Thought,* III, No. 4 (December, 1963), 251-269; John Rue, "Is Mao Tse-tung's 'Dialectical Materialism' a Forgery," *Journal of Asian Studies,* XXVI, No. 3 (May, 1967), 464-468 (the author of this article holds the interesting position that Mao did not write the article—Mao himself apparently admitted as much in an interview with Edgar Snow). Translations of portions of this document appear in Schram, *The Political Thought,* pp. 180-190 and Mao Tse-tung, "Dialectical Materialism," *China Quarterly,* trans. by Dennis J. Doolan and Peter J. Golas, No. 19 (July-September, 1964), pp. 38-46.

28. Mao Tse-tung, "Interview with British Journalist James Bertram" [October, 1937], *SW,* II, 50; Mao Tse-tung, "Tasks of the Chinese Communist Party in the Period of Resistance to Japan" [May 3, 1937], *SW,* I, 267.

29. Mao Tse-tung, "Policies, Measures, and Perspectives for Resisting the Japanese Invasion" [July 23, 1937], *SW,* II, 18.

30. Mao Tse-tung, "On The New Stage" [November, 1938], in *Chinese Education,* II, Nos. 1-2 (Spring-Summer, 1969), 62.

31. Mao Tse-tung, "Problems of War and Strategy" [November, 1938], *SW,* II, 228.

32. Mao, "On Protracted War," p. 143.

33. Mao Tse-tung, "The Situation and Our Policy After the Victory in the War of Resistance Against Japan" [August, 1945], *SW,* IV, 19.

34. Mao Tse-tung, "Instruction on the Question of Consolidating the Anti-Japanese Military and Political College" [July, 1939], *Current Background,* No. 897 (December 10, 1969), p. 10; statement originally appeared in *Chieh-fang chun-pao* (October 6, 1966.)

35. Mao Tse-tung, *To Be Attacked by the Enemy is Not a Bad Thing But a Good Thing* [May, 1939] (Peking: Foreign Languages Press, 1966), p.3.

36. Mao Tse-tung, "Instruction of the Military Affairs Committee of the Chinese Communist Party Central Committee on the Question of Consolidating the Anti-Japanese Military and Political College" [July, 1939], *CB,* No. 888 (August 22, 1969), pp. 3-4.

37. Mao Tse-tung, "Urgent Tasks Following the Establishment of Kuomintang-Communist Co-operation" [September, 1939], *SW,* II, 40.

38. Mao, "Problems of War and Strategy," p. 225.

39. Mao Tse-tung, "On New Democracy" [January, 1940], *SW*, II, 340.

40. Mao, "On New Democracy," p. 340.

41. Mao, "On New Democracy," p. 342.

42. Mao, "On New Democracy," p. 350.

43. Mao, "On New Democracy," p. 371.

44. Lu Hsun (Chou Shu-jen: 1881-1936) was China's most outstanding satirist and social critic during this period. His essays attacked Chinese society and mores on several levels and he later came to support the communist cause though he did not join the Party. Mao, "On New Democracy," p. 372.

45. Mao, "On New Democracy," p. 389.

46. While Mao realized that such an "open door" policy with regard to intellectuals would result in allowing a few "counter-revolutionaries" to penetrate the red base areas he was nevertheless willing to take the risk: "We should not be overcautious or too afraid of reactionaries sneaking in. Unavoidably, some such elements will creep in, but there will be time to comb them out in the course of study and work." Mao Tse-tung, "On Policy" [December, 1940], *SW*, II, 448.

47. Mao Tse-tung, "Wei tung-yun yi-ch'ieh li-liang cheng-ch'u k'ang-chan sheng-li er tou-cheng" [August 25, 1937], *MC*, V, 255. This article appears in translation in *SW*, II under the title: "For the Mobilization of All The Nation's Forces for Victory in The War of Resistance," 23-29; however, some segments of the educational program which are included in the *MC* original version are excluded in the translation.

48. Mao Tse-tung, "Conclusions on the Repulse of the Second Anti-Communist Onslaught" [May, 1941], *SW*, II, 466-467.

49. Mao Tse-tung, "Our Tasks for 1945" [December 15, 1944], in *Chinese Education*, II, Nos. 1-2 (Spring-Summer, 1969), 65.

50. Mao Tse-tung, "On Coalition Government" [April, 1945], *SW*, III, 300.

51. Mao Tse-tung, "We Must Learn To Do Economic Work" [January, 1945], *SW*, III, 239.

52. Mao, "On Coalition Government," pp. 287-288.

53. Yen Chang-lin, *In His Mind a Million Bold Warriors* (Peking: Foreign Languages Press, 1972), p. 14.

54. Mao Tse-tung, "Manifesto of the Chinese People's Liberation Army" [October, 1947], *SW*, IV, 150.

55. Mao Tse-tung, "Report to the Second Plenary Session of the Seventh Central Committee of the Chinese Communist Party" [March, 1949], *SW*, IV, 365.

56. Mao Tse-tung, "Proclamation of the Chinese People's Liberation Army" [April, 1949], *SW*, IV, 398.

57. Mao Tse-tung, "On the People's Democratic Dictatorship" [June, 1949], *SW*, IV, 143.

58. Possibly in connection with the agricultural collectivization program emphasized by Mao in 1955, a campaign against bourgeois tendencies in the arts was launched the main target of which was the writer Hu Feng. For an in-depth study of this particular incident see: Merle Goldman, "Hu Feng's Conflict with the Communist Literary Authorities," *Papers on China, Harvard University*, III (December, 1957), 149-191.

59. Mao Tse-tung, "Introductory Note to the Second Lot of Material on the Hu Feng Counter-revolutionary Clique" [May, 1955], *CB*, No. 891 (October 8, 1969), pp. 19-20.

60. Mao Tse-tung, "On the Correct Handling of Contradictions Among the People" [February, 1957], *Four Essays on Philosophy* (Peking: Foreign Languages Press, 1968), p. 110. One of the first official pedagogical documents issued following the establishment of the People's Republic in 1949 was authored by the then Vice-Minister of Education, Ch'ien Chun-jui. Ch'ien suggested that education had two basic aims: It should serve the class interests of the workers and peasants and it should provide a mechanism for economic reconstruction. While this statement might seem to coincide with views held by Mao, Ch'ien continued in the article to describe a set of controls and procedures which could not encompass the essential ideals of such goals. For a discussion of Ch'ien's document and its relation to current educational policy and practice in China see: John N. Hawkins, *Educational Theory in the People's Republic of China: The Report of Ch'ien Chun-jui* (Honolulu: University of Hawaii Press, 1971).

61. Mao reasserted the necessity of striking a balance between unity and diversity particularly against the background of the Hungarian—Polish situation: "Letting a hundred flowers blossom and a hundred schools of thought contend is the policy for promoting the progress of the arts and the sciences and a flourishing socialist culture in our land. Different forms and styles in art should develop freely and different schools in science should contend freely." See Mao, "On the Correct Handling of Contradictions Among the People," pp. 113-114. Stuart Schram suggests the connection between the Hundred Flowers movement and Soviet difficulties in Eastern Europe in, *Mao Tse-tung* (London: Penguin Press, 1966), p. 288.

62. For a discussion of the "Hundred Flowers Movement" and the rectification anti-rightist campaign which followed see Roderick MacFarquhar, *The Hundred Flowers Campaign and the Chinese Intellectuals* (New York: Praeger Press, 1960).

63. Mao Tse-tung, "A Talk Delivered in 1958" [1958], *CB*, No. 888 (August 22, 1969), p. 7.

64. Mao Tse-tung, "Instruction on the Question of 'Redness and Expertness' " [January, 1958], *CB*, No. 891, (October 8, 1969), p. 28.

65. Mao Tse-tung, "Under the Red Flag of Mao Tse-tung" [July, 1958], *Chinese Education*, II, No. 3 (Fall, 1969), 44.

66. Mao Tse-tung, "Outline for National Agricultural Development, 1956-1957" [1956?], *Chinese Education*, II, No. 3 (Fall, 1969), 53-54.

67. Mao, "Where Do Correct Ideas Come From" [May, 1963], *Four Essays on Philosophy* (Peking: Foreign Languages Press, 1968), p. 134.

68. Mao Tse-tung, "Instruction Given at the Spring Festival Concerning Education Work (excerpts)" [February, 1964], *CB*, No. 891 (October 8, 1969), p. 44.

69. Mao, "Instruction given at the Spring Festival," pp. 42-44.

70. In a talk with an educational delegation from Nepal Mao, probably to the surprise of the delegation, suggested that the Chinese educational system had several defects: "There are many problems in our education, and the most important one is dogmatism. . . . Therefore, I advise against your having blind faith in China's educational system." See: Mao Tse-tung, "Talk with the Nepalese Educational Delegation on Educational Problems" [1964], *CB*, No. 891 (October 8, 1969), p. 46.

71. Mao Tse-tung, "Comment on the 'Instruction Concerning Learning to Strengthen Political Work from the Liberation Army' " [1964], *CB*, No. 891 (October 8, 1969), p. 48.

72. Mao Tse-tung, "The Intelligence of the People" [February 11, 1966], *MP*, p. 103.

73. Mao Tse-tung, "The Anti-Japanese Military and Political University" [August 2, 1966], *MP*, 116.

74. Mao Tse-tung, "Proletarian Dictatorship and Renegade China's Khrushchev" [August 20, 1967], *CB*, No. 885 (July 31, 1969), p. 34.

75. Mao Tse-tung, cited in a *Jen-min jih-pao* editorial entitled, "The Whole Country Should Become a Great School in Mao Tse-tung Thought," (August 1, 1966), p. 1; also available in translation in *The Whole Country Should Become a Great School of Mao Tse-tung's Thought* (Peking: Foreign Languages Press, 1966), pp. 1-2.

76. Mao Tse-tung, "Instruction on the Question of Consolidating the Anti-Japanese Military and Political College" [October 6, 1966], *CB*, No. 897 (December 10, 1969), p. 10.

77. During the Cultural Revolution work-teams were formed to investigate local Party affairs and were given the responsibility of directing the reforms at the local level. In some cases, the teams were controlled by anti-Mao forces in the Party and therefore came under criticism. For a discussion of the complexities of the period leading up to the Cultural Revolution see: Richard Baum and Fredrick C. Teiwes, *Ssu-ch'ing: The Socialist Education Movement of 1962-1966* (Berkeley: Center for Chinese Studies, 1968). Mao's statement on work-teams appears in Mao Tse-tung, "Work Teams" [August 26, 1966], *MP*, 128. "It will not do to depend on the work teams coming from the Navy, Air Force, and governmental agencies. They neither teach nor learn. How can they understand the conditions in the schools. . . ? The Cultural Revolution at the schools must not depend on work teams. . . . It must depend on the revolutionary teachers and students at schools."

78. Mao Tse-tung, "Talk at the Hangchow Conference" [December, 1965], *CB*, No. 891 (October 8, 1969), p. 52. Mao's concern with physical education again re-appears almost fifty years after he first indicated the value of correct physical education in the schools: Mao Tse-tung, "A Study of Physical Education" [April, 1917], *The Political Thought of Mao Tse-tung*, ed. and trans. by Stuart R. Schram, 2nd ed. (New York: Praeger Press, 1963), pp. 152-160.

79. Mao Tse-tung, "Scientific and Technological Training" [July 21, 1968], *MP*, p. 154. The Shanghai Machine Tools Plant continues to be the model for higher technical education. The plant trains technicians from among its own work force and has established a college within the plant. It is still unclear whether Mao feels that the standard polytechnical colleges and universities will one day be completely replaced by worker-colleges of this type or will still have some use. For a brief discussion of the Shanghai Machine Tools Plant college see: Stewart E. Fraser and John N. Hawkins, "Chinese Education: Revolution and Development," *Phi Delta Kappan*, LIII, No. 8 (April, 1972), 498.

80. More recently Mao has expressed admiration for the level of universal education present in the United States. Edgar Snow, "A Conversation with Mao Tse-tung," *Life*, 70, No. 16 (April 30, 1971), 47.

Notes to Chapter 5

1. The very complicated struggle between Mao and other CCP factions is discussed at length in the following books: Harold R. Isaacs, *The Tragedy of the Chinese Revolution* (Stanford: Stanford University Press, 1961), pp. 323-349; Jerome Ch'en, *Mao and the Chinese Revolution* (New York: Oxford University Press, 1967), pp. 138-184; Benjamin I. Schwartz, *Chinese Communism and the Rise of Mao* (Cambridge: Harvard University Press, 1964), chapters 9-12.

2. On the reference to land-reform structure see Franz Schurmann, *Ideology and Organization in Communist China*, 2nd ed., enlarged; (Berkeley: University of California Press, 1968), p. 415; for the reference to a central authority for education see Mao Tse-tung, "Shih-hsing kuang-fan shen-ju ti ch'a-t'ien yun-tung," [June 20, 1933], *MC*, III, 224.

3. This criticism came from Chief of the General Staff of the PLA Lo Jui-ching in 1957. Mao and Lo clashed over administrative control of the People's Liberation Army in 1959 and Lo was later purged. See, Schurmann, *Ideology and Organization in Communist China*, p. 193.

4. Schurmann, *Ideology and Organization in Communist China*, p. 416.

5. Mao Tse-tung, "Hunan tse-hsiu ta-hsueh chuang-li hsuan-yen" [March 1, 1923], in *MC*, I, 82.

6. Mao Tse-tung, "Report on an Investigation of the Peasant Movement in Hunan" [March, 1927], *SW*, I, 54.

7. Mao Tse-tung, "Hsing-kuo tiao-ch'a" [January 26, 1931], *MC*, II, 249-250.

8. Mao, "Shih-hsing kuang-fan shen-ju ti ch'a-t'ien yun-tung," p. 224.

9. Mao Tse-tung, "Ba hsien ch'u yi-shang ssu-wei-ai fu-tse jen-yuan ch'a-tien yun-tung ta-hui suo t'ung-kuo ti chieh-lun," [June 21, 1933], *MC*, III, 262.

10. Stephen J. Knezevich, *Administration in Public Education* (New York: Harper and Row Publishers, 1962), p. 83. The author lists several elements common to most administrative structures. Further evidence of the organizational and administrative authority of the new Soviet government is revealed in a document by Mao regulating entrance policies and delegating authority in educational matters to the local village soviets, see Mao Tse-tung, "Chih-hsing yu-tai hung-chun t'iao-li ti shih-shih pan-fa," [February 1, 1932], *MC*, III, 90.

11. Mao, "Hsing-kuo tiao-ch'a," pp. 249-250.

12. Mao Tse-tung, "Ch'ang-kang hsiang tiao-ch'a," [March 15, 1933], in *MC*, IV, 158. Mao also encouraged women to take an active role in administration of education and noted approvingly that this was becoming a trend. See Mao Tse-tung, "Chung-hua ssu-wei-ai kung-ho-kuo chung-yang chih-hsing wei-yuan-hui yu jen-min wei-yuan-hui tui ti-er-ts'e ch'uan-kuo ssu-wei-ai tai-piao ta-hui ti pao-kao," [March 15, 1933], *MC*, IV, 262-263.

13. The human relations approach to management is outlined in Jacob W. Getzels, James M. Lipham and Roald F. Cambell, *Educational Administration as a Social Process* (New York: Harper and Row Publishers, 1968), pp. 30-39.

14. Mao, "Chung-hua ssu-wei-ai kung-ho-kuo chung-yang," pp. 262-263.

15. Administrative practices during the Yenan period are discussed in Schurmann, *Ideology and Organization in Communist China* and especially in the excellent study by Mark Selden, *The Yenan Way in Revolutionary China* (Cambridge: Harvard University Press, 1971), pp. 144-160, 274.

16. Mao Tse-tung, "For the Mobilization of all the Nation's Forces for Victory in the War of Resistance" [August 25, 1937], in *SW*, II, 27. A statement to this effect was contained in a general document outlining policy for the nation as a whole including the KMT: it also represented the CCP's own educational policy.

17. Mao Tse-tung, "Rectify the Party's Style of Work" [February, 1942, in *SW*, III, 39.

18. Mao Tse-tung, "Economic and Financial Problems in the Anti-Japanese War" [December, 1942], in *SW*, III, 114; Mao Tse-tung, "Spread the Campaigns to Reduce Rent, Increase Production and 'Support the Government and Cherish the People' in the Base Areas" [October, 1943], in *SW*, III, 132.

19. This statement appears in a document published by the Shen-kan-ning Border Region Government and contained in a collection of Mao's writings on education published in Japan: "Hanrei Kenkyu no teisho oyobi mintei shogaku shiko ni kansuru no tegami" [April, 1943], in *Mo Taku-to kyoiku ron*, ed. and trans. by Saito Akio and Niijima Atsuyoshi (Tokyo: Aoki Shoten, 1957), p. 258. The authorship of the article is not clear in the Japanese edition. The article has also been translated into English and is attributed to a commit-

tee of the Civil Affairs Office of the Shen-kan-ning Border Region Government but is dated one year later: "Border Region Government Directive on Promoting the Study of Model Schools and on Experimentation with Popular Management Primary Schools" [April 18, 1944], in *Chinese Education,* IV, No. 4 (Winter, 1971-1972), 271-272. The two versions are slightly different and it is not known who participated in the drafting of the original document. It is known that at this time (1942-1944) a Party rectification campaign was in progress and Mao was presiding over the writing of most official documents sometimes writing them himself and having them published under a different name or committee (Stuart Schram, *Mao Tse-tung* (London: Penguin Press, 1966), p. 233). In any case, the concept of popular management of schools was part of Mao's educational philosophy and it is likely that he had a strong influence on the document in question; the 1943, unauthored Japanese version strengthens this possibility. This document will be considered in this light.

20. "Hanrei kenkyu no teisho," p. 260; "Border Region Government Directive," p. 274.

21. Mao Tse-tung, "Some Questions Concerning Methods of Leadership" [June 1, 1943], in *SW,* III, 118-119.

22. This is suggested in "Hanrei kenkyu no teisho, p. 260; "Border Region Government Directive," pp. 273-274.

23. Mao, "Some Questions Concerning Methods of Leadership," p. 119; on the eve of the establishment of the People's Republic Mao suggested that CCP committees attached to leading groups (e. g. schools) be tightened up organizationally, hold more meetings and more discussions, and eliminate one-man domination of decision-making within the committees: "On strengthening the Party Committee System" [September, 1948], in *SW,* IV, 268.

24. The "mass-line" concept is discussed in John Wilson Lewis, *Leadership in Communist China* (Ithaca: Cornell University Press, 1963), pp. 70-100 and Mao in "Some Questions Concerning Methods of Leadership," pp. 120-121.

25. Mao Tse-tung, "On the September Meeting—Circular of the Central Committee of the Communist Party" [October, 1948], in *SW,* IV, 274.

26. Mao Tse-tung, "Turn the Army into a Working Force" [February, 1949], in *SW,* IV, 338-339.

27. Mao Tse-tung, "Methods of Work of Party Committees" [March, 1949], in *SW,* IV, 377-381.

28. Policy-making since 1949 and Mao's role as leader of the state are discussed at length in: Michel C. Oksenberg, "Policy Making Under Mao: 1949-1968-An Overview," in *China: Management of a Revolutionary Society* ed. by John M. H. Lindbeck (Seattle: University of Washington Press, 1971), pp. 79-115. The author notes the various constraints on Mao as an administrator especially those imposed by the Party, bureaucracy and mass opinion.

29. Those ministries and committees related to education before the Cultural Revolution are discussed in: Tsang Chiu-sam, *Society Schools and Progress in China* (New York: Pergamon Press, 1968), p. 80.

30. Schurmann has outlined five steps in the development of administrative practices in China before the Cultural Revolution with special reference to industrial management: Franz Schurmann, *Ideology and Organization in Communist China*, 2nd ed. (Berkeley: University of California Press, 1968), p. 308.

31. Schurmann, *Ideology and Organization in Communist China*, p. 308.

32. Mao Tse-tung, "On the Correct Handling of Contradictions Among the People" [February, 1957], *Four Essays on Philosophy* (Peking: Foreign Languages Press, 1968), p. 112.

33. In his characteristically down-to-earth fashion Mao criticized the prevailing pedagogical wisdom of educational planners in Peking with specific reference to colleges of agriculture: "Why the deuce are agricultural universities run in cities? All agricultural universities should be removed to the countryside." Mao Tse-tung, "Talk Delivered in August 17, 1958" [August 17, 1958], *CB*, No. 888 (August 22, 1969), p. 8.

34. Mao Tse-tung, "Summary of Talk to Heads of Education Departments and Bureaus of Seven Provinces and Municipalities [March 7, 1957], *CB*, No. 888 (August 22, 1969), p. 7.

35. Mao Tse-tung, "Sixty Points on Working Methods—A Draft Resolution from the Office of the Centre of the CCP" [February, 1958], *MP*, p. 69.

36. Mao Tse-tung, "Instruction Given on an Inspection Tour of Tientsin University (excerpts)" [August, 1958], *CB*, No. 891 (October 8, 1969), p. 30.

37. Mao Tse-tung, "The Experience of the Liu-kou Village Branch of Chu-nan County Communist Youth Corps in Organizing Recording Work Study Classes" [1956], *Chinese Education*, II, No. 3 (Fall, 1969), 54-55.

38. Mao, "Instruction Given on an Inspection Tour of Tientsin University," p. 30.

39. Mao Tse-tung, "Instruction on Part-Work, Part-Study" [February, 1958], *CB*, No. 891 (October 8, 1969), p. 29.

40. Mao, "Sixty Points on Working Methods," p. 73.

41. The change in bureaucratic compliance in the 1950's and the 1960's with Mao's goals is noted by Oksenberg, "Policy Making Under Mao," pp. 110-111.

42. Tsang, *Society, School and Progress in China*, p. 81.

43. Mao Tse-tung, "Instructions Given at the Spring Festival Concerning Educational Work (excerpts)" [February, 1964], *CB*, No. 891 (October 8, 1969), p. 43.

44. Mao Tse-tung, *The Whole Country Should Become a Great School of Mao Tse-tung's Thought* (Peking: Foreign Languages Press, 1966), p. 2.

45. Mao Tse-tung, "Talk with the Guinean Educational Delegation" [August 8, 1965], *CB*, No. 888 (August 22, 1969), p. 15.

46. Mao Tse-tung, "Address to Regional Secretaries and Members of the Cultural Revolution Group Under the Central Committee" [July, 1966], *CB*, No. 891 (October 8, 1969), p. 60.

47. Mao Tse-tung, "The Resolutions of the Eleventh Plenum of the Central Committee of the CCP—the Sixteen Articles" [August 8, 1966], *MP*, p. 124.

48. Mao, *The Whole Country Should Become a Great School,* p. 10.

49. Mao Tse-tung, "More on the Need for All Universities, Middle Schools and Primary Schools to Resume Class and Carry Out the Revolution" [November 26, 1967], *CB*, No. 897 (December 10, 1969), 38.

50. Mao Tse-tung, "Notice on Forging Revolutionary Great Alliances According to Systems" [October 18, 1967], *CB*, No. 897 (December 10, 1969), p. 34.

51. Mao Tse-tung, "Firmly Carry Out Chairman Mao's Latest Instruction and Rely on the Masses to Make Revolution in Education on a Large Scale" [November 6, 1967], *CB*, No. 897 (December 10, 1969), p. 35.

52. Mao Tse-tung, "Educational Revolution" [August 27, 1968], *MP*, p. 155.

53. Early in 1972 it was found that in both rural and urban schools administrative three-in-one committees of the type described by Mao were in operation in various parts of China. The committees appeared to be operating effectively and morale in the schools was high. See: Stewart E. Fraser and John N. Hawkings, "Chinese Education: Revolution and Development," *Phi Delta Kappan*, LII, No. 8 (April, 1972), 487-500.

54. At the school level the "three-in-one" revolutionary committees along with a separate Party committee are the basic decision-making structure. City, county and provincial committees also exist but their relationship to the local school committees is unclear. In place of the former Ministry of Education a new organization called the Science and Education Group (*K'e-chiao-tsu*) formulates high level decisions. The communication between the various levels and the degree of authority and autonomy accorded each seems to have increased in comparison to the pre-Cultural Revolution period. (I am indebted to Dr. Fan Kuang-ti of York University for much of this information. Dr. Fan visited China and talked with high level educational officials in the Fall of 1972).

55. Educational administrators interviewed by the author in China in January 1972 all quoted Mao's views on leadership and cadre behavior as providing the major guidelines to inter-level communication. Many of these quotes can be found in chapters ten and twenty-nine of *Quotations From Chairman Mao Tse-tung* (Peking: Foreign Languages Press, 1966), pp. 104-117, 276-287.

56. Most standard views of leadership types identify them in terms of mutually exclusive categories: democratic, autocratic etc. However, other categories have been identified including the "transactional" model which seems to offer a closer parallel to the Chinese situation: Stephen J. Knezevich, *Administration in Public Education* (New York: Harper and Row Publishers, 1962), p. 100.

Notes to Chapter 6

1. Curricular revision and curricular development are distinct processes. In the former, existing curricular practices are reconsidered in light of changed social conditions, or an increase in the availability of new information (or technology). In the latter, a systematic, sustained, on-going process is engaged in to quantitatively and qualitatively change the teaching-learning process. The Kiangsi Soviet period appears to exhibit characteristics more in the direction of curricular revision whereas in the Yenan period the roots of curricular development are observable. For a discussion of curricular revision and curricular development see: G. Robert Koopman, *Curriculum Development* (New York: The Center for Applied Research in Education, Inc., 1966), p. 9.

2. Mao Tse-tung, "A Study of Physical Education," in *The Political Thought of Mao Tse-tung,* ed. by Stuart R. Schram, 2nd ed. (New York: Praeger, 1970), p. 154.

3. "Chairman Mao's Activities in Revolutionary Practice," *CB,* No. 900 (January 30, 1970), p. 20.

4. The May Fourth Movement refers specifically to the student protest which occurred on May 4, 1919 in Peking in response to a series of humiliating demands made upon the Chinese government by Japan. See: Chow Tse-tung, *The May Fourth Movement: Intellectual Revolution in Modern China* (Cambridge: Harvard University Press, 1964).

5. Mao Tse-tung, "Hunan tse-hsiu ta-hsueh chuang-li hsuan-yen" [March 1, 1923], *MC,* I, 81.

6. Mao, "Hunan tse-hsiu ta-hsueh," p. 82.

7. It is not known how many students attended the Self-Study University nor where Mao obtained sufficient teaching staff to provide instruction for such a variety of courses. The author was told by educational authorities in Ch'ang-sha (1971) that teachers from nearby colleges, such as the teacher's training school, volunteered their services to Mao and that the student body changed its composition regularly. It was not a large enterprise. For Mao's description of the facilities see: Mao, "Hunan tse-hsiu ta-hsueh," pp. 81-84.

8. Mao Tse-tung, "Report on an Investigation of the Peasant Movement in Hunan" [March, 1927], *SW,* I, 54.

9. Chairman Mao's Activities in Revolutionary Practice," p. 26.

10. Mao Tse-tung, "Chung-kuo kung-ch'an-tang hung-chun ti-ssu-chun ti-chiu-ts'e tai-piao ta-hui chu-yi-an" [1929], *MC,* II, 117.

11. Mao Tse-tung, "Ch'ang-kang hsiang tiao-ch'a" [March 15, 1933], *MC,* I, 158.

12. This requirement extended to government and Party work as well. See Mao Tse-tung, "Shih-hsing kuang-fan shen-ju ti ch'a-t'ien yun-tung" [June 20, 1933], *MC,* III, 224.

13. Mao suggested in an article late in 1933 that progress in the establishment of educational facilities, elimination of illiteracy, etc. had lagged behind expectations. See Mao Tse-tung, "Kuan-yu chiao-yu kung-tso" [September 15, 1933], *MC*, IV, 29-31.

14. "Hanrei kenkyu no teisho oyobi-mintei shogaku shiko ni kansuru no tegami" [April, 1943], in *Mo Taku-to kyoiku ron*, ed. and trans. by Saito Akio and Niijima Atsuyoshi (Tokyo: Aoki Shoten, 1957), p. 259; also see "Border Region Government Directive, on Promoting the Study of Model Schools and on Experimentation with Popular-Management Primary Schools" [April, 1944], translated in *Chinese Education*, IV. No. 4 (Winter 1971-1972), 273.

15. "Hanrei kenkyu no teisho." p. 259; "Border Region Government Directive," p. 273.

16. Mao Tse-tung, "For the Mobilization of all the Nation's Forces for Victory in the War of Resistance" [August 25, 1937], *SW*, II, 27. This was a policy suggested for the Nationalist government (KMT) as well as the Border Region government (CCP).

17. Mao Tse-tung, "On Policy" [December, 1940], *SW*, II, 441.

18. Mao Tse-tung, "Rectify the Party's Style of Work" [February, 1942], *SW*, III, 39.

19. Mao Tse-tung, "The Orientation of the Youth Movement" [May, 1939], *SW*, II, 248.

20. See interview with Edgar Snow in *Red Star Over China*, 2nd ed. (New York: Grove Press, 1968), p. 446. At present (1973) attempts are being made to introduce into the primary school curriculum a romanized form of Chinese (P'in-yen).

21. Mao Tse-tung, "Letter to Comrade Lin Piao" [1936], *CB*, No. 891 (October 8, 1969), p. 3.

22. See chapter two of Mao Tse-tung, "Chung-kuo ko-ming ho chung-kuo kung-ch'an-tang" [December, 1939], *Mao Tse-tung hsuan-chi*, II, (Peking: People's Publishing House, 1967), 595-617. An English translation is available in Mao Tse-tung, "The Chinese Revolution and the Chinese Communist Party" [December, 1939], *SW*, II, 314-334.

23. Mao Tse-tung, "Oppose Stereotyped Party Writing" [February, 1942], *SW*, III, 53-68.

24. In a letter to Lin Piao [1936] Mao expressed agreement with the idea that reality and theory are and must be linked in the educational process; Mao, "Letter to Comrade Lin Piao," p. 3.

25. Mao Tse-tung, "Reform Our Study" [May, 1941], *SW*, III, 20.

26. Mao Tse-tung, "Talk at the Yenan Forum on Literature and Art" [May, 1942], *SW*, III, 69-98. This lengthly article is the most complete exposition by Mao of his ideas concerning the relationship between politics and culture (including education).

27. Mao, "Talks at the Yenan Forum," p. 72.

28. Mao, "Talks at the Yenan Forum." p. 84. In the GPCR these demands were again raised and acted upon.

29. Mao, "Talks at the Yenan Forum," p. 86.

30. "On Regulations and Curriculum in General Education" [May 27, 1944], translated in *Chinese Education,* IV, No. 3 (Fall, 1971), 196-197.

31. "On Regulations and Curriculum," p. 202.

32."On Regulations and Curriculum," p. 204.

33. "Regarding the New Curriculum for Middle Schools" [May 27, 1944], translated in *Chinese Education,* IV, No. 4 (Winter 1971-1972), 280-281.

34. See the report by two United Nations Relief and Rehabilitation Administration [UNRRA] representatives who visited Yenan in 1947-1949 and noted the democratic and practical nature of the higher education curriculum; in the appendix of Michael Lindsay, *Notes on Educational Problems in Communist China* (New York: Institute of Pacific Relations, 1950), pp. 162-169.

35. Tsang Chiu-sam, *Society, Schools and Progress in China* (New York: Pergamon Press, 1968), p. 183.

36. R.F. Price, *Education in Communist China* (New York: Praeger Publishers, 1970), p. 115.

37. Mao Tse-tung, "Summary of Talks to Heads of Education Departments and Bureaux of Seven Provinces and Municipalities" [March 7, 1957], *CB*, No. 888 (August 22, 1969), p. 7.

38. Mao, "Summary of Talks to Heads of Education Departments," p. 7.

39. Mao Tse-tung, "On the Correct Handling of Contradictions Among the People" [February, 1957], *Four Essays on Philosophy* (Peking: Foreign Languages Press, 1968), p. 79.

40. Mao Tse-tung, "Instruction on Part-Work, Part-Study" [February, 1958], *CB*, No. 891 (October 8, 1969), p. 29.

41. Mao, "Instruction on Part-Work, Part-Study," p. 29.

42. Mao Tse-tung, "Instruction Given on an Inspection Tour of Tientsin University (excerpts)" [August, 1958], *CB*, No. 891 (October 8, 1969), p. 30.

43. Mao Tse-tung, "Instructions Given at the Spring Festival Concerning Educational Work (excerpts)" [February, 1964], *CB*, No. 891 (October 8, 1969), pp. 42-44.

44. Mao Tse-tung, "Comment on Courses of Study and Examination Method" [March, 1964], *CB*, No. 891 (October 8, 1969), p. 45. Mao also suggested that both teachers and students be involved in any new curricular reform program: Mao Tse-tung, "Comment on Peking Normal College's Investigation Material Report" [July, 1965], *CB*, No. 891 (October 8, 1969), p. 50.

45. Mao Tse-tung, "Talk at the Hangchow Conference" [December, 1965], *CB*, No. 891 (October 8, 1969), p. 52.

46. Mao, "Talk at the Hangchow Conference," p. 52.

47. Mao, "Talk at the Hangchow Conference," p. 52.

48. Mao, "Instructions Given at the Spring Festival," p. 42.

49. Mao Tse-tung, "Summary of Talk with Mao Yuan-hsin" [July 5, 1964], *CB*, No. 888 (August 22, 1969), p. 14.

50. Mao was commenting on an issue of the prominant *Che-hsueh yen-chiu* (Philosophical Research) journal (1965, No. 6) which contained articles written solely by industrial workers. Mao praised the "popular and plain. . . language of the working people" as revealed in the articles and suggested that this journal might serve as a model for other instructional materials: Mao, "Talk at the Hangchow Conference," p. 54.

51. Mao Tse-tung, "Address to Regional Secretaries and Members of the Cultural Revolution Group Under the Central Committee" [July, 1966], *CB*, No. 891 (October 8, 1969), p. 61.

52. This information was received by the author while interviewing educational authorities at Peking and Tsinghua Universities in December, 1971.

53. Mao Tse-tung, "Talk with the Nepalese Educational Delegation on Educational Problems" [1964], *CB*, No. 891 (October 8, 1969), p. 47.

54. Mao, "Summary of Talk With Mao Yuan-hsin," p. 16.

55. Mao, "Summary of Talk With Mao Yuan-hsin," p. 16. The Socialist Educational Movement is described in detail in Richard Baum and Frederick C. Teiwes, *Ssu-Ch'ing: The Socialist Education Movement of 1962-1964* (Berkeley: Center for Chinese Studies, 1968). Its urban counterpart was called the "Five-anti movement" and was designed to combat bribery, tax evasion, fraud, theft of state property, and theft of state economic secrets. Mao's concern with the political development of the nations's youth was re-stated in 1966: "For our youth, the major subject of study is class struggle." Mao Tse-tung, "Class Struggle" [August 2, 1966], *MP*, p. 116. Student involvement in the Socialist Education Movement was significant at least at one of the major universities in China (Peking University) but was secondary to the larger political struggle taking place within the Party hierarchy. See: Victor Nee, *The Cultural Revolution at Peking University* (New York: Monthly Review Press, 1969), pp. 42-43.

56. Mao Tse-tung, "The Resolutions of the Eleventh Plenum of the Central Committee of the Chinese Communist Party—The Sixteen Articles" [August 8, 1966], *MP*, p. 124.

57. The structure and shape of the new educational curriculum is described in: Stewart E. Fraser and John N. Hawkins, "Chinese Education: Reform and Development," *Phi Delta Kappan*, LIII, No. 8 (April, 1972), 494-498.

Notes to Chapter 7

1. Mao Tse-tung, "To Hakuro Toten (Miyazaki Toten)" [April, 1917], MP, p.3. "Chih-fan [a school-mate] and Tse-tung are school boys in Hunan who have acquired some knowledge of the classics and have disciplined their aspirations. We long to have an opportunity to meet you, to learn deportment and receive instructions from you. We shall feel extremely honoured if our request is granted."

2. Mao Tse-tung, "The Great Union of the Popular Masses" [1919], *The China Quarterly*, trans. by Stuart R. Schram, No. 49 (January-March, 1972), p. 80. This article appears in the original Chinese in, Mao Tse-tung, "Min-chung ti ta-lien-ho" [July 21, 1919], *MC*, I, 61-62.

3. Mao, "The Great Union," p. 81.

4. Mao, "The Great Union," pp. 80-81.

5. Mao, "The Great Union," pp. 81-82.

6. Mao, "The Great Union," pp. 81-82. The Chinese Communists have made considerable use of "models" in attempting to communicate ideals of social behaviour. This may relate somewhat to the Confucian concept of ruling by example. In any case, it is clear that Mao was thinking in these terms early in his career.

7. Mao Tse-tung, "Analysis of Classes in Chinese Society" [1926], *SW*, I, 15-16.

8. Mao Tse-tung, "Ch'ang-kang hsiang tiao-ch'a" [March 15, 1933], *MC*, IV, 157.

9. Mao Tse-tung, "Chung-hua ssu-wei-ai kung-ho-kuo chung-yang chih-hsing wei-yuan-hui yu jen-min wei-yuan hui tui ti-er-ts'e ch'uan-kuo ssu-wei-ai tai-piao ta-hui ti pao-kao" [January 26, 1934], *MC*, IV, 264.

10. This quote appears in a pamphlet originally entitled, "Material for Study," released in 1966 and translated in "Chairman Mao's Activities in Revolutionary Practice," *CB*, No. 900 (January 30, 1970), p. 20. The excerpt is probably dated 1917.

11. Mao Tse-tung, "Resolution of the Ninth Congress of the Fourth Army of the Red Army of the Communist Party of China" [December, 1929], *CB*, No. 888 (August 22, 1969), p. 2. Many of these points were heard by the author in 1971 as still representing a useful guide to teaching method.

12. Mao Tse-tung, "Hunan tse-hsiu ta-hsueh chuang-li hsuan-yen" [March 1, 1923], *MC*, I, 82.

13. Mao, "Ch'ang-kang hsiang," pp. 156-157.

14. Mao Tse-tung, "Report on an Investigation of the Peasant Movement in Hunan" [March, 1927], *SW*, I, 54. Political loyalty and enthusiasm were important considerations during the Kiangsi period as well. See Mao Tse-tung, "Kuan-yu chiao-yu kung-tso" [September 15, 1933], *MC*, IV, 30.

15. Mao Tse-tung, "Kuan-yu t'u-ti tou-cheng chung yi-hsieh wen-t'i ti chueh-ting" [October 10, 1933], *MC*, IV, 56-57.

16. See fn. no. 1 in Mao Tse-tung, "Recruit Large Numbers of Intellectuals" [December, 1939], *SW*, II, 303.

17. Mao Tse-tung, "The Chinese Revolution and the Chinese Communist Party," [December, 1939], *SW*, II, 321.

18. Mao, "The Chinese Revolution and the Chinese Communist Party," pp. 321-322.

19. Mao, "The Chinese Revolution and the Chinese Communist Party," pp. 321-322.

20. Mao Tse-tung, "On Tactics Against Japanese Imperialism" [December 27, 1935], *SW*, I, 154, 161, 164. Mao was specifically referring to the December 9, 1935 demonstration of students in Peking urging resistance to Japanese aggression. Mao also encouraged student unions in KMT controlled portions of China to form a "national defense unit." See: Mao Tse-tung, "The Tasks of the Chinese Communist Party in the Period of Resistance to Japan" [May 3, 1937], *SW*, I, 277.

21. Mao Tse-tung, "Policies, Measures and Perspectives for Resisting the Japanese Invasion" [July 23, 1937], *SW*, II, 17; also see, Mao, "Recruit Large Number of Intellectuals," pp. 301-303. These arguments are also presented later in, Mao Tse-tung, "Current Problems of Tactics in the Anti-Japanese United Front" [March 11, 1940], *SW*, II, 428.

22. Mao Tse-tung, "Comrade Mao Tse-tung's Speech at the Opening Ceremony of the Women's University of China" [July 25, 1939], *Chinese Education*, II, No. 3 (Fall, 1969), 37-38.

23. For discussions of the workings of the 1942-1944 *cheng-feng* or "rectification movement" see Boyd Compton, *Mao's China: Party Reform Documents 1942-1944* (Seattle: University of Washington Press, 1952) and Mark Selden, *The Yenan Way in Revolutionary China* (Cambridge: Harvard University Press, 1971), pp. 188-200.

24. Mao Tse-tung, "Talks at the Yenan Forum on Literature and Art" [May, 1942], *SW*, III, 90.

25. The importance of productive labor for re-education is cited in Mao Tse-tung, "Yi-chiu ssu-wu-nien ti jen-wu" [December 15, 1949], *MC*, IX, 148; also see Mao Tse-tung, "Our Tasks for 1945" [December 15, 1944], *Chinese Education*, II, Nos. 1-2 (Spring-Summer, 1969), 64-65.

26. "Hanrei kenkyu no teisho oyobi mintei shogaku shiko ni kansuru no tegami" [April, 1943], in *Mo Taku-to kyoiku ron*, ed. by Saito Akio and Niijima Atsuyoshi (Tokyo: Aoki Shoten, 1957), p. 260; the document also appears in translation in "Border Region Government Directive on Promoting the Study of Model Schools and on Experimentation with Popular Management Primary Schools" [April 18, 1944], trans. in *Chinese Education*, IV, No. 4 (Winter, 1971-1972), 273-274.

27. Mao Tse-tung, "Greet the New High Tide of the Chinese Revolution" [February 1, 1949], *SW*, IV, 120; also see, Mao Tse-tung, "The Chiang Kai-shek Government is Besieged by the Whole People" [May 30, 1947], *SW*, IV, 136.

28. Mao Tse-tung, "Correct the 'Left' Errors in Land Reform Propaganda" [February 11, 1948], *SW*, IV, 197.

29. Mao Tse-tung, "On Some Important Problems of the Party's Present Policy" [January 18, 1948], *SW*, IV, 184.

30. Mao Tse-tung, "Speech at a Conference of Cadres in the Shansi-Suiyuan Liberated Area" [April 1, 1948], *SW*, IV, 231.

31. Mao Tse-tung, "Essential Points in Land Reform in the New Liberated Areas" [February 15, 1948], *SW*, IV, 202.

32. Mao Tse-tung, "Cast Away Illusions, Prepare for Struggle" [August 14, 1949], *SW*, IV, 426-427.

33. Mao Tse-tung, "Inscription for the Anti-Japanese Military and Political College" [April, 1939], *CB*, No. 897 (December 10, 1969), p. 5; this criteria is also expressed in: Mao Tse-tung, "The May Fourth Movement" [May, 1939], *SW*, II, 238.

34. Mao Tse-tung, "The Orientation of the Youth Movement" [May 4, 1939], *SW*, II, 245. ". . . In assessing the youth movement of the past . . . we should call attention to a wrong tendency. In the youth movement of the last few decades, a section of the young people have been unwilling to unite with the workers and peasants and have opposed their movements; this is a counter-current in the youth movement."

35. Mao Tse-tung, "Rectify the Party's Style of Work" [February 1, 1942], *SW*, III, 39.

36. Mao, "Talks at the Yenan Forum," p. 73.

37. Mao, "Talks at the Yenan Forum," p. 73.

38. Mao Tse-tung, "For the Mobilization of all the Nation's Forces For Victory" [August 25, 1937], *SW*, II, 27.

39. Mao Tse-tung, "Kuan-yu mu-ch'ien cheng-chih hsing-shih yu tang ti jen-wu chueh-yi" [December 25, 1935], *MC*, V, 28.

40. Mao Tse-tung, "Kuan-yu t'u-ti cheng-ts'e ti chih-shih" [July 22, 1937], *MC*, V, 64.

41. Mao Tse-tung, "Ten Demands on the Kuomintang" [February 1, 1940] *SW*, II, 398. This statement obviously referred to the extremely repressive practices of the KMT particularly with regard to students and teachers in the cities. It does not mean that Mao and the CCP never used force to maintain their own stability but rather represents Mao's general belief that education and re-education were far more effective tools for changing ideas and beliefs.

42. Mao Tse-tung, "On New Democracy" [January, 1940], *SW*, II, 378.

43. Mao Tse-tung, "Preface and Postscripts to 'Rural Survey's' " [March and April, 1941], *SW*, III, 13.

44. Mao, "Rectify the Party's Style of Work," p. 40. Toward the end of the 1942-1944 rectification movement Mao reiterated this position at a meeting of educational personnel of the Border Region Government: "All intellectuals undoubtedly must discard the bad habit of cutting themselves off from the masses. They must dedicate themselves to the people with the spirit of giving their all and must closely integrate themselves with the workers, peasants, and soldiers. The worker-peasant-soldier-cadre should also think highly of and trust such revolutionary intellectuals." See Mao Tse-tung, "Speech Delivered in November, 1944 at a Conference of Cultural and Educational Workers of the Border Region" [November, 1944], *CB*, No. 897 (December, 1969), p. 45.

45. Mao Tse-tung, "Reform Our Study" [May, 1941], *SW*, III, 23-24.

46. Mao Tse-tung, "Kai-tsao wo-men ti hsueh-hsi" [May, 1941], *MC*, VII, 317.

47. Mao Tse-tung, "Letter to Venerable Comrade Hsu" [February, 1937], *CB*, No. 891, p. 4. Hsu T'e-li (1876-1967) was a Hunanese who instructed Mao in mathematics at the Hunan First Normal School. He joined the CCP in 1927 and in 1935 headed the educational section in the Border Region Government. He continued to remain active in educational affairs up to his death in 1967. For a biographical sketch see: Howard L. Boorman, ed., *Biographical Dictionary of Republican China,* II (New York: Columbia University Press, 1968), 149; for a colorful account of Hsu's activities in the Border Regions and some interview material see Part Six, Chapter Five of Edgar Snow, *Red Star Over China,* 2nd ed., (New York: Grove Press, Inc., 1968), pp. 233-237.

48. Mao Tse-tung, "On the Spirit of Lu Hsun—Talk at a Meeting of the North Shensi Public School Marking the Anniversary of the Death of Lu Hsun" [October, 1937], *CB*, No. 891 (October 8, 1969), pp. 6-7

49. Mao Tse-tung, "Inscription in Memory of the Founding and Opening of the North Shensi Public School" [October, 1937], *CB*, No. 891 (October 8, 1969), p. 8.

50. Mao Tse-tung, "On Coalition Government" [April 24, 1945], *SW*, III, 302-305.

51. Mao Tse-tung, "Give Serious Attention to the Discussion of the Film *The Life of Wu Hsun*" [1951], *CB*, No. 891 (October 8, 1969), p. 15.

52. Mao Tse-tung, "Talk at the Reception for the Presidium of the Second National Congress of the Youth League" [June, 1953], *CB*, No. 891 (October 8, 1969), p. 16.

53. This sentiment was expressed most vividly in a speech to Chinese students in Moscow in 1957 and quoted widely by Red Guards in the summer of 1966: "The world is yours as well as ours, but in the last analysis, it is yours. You young people, full of vigour and vitality, are in the bloom of life, like the sun at eight or nine in the morning. Our hope is placed in you. . . . The world belongs to you. China's future belongs to you." *Quotations of Mao Tse-tung* (Peking: Foreign Languages Press, 1966), p. 288.

54. The relationship of these campaigns to education is discussed in Stewart E. Fraser, ed., *Chinese Communist Education: Records of the First Decade* (New York: John Wiley and Sons, 1965), pp. 22-32.

55. Mao Tse-tung, *Speech at the Chinese Communist Party's National Conference on Propaganda Work* (Peking: Foreign Languages Press, 1966), p. 5. The excerpt quoted is dated March, 1957.

56. Mao, *Speech at the Chinese Communist Party's National Conference on Propaganda Work,* p. 5.

57. This has been suggested by Stuart Schram in *Mao Tse-tung* (London: Penguin Press, 1966), p. 289.

58. Mao, *Speech at the Chinese Communist Party's National Conference on Propaganda Work,* p. 7.

59. Mao, *Speech at the Chinese Communist Party's National Conference on Propaganda Work,* p. 8.

60. Mao Tse-tung, "Summary of Talk to Heads of Education Departments and Bureaux of Seven Provinces and Municipalities" [March 7, 1957], *CB,* No. 888 (August 22, 1969), p. 7.

61. Mao Tse-tung, "Instruction on Part-Work, Part-Study" [February, 1958], *CB,* No. 891 (October 8, 1969), p. 29. The role of teachers was also expected to change during this period as evidenced in this statement by Mao: "Teachers should also take part in labor and they cannot just give lip service to the matter without giving a hand to it." Mao Tse-tung, "Instruction Given on an Inspection Tour of Tientsin University" [August, 1958], *CB,* No. 891 (October 8, 1969), p. 30.

62. Mao, "Instruction on Part-Work, Part-Study," p. 29.

63. Mao Tse-tung, "Things are Changing" [May, 1957], *CB,* No. 891 (October 8, 1969), p. 24.

64. Mao Tse-tung, "Sixty Points on Working Methods—A Draft Resolution from the Office of the Centre of the CCP" [February, 1958], *MP,* p. 71.

65. Mao, "Speech at the Chinese Communist Party's National Conference on Propaganda Work," p. 9.

66. Mao, "Speech at the Chinese Communist Party's National Conference on Propaganda Work," p. 10.

67. Stuart Schram suggests that opposition to "romanticism" was official until the Great Leap Forward of 1958. Revolutionary romanticism then became permissible. However, it is unlikely that all members of the Party shifted easily to this new position. See, Schram, *Mao Tse-tung,* p. 293.

68. Mao Tse-tung, "Talk at the Second Session of the Eighth National Congress" [May 8, 1958], *CB*, No. 888 (August 22, 1969), p. 9.

69. Mao Tse-tung, "Talk at the Conference of Heads of Delegations to the Second Session of the Eighth Congress, May 18, 1958" [May 18, 1958], *CB*, No. 888 (August 22, 1969), p. 9.

70. Mao Tse-tung, "Instruction Given on an Inspection Tour of Wuhan University (excerpts)" [September, 1958], *CB*, No. 891 (October 8, 1969), p. 31.

71. Edgar Snow, "A Conversation with Mao Tse-tung," *Life*, LXX, No. 16 (April 30, 1971), 46.

72. Mao Tse-tung, "His Wish" [July 29, 1966], *MP*, p. 115.

73. These terms were ascribed to Mao during the height of the GPCR by Red Guards and other supporters. Mao has since indicated that this level of adulation was unfortunate but necessary and he now hopes that all terms but "Great Teacher" will be dropped. Snow, "A Conversation with Mao Tse-tung," p. 46.

74. Andre Malraux, *Anti-Memoirs* (New York: Holt, Rinehart and Winston, 1968), p. 365.

75. Mao Tse-tung, "Comment on Courses of Study and Examination Method" [March, 1964], *CB*, No. 891 (October 8, 1969), p. 45.

76. Mao Tse-tung "Instructions Given at the Spring Festival Concerning Educational Work" [February, 1964], *CB*, No. 891 (October 8, 1969), p. 43.

77. Mao Tse-tung, "Summary of a Talk with Mao Yuan-hsin" [July 5, 1964], *CB*, No. 888 (August 22, 1969), p. 14.

78. Mao Tse-tung, "Talk at the Hangchow Conference" [December, 1965], *CB*, No. 891 (October 8, 1969), p. 53.

79. Mao, "Talk at the Hangchow Conference," pp. 51, 53. Also see, *The Whole Country Should Become a Great School of Mao Tse-tung's Thought* (Peking: Foreign Languages Press, 1966), p. 2.

80. Mao Tse-tung, "A Letter to the Red Guards of the Middle School Attached to Tsinghua University" [August, 1966], *CB*, No. 891 (October 8, 1969), p. 63.

81. It is clear that various leading governmental bodies and some members of the Central Committee were dissatisfied with the developing student movement. Mao clearly supported the students in this respect and criticized those in opposition to the GPCR: "It is anti-Marxist for the Communist Party to fear the student movement" (see, Mao Tse-tung, "Talks to Central Committee Leaders" [1966], *CB*, No. 891 (October 8, 1969), p. 58.). "I firmly believe that a few months of disturbances will be mostly for the good. . . if the students want to be on the streets, let them." (See: Mao Tse-tung "A Talk Before the Central Committee Work Conference" [August, 1966], *CB*, No. 891 (October 8, 1969), p. 68.

82. Mao Tse-tung, "Instruction on the Problems of Tsingtao, Changsha and Sian" [September, 1966], *CB*, No. 891 (October 8, 1969), p. 69. Mao also cautioned against any attempts to forcibly repress the student movement and cited

past history as an example of the result of such action: "None of those who repressed student movements has ended well. The Manchu government repressed them; how did it end? The northern warlords did the same. How did they end? Chiang Kai-shek repressed them; how did he end? Lu P'ing of Peking University and Chiang Nan-hsiang of Tsinghua University did exactly the same; how did they end? The work teams sent out later also repressed them. Now they have met their doom. . . . Of course we must add that the blame goes to those who sent them." Mao Tse-tung, "Repressing Students" [September 2, 1966], *MP*, p. 129.

83. On several occasions Mao clearly urged rebellious Red Guards to form as broad a united front as possible. See, Mao, "A Letter to the Red Guards of the Middle School Attached to Tsinghua University," p. 63; Mao Tse-tung, "Speech at Enlarged Work Conference of the Central Committee" [1966] *CB*, No. 891 (October 8, 1969), p. 66; Mao Tse-tung, "The Resolutions of the Eleventh Plenum of the Central Committee of the CCP—the Sixteen Articles" [August 8, 1969], *MP*, p. 124. Students who were later termed "ultra-left" were precisely those who were urging that no alliance be made with any segment of the population who had made ideological mistakes or had been misled by the anti-Mao forces. Their failure to come to terms with their own elitism and ideological shortcomings is discussed in an enlightening case study by William Hinton. "Hundred Day War: The Cultural Revolution at Tsinghua University," *Monthly Review*, XXIV, No. 3 (July-August, 1972) pp. 1-288.

84. The role of the PLA is discussed in, Mao Tse-tung, "The PLA and Schools" [March 7, 1967], *MP*, p. 136; Mao Tse-tung, "Military and Political Training is Good" [March 16, 1967], *CB*, No. 897 (December 10, 1969), p. 17.

85. Mao Tse-tung "Talk with the Nepalese Educational Delegation on Educational Problems" [1964], *CB*, No. 891 (October 8, 1969), p. 46.

86. Mao Tse-tung, "Comment on Peking Normal College's Investigation Material Report" [July, 1965], *CB*, No. 891 (October 8, 1969), p. 50.

87. For examples of these sentiments see, Mao Tse-tung, "Quotations From Chairman Mao" [May 4, 1968], *CB*, No. 897 (December 10, 1969), p. 45; Mao Tse-tung, "Re-educating Intellectuals" [September 12, 14, 1968], *MP*, p. 155; Mao Tse-tung, "The Orientation of the Revolution in Medical Education as Seen from the Maturing of 'Barefoot Doctors' " [September 14, 1968], *CB*, No. 897 (December 10, 1969), p. 49.

88. Mao Tse-tung, "Re-Educating the Young" [December 22, 1968], *MP*, p. 157.

89. Karl Marx and Frederick Engels, *The German Ideology* (New York: International Publishers, 1970), p. 53.

Notes to Chapter 8

1. Mao Tse-tung, "Hunan tse-hsiu ta-hsueh chuang-li hsuan-yen" [March 1, 1923], *MC*, I, 83. The curriculum of the "Self-Study University is discussed in Chapter Six.

2. Mao Tse-tung, "Report on an Investigation of the Peasant Movement in Hunan" [March, 1927], *SW*, I, 54.

3. Mao Tse-tung, "Chung-kuo kung-ch'an-tang hung-chun ti-ssu-chun ti-chiu-ts'a tai-piao ta-hui chu-yi-an" [1929], *MC*, II, 117.

4. During Edgar Snow's visit to Yenan in 1936 he found the following conditions among the First Front Army: "Between sixty and seventy per cent of the soldiers were literate—that is, they could write simple letters and texts, posters, handbills, etc. This was much higher than the average among ordinary troops in the White districts [KMT] and it was very much higher than the average in the peasantry of the Northwest." Edgar Snow, *Red Star Over China*, 2nd ed., (New York: Grove Press, Inc., 1968), p. 258. Also see: Michael Lindsay, *Notes on Educational Problems in Communist China* (New York: Institute of Pacific Relations, 1950); Jack Belden, *China Shakes the World* (New York: Monthly Review Press, 1970), pp. 237-242.

5. Mao Tse-tung, "Ch'ang-kang hsiang tiao-ch'a" [March 15, 1933], *MC*, IV, 158. Mao was also very impressed with the extent of women's education and stated that the elimination of illiteracy among women was "the first step toward their liberation." Mao encouraged women to take an active role in the administration of education. See: Mao Tse-tung, "Chung-hua ssu-wei-ai kung-ho-kuo chung-yang chih-hsing wei-yuan-hui yu jen-min wei-yuan-hui tui ti-er-ts'e ch'uan-kuo ssu-wei-ai tai piao ta-hui ti pao-kao" [January 26, 1934], *MC*, IV, 262.

6. Mao, "Ch'ang-kang hsiang tiao-ch'a," p. 159.

7. The startling contrast between peasants in the "liberated" areas of China who were keenly interested in national and international affairs and the traditional, conservative peasants of North China was noted by Lindsay, *Notes on Educational Problems in Communist China*, p. 43.

8. Mao, "Ch'ang-kang hsiang tiao-ch'a," pp. 159-160. The students would contribute roughly eighty percent of the material for the newspaper and the community groups the remaining twenty percent.

9. See ethnolinguistic maps and discussion in: *People's Republic of China: Atlas* (Washington D.C.: United States Government Printing Office, 1971), pp. 40-45. For a brief discussion of overall Chinese Communist policy toward national minorities see: Edgar Snow, *Red China Today*, 2nd ed., (New York: Vintage Books, 1971), pp. 568-572.

10. For an account of the Long March and the problems with the minorities encountered on the way see: Snow, *Red Star Over China*, pp. 185-208.

11. This was the first reference the author was able to find by Mao on the educational needs of the national minorities. Mao Tse-tung, "Lun hsin chieh-tuan" [October 12-14, 1938], *MC*, VI, 220.

12. For a more detailed discussion of the cadre concept in Chinese Communist politics see: Franz Schurmann, *Ideology and Organization in Communist China*, 2nd ed., (Berkeley: University of California Press, 1968), pp. 162-172.

13. Mao Tse-tung, "The Role of the Chinese Communist Party in the National War" [October, 1938], *SW*, II, 203.

14. Mao, "The Role of the Chinese Communist Party," p. 208.

15. Mao, "The Role of the Chinese Communist Party," p. 210.

16. In the introduction to a newly founded CCP journal Mao suggested that this kind of journal could ". . . become a school for educating the workers and for training cadres from their midst. . . ". Mao Tse-tung, "Introducing The Chinese Worker" [February 7, 1940], *SW*, II, 403-404.

17. Mao Tse-tung, "The Experience of the Liu-kou Village Branch of Chu-nan County Communist Youth Corps in Organizing Record Work Study Classes" [1956], *Chinese Education*, II, No. 3 (Fall, 1969), 54-55.

18. Mao Tse-tung, "A Welcome Evening Agricultural Technical School" [1956], *Chinese Education*, II, No. 3 (Fall, 1969), 56.

19. Mao Tse-tung, "On the Ten Great Relationships" [April, 1956], *Mao*, ed. by Jerome Ch'en (New Jersey: Prentice Hall, 1969), p. 70.

20. Mao, "On the Ten Great Relationships," p. 70.

21. E.L. Wheelwright and Bruce McFarlane, *The Chinese Road to Socialism* (New York: Monthly Review Press, 1970), p. 41.

22. Mao Tse-tung, "Sixty Points on Working Method—A Draft Resolution From the Office of the Centre of the CCP" [February, 1958], *CB*, No. 891 (October 8, 1969), p. 29.

23. Robert D. Baredsen [sic], "The Innovation of Half-Work and Half-Study Schools," *Chinese Society Under Communism: A Reader*, ed. by William T. Liu (New York: John Wiley and Sons, 1967), pp. 345-362.

24. Mao Tse-tung, "A Letter to Kiangsi Communist Labor University" [July 30, 1961], *CB*, No. 891 (October 8, 1969), p. 36.

25. This discussion is abstracted from an article by the author. See, John N. Hawkins, "Mao Tse-tung and Bureaucracy: The May 7 Cadre Schools," *Journal of Continuing Education and Training*, I, No. 4 (May, 1972), 259-266.

26. Seymour Martin Lipset, *Political Man* (New York: Doubleday and Co., 1963), p. 10.

27. In the early 1950s a rectification campaign was carried out (the *cheng-feng* movement) to correct such tendencies among cadres; in 1955 another campaign was launched (the *szu-fan* movement) also directed against the bureaucracy; in 1957 in connection with the Hundred Flowers Movement another rectification of cadres took place with cadres being sent down to the countryside to participate in manual labor; and finally, the massive anti-bureaucratic movement of 1966 known as the Great Proletarian Cultural Revolution climaxed the attempt at cadre rectification. For descriptions of

these movements see, Schurmann, *Ideology and Organization in Communist China.*

28. *The Whole Country Should Become a School For Mao Tse-tung's Thought* (Peking: Foreign Languages Press, 1966), p. 1. For further information on the operation of May Seventh Cadre Schools see, *CB*, No. 888 (August 22, 1969), p. 17; Li Teh, "Wu-ch'i kan-hsiao yu kung-kan lun-hsun," *Chung-kuo ta-lu yen-chiu,* No. 4 (April 25, 1971), p. 19; *The Great Power Struggle in China* (Hong Kong: Asia Research Center, 1969), p. 464.

29. Stewart E. Fraser and John N. Hawkins, "Chinese Education: Revolution and development," *Phi Delta Kappan,* LIII, No. 8 (April, 1972), 498-499.

Notes to Chapter 9

1. The bulk of what is known about the Chinese communist economy can be found in five major studies: T.C. Liu and K.C. Yeh, *The Economy of the Chinese Mainland: National Income and Economic Development 1933-1959* (Princeton: Princeton University Press, 1965); *An Economic Profile of Mainland China,* 2 vols. (Washington D.C.: Joint Economic Committee of the U.S. Congress, 1967); A. Eckstein, T.C. Liu and W. Galenson eds., *Economic Trends in Communist China* (Chicago: Aldine Publishing Company, 1968); Barry M. Richman, *Industrial Society in Communist China* (New York: Vintage Books, 1969); E. L. Wheelwright and Bruce McFarlane, *The Chinese Road to Socialism* (New York: Monthly Review Press, 1970).

2. Richman, *Industrial Society in Communist China,* p. 597.

3. Richman, *Industrial Society in Communist China,* pp. 603-615.

4. Richman, *Industrial Society in Communist China,* pp. 610-618 and Wheelwright, *The Chinese Road to Socialism,* pp. 13-95.

5. Richman, *Industrial Society in Communist China,* pp. 214-215.

6. Wheelwright, *The Chinese Road to Socialism,* pp. 66-77, and Richman, *Industrial Society in Communist China,* p. 614.

Partially Annotated Bibliography

Bibliographic Note

A complete collection of Mao Tse-tung's writings is not yet available. Only a small portion of his works has been officially released by Peking, consisting primarily of the four volumes of the *Selected Works of Mao Tse-tung* and several miscellaneous pamphlets. The Chinese acknowledge the existence of additional materials and future volumes are in the planning stage. The selection of Mao's writings utilized in this study draws heavily from both official and nonofficial collections of Mao's works. In both, primary consideration has been given to the degree of authenticity, historical period, intended audience, and degree of editing (to the extent that this could be determined). Unless other factors intervened, documents were avoided which did not have a legitimate source or could not be reasonably ascribed to Mao. The annotations in the bibliography were for the most part restricted to Mao's works or secondary sources directly related to Mao's educational thought.

Each bibliographic entry authored by Mao shows the original date of publication in brackets immediately following the title unless it is the same as the date of the original source of the document, in which case it appears in the parenthetical entry along with the citation of the original publication.

The information following the words "Originally published in . . ." does not necessarily mean that the only source is the one listed in the parentheses following the main entry. Rather it is intended to represent the original source from which the editor of the collection derived the document.

Several major collections of Mao's works were invaluable in searching out and isolating his thoughts on education. The ten-volume collection compiled by a Japanese team of scholars headed by Takeuchi Minoru is the most complete down to 1949 (*Mao Tse-tung chi*). Each document appears in Chinese and where possible the original source appears at the end of each document. The four volumes of the Peking 1965 edition of the *Selected Works of Mao Tse-tung* complements the Japanese collection for the same time period. Beyond 1949 Jerome Ch'en's collection (*Mao Papers*) along with documents contained in various editions of *Current Background* provide a major source. The editors of both relied heavily upon statements and quotations by Mao obtained during the Great Proletarian Cultural Revolution and verified in most instances as actually belonging to Mao by several scholars specializing in this subject. (See *Time Magazine*, No. 24, December 12, 1969. pp. 32-33.) One collection in particular appearing in Ch'en and *Current Background* is entitled *Mao Tse-tung ssu-hsiang wan-sui* and contains no additional publication data. This pamphlet was distributed during the GPCR and contains several previously verified documents and statements as well as a number of new entries.

The following bibliography is organized according to major topics and historical periods. The Wade-Giles romanization system has been used for all Chinese titles and terms except those where common usage has been established (e.g., Peking).

I. MARXISM, LENINISM, AND EDUCATION

Bauer, Raymond H.; Inkeles, Alex; and Kluckholn, Clyde. *How the Soviet System Works: Cultural, Psychological and Social Themes.* Cambridge, Mass.: Harvard University Press, 1956. xiv+274 pp.

Based on refugee accounts this book attempts with some success to provide an overview of Soviet society and the individual in that society.

Bauer, Raymond H. *The New Man in Soviet Psychology.* Cambridge, Mass.: Harvard University Press, 1959. xv+229 pp.

This book traces the history of the theory and practice of psychology in the Soviet Union from 1917 up through the fifties.

Bereday, G. *The Politics of Soviet Education.* New York: Praeger, 1960. vi+217pp.

Bowen, James. *Soviet Education: Anton Makarenko and the Years of Experiment.* Madison: University of Wisconsin, 1962. 232 pp.

This book analyzes Makarenko's educational ideas and practices particularly as they were derived from and related to his experiments in the orphan colonies—behavior modification.

Cameron, Meribeth H. *The Reform Movement in China: 1898-1912.* New York: Octagon Books, 1963. 233 pp.

Counts, George S. *The Challenge of Soviet Education.* New York: McGraw-Hill, 1957. xi+330 pp.

A polemical account of Soviet educational practice up to the 1950s.

d'Encausse, Helene Carrere, and Schram, Stuart R. *Marxism and Asia: An Introduction with Readings.* Baltimore: Penguin Press, 1969. 404 pp.

A very important, unique account of the coming of Marxism to Asia; gives a clear account with many documents of Mao's understanding of Marxism—Leninism.

Easton, Loyd D., and Guddat, Kurt H. eds. *Writings of the Young Marx on Philosophy and Society.* New York: Doubleday and Co., 1967. ix+506.

This collection presents seminal writings of Karl Marx in the early period of his career in 1830-50; much of his later work can be traced to this period including his ideas on education.

Engels, Fredrick. *Anti-Duhring.* New York: International Publishers, 1939. vi+365 pp.

———. *Socialism: Utopian and Scientific.* Translated by Edward Aveling. New York: International Publishers, 1935. 96 pp.

Hawkins, John N. *Educational Theory in the People's Republic of China: The Report of Ch'ien Chun-jui.* No. 6. Honolulu; Univer-of Hawaii Press, 1971. 122 pp.

A commentary and translation of the first official document on education to emerge following the communist victory in 1949; contains a brief section on the pre-1949 educational thought of Mao.

Hessen, Sergio, and Han, Nicholas. *Educational Policy in Soviet Russia.* London: P. S. King and Son, 1930.

Isaacs, Harold R. *The Tragedy of the Chinese Revolution.* Stanford: Stanford University Press, 1961. xix+392 pp.

This book examines the establishment of the Communist Party of China focusing particularly on the relationship between that body and the Comintern in Moscow.

Johnson, W.H. *Russia's Educational Heritage.* Pittsburgh: Carnegie Press, 1950.

Kalinin, Mikhail Ivanovich. *On Communist Education: Selected Speeches and Articles.* Moscow: Foreign Languages Publishing House, 1950. 479 pp.

A collection of speeches and excerpts of speeches by a leading Soviet educational authority during the war years. It is an example of the kind of retrenchment characteristic of this period.

Kuusinen, O.V., et. al. *Fundamentals of Marxism—Leninism.* Moscow: Foreign Languages Publishing House, 1963. 735 pp.

Although an official Soviet handbook of Marxist ideology this volume provides a handy reference for almost any aspect of Marxism—Leninism.

Lenin, V.I. *Collected Works.* Vols. 14 and 38. Moscow: Foreign Languages Publishing House, 1962. 498 and 565 pp.

______. *On Socialist Ideology and Culture.* Moscow: Foreign Languages Publishing House, n.d. 136 pp.

This pamphlet contains several excerpts from articles by Lenin on the topic of the relationship between socialist ideology and culture particularly in the realms of religion and education.

Levin, Deana. *Soviet Education Today.* Rev. ed. New York: Monthly Review Press, 1963. 179 pp.

Li Yu-ning. *The Introduction of Socialism into China.* New York: Columbia University Press, 1971. 138 pp.

This monograph traces the earliest instances of socialist ideas and literature in China noting that the Japanese had more influence on early Chinese socialist thought than did the Russians.

Lilge, Frederick. "Lenin and the Politics of Education," *Slavic Review,* No. 2 (June, 1968), 230-257.

Marx, Karl. *Capital.* Vol. I. New York: International Publishers, 1967. xii+805 pp.

______, and Engels, Frederick. *The Communist Manifesto.* New York: International Publishers, 1948. 48 pp.

______. *Critique of Political Economy.* Chicago: Charles H. Kerr and Co., 1904. 276 pp.

______. *Critique of the Gotha Program.* New York: International Publishers, 1938. vii+116 pp.

______, and Engels, Frederick. *The German Ideology.* New York: International Publishers, 1970. viii+158 pp.

A classical treatise which makes comparisons between capitalist and communist type societies focusing on questions related to division of labor and education.

Pinkevich, Albert. *The New Education in the Soviet Republic.* New York: The John Day Co., 1929. 401 pp.

The author, a leading educational theorist in the USSR in the 1920's provides a fairly complete exposition of the experimental phase of Soviet education.

Schlesinger, Ina. "Soviet Educational Change," *School and Society,* C, No. 2338 (January, 1972), 43-48.

A clear and concise analysis and description of post-1950 educational reforms primarily at the secondary level.

Schwartz, Benjamin I. *Chinese Communism and the Rise of Mao.* Cambridge, Mass.: Harvard University Press, 1964. ix+258 pp.

An important account of Mao's rise in the CCP and the development of that organization.

Shore, Maurice. *Soviet Education: Its Psychology and Philosophy.* New York: Philosophical Library, 1947. 346 pp.

The author discusses the basic pedagogical principles of Marx, Engels and Lenin down to 1940 in terms of practical application.

Snow, Edgar. *Red Star Over China.* Rev. and enlarged ed. New York: Grove Press, 1968. 543 pp.

This is a classic account of Mao Tse-tung's life and also contains useful information on the development of Marxism—Leninism in a Chinese setting.

Widmayer, Ruth. "A Historical Survey of Soviet Education," in Alex Inkeles and Kent Geiger, eds. *Soviet Society: A Book of Readings*, pp. 429-439. Boston: Houghton Mifflin Co., 1961.

The author traces Soviet educational theory and practice from the pre-Bolshevic period down to the late 1950s.

Wingo, Max. *The Philosophy of American Education*. Lexington, Mass. D.C. Heath and Co., 1965. 438 pp.

Zepper, John T. "Recent and Contemporary Soviet Educational Thought," *School and Society*, C, No. 2338 (January, 1972), 31-43.

A concise and analytical article summing up Soviet educational thought down to 1972.

II. EDUCATIONAL THOUGHT IN TRADITIONAL AND REPUBLICAN CHINA

Balazs, Etienne. *Chinese Civilization and Bureaucracy: Variations on a Theme*. Edited by Arthur F. Wright; translated by H.M. Wright. New Haven: Yale University Press, 1964. 309 pp.

A collection of Professor Balazs's writings on the nature of Chinese institutional history. The subjects are all cogently argued including discussions of feudalism, the rise and failure of capitalism etc. A valuable selection for anyone desiring a background in traditional Chinese thought and practice.

Biggerstaff, Knight. *The Earliest Modern Government Schools in China*. Ithaca, N.Y.: Cornell University Press, 1961. xi+276 pp.

This book describes the first attempts by the Ch'ing dynasty to modernize the educational system by examining three of the schools established for this purpose.

deBary, William Theodore, Wing-tsit Chan, and Watson, Burton, eds. *Sources of Chinese Tradition*. Vol. I. New York: Columbia University Press, 1960. 578 pp.

An excellent source book for an introduction to some of the original writings in English of Chinese philosophy.

Eichhorn, Werner. *Chinese Civilization: An Introduction*. Translated by Janet Seligman. New York: Praeger, 1969. 360 pp.

A fairly complete introductory treatment of early Chinese civilization up through the Sung dynasty—the Yuan, Ming, and Ch'ing periods are treated only slightly. Education is covered only during the Sung when Wang An-shih attempted reform of the existing educational system. (P. 258)

Ho Ping-ti, and Tang Tsou. "Salient Aspects of China's Heritage." *China in Crisis: China's Heritage and the Communist Political System.* Vol. I, Book 1. Chicago: University of Chicago Press, 1968. Pp. 1-92.

A wide-ranging and provocative analysis of those aspects of China's traditional past which persist and influence her present. The paper is followed by critical comments by Wright, Franke, Bodde, and Creel which nicely balance the rather one-sided picture given by Ho of a modern China which is in many ways a carbon copy of the past. Ho adds an addendum which concedes on some points while basically standing firm.

Kuo, Ping-wen. *The Chinese System of Public Education.* New York: Teachers College, Columbia University, 1915. xii+209 pp.

This study traces educational theory and practice from earliest times in China to the advent of Republican China.

Kusumoto, M. "Educational Thought of the People of China." *Year Book of Education, 1957.* New York: World Book Co., 1957. Pp. 113-127.

A provocative article which discusses the nature of traditional educational thought with some discussion of educational institutions.

Levenson, Joseph R. *Modern China: An Interpretive Anthology.* London: Macmillan Co., 1971. 236 pp.

An important anthology of writings by China scholars the primary purpose being to link traditional China with its modern form. Education is dealt with only incidentally especially in the articles by Levenson.

———. *Modern China and Its Confucian Past.* New York: Doubleday Anchor Book, 1964. 246 pp.

An engaging attempt to account for continuity and change in Chinese history and culture. Basically concludes that while continuity (intellectual) exists, China had been undergoing slow change and rejection of traditional values and institutions (i.e., the Confucian educational institution) and Marxism was a rejection of these values while maintaining some traditionalistic elements.

Loewe, Michael. *Imperial China: The Historical Background to the Modern Age.* New York: Praeger, 1965. 325 pp.

The author uses the topical approach to the study of Imperial China rather than chronological. The chapter on "The Basis and Practice of Imperial Sovereignty" provides the necessary background to the understanding of traditional Chinese attitudes and practices with regard to education.

Lund, Renville Clifton. "The Imperial University of Peking." Unpublished Ph. D. dissertation. Ann Arbor, Mich. University Microfilm, 1957. 353 pp.

A complete and thorough analysis of the origin and operation of the Imperial University of Peking from the period 1898 to 1911. Provides a good description of Chinese traditional theory and practice of education and the effect of the impact of the West.

McAleavy, Henry. *The Modern History of China.* New York: Praeger Publishers. 1967, x+392 pp.

A concise historical analysis of events following the fall and decline of the Ch'ing dynasty up through the establishment and development of the People's Republic of China.

Miles, John "Tung-lung-men: An Introduction to the Civil Service Examination in Traditional China." Unpublished Honor's Thesis for Howard Boorman, Vanderbilt University May, 1970. 129 pp.

An useful outline of development of the examination system but questions conclusions with regard to the efficacy of the system.

Mote, Frederick W. *Intellectual Foundations of China.* New York: Alfred A. Knopf, 1971. xiii+135 pp.

Peake, Cyrus H. *Nationalism and Education in Modern China.* New York: Columbia University Press, 1932. xiv+240 pp.

This dated but informed book on early Republican education in China traces the movements of educational theory and practice from the elimination of the Civil Service Examinations in 1905 to the rise of KMT nationalism in the 1930's.

Schurmann, Franz, and Schell, Orville. *Imperial China: The Decline of of the Last Dynasty and the Origins of Modern China. The 18 and and 19th Centuries.* The China Reader, 1. New York: Random House, Vintage Books, 1967. 322 pp.

Book one of a three-book reader series dealing with Imperial China, Republican, and Communist China respectively. This volume contains selections from many China specialists on Chinese society with editorial comments designed to provide continuity between the past and the present—good selections and very useful commentaries.

Schwartz, Benjamin. "Some Polarities in Confucian Thought. Chapter 1: Ideas and Values." *Confucianism and Chinese Civilization.* Edited by Arthur F. Wright. New York: Atheneum, 1964. Pp. 3-15.

A discussion of three polarities which Confucian scholars attempted over the years to reconcile or at least come to terms with (self-cultivation vs. ordering of society; inner vs. outer realms; knowledge vs. action). The discussion is useful in finding parallels within the experience of the Chinese Communists in their attempt to apply Marxism to a formerly Confucian intellectual tradition.

Solomon, Richard H. "Educational Themes in China's Changing Culture." *Education in Comparative and International Perspective.* Edited by Kalil T. Gezi. New York: Holt, Rinehart and Winston Inc., 1971. Pp. 158-179.

III. MAO TSE-TUNG A BIOGRAPHICAL SKETCH

Boorman, Howard L. *Mao Tse-tung: The Lacquered Image,* Bombay: Manktalas, 1965. 75 pp.

First published in *The China Quarterly,* October-December, 1963. Boorman's essay analyzes Mao's life in an attempt to separate the historical Mao from the image.

Chang Kuo-t'ao. "Mao—A New Portrait by an Old Colleague." *New York Times Magazine,* August 2, 1953.

A personal insight into Mao's personality.

Ch'en, Jerome. *Mao and the Chinese Revolution.* New York: Oxford University Press, 1967. xi+419 pp.

One of the best histories of Mao and his role in the formation and development of the CCP.

"The Flame Over the Hsiang River." *Selections from China Mainland Magazines,* No. 621 (July 29, 1968), pp. 1-37. (Originally published in *Chieh-fang-chun wen-i,* No. 6, March 25, 1968.)

The article is on the early life of Mao Tse-tung.

"The Great Voyage." *Selections from China Mainland Magazines.* No. 614 (February 12, 1968), pp. 23-26. (Originally published in *Chieh-fang-chun wen-i,* Nos. 20-21, 1967.)

This article is on the early life of Mao Tse-tung.

"The Hsiang River is Roaring." *Selections from China Mainland Magazines,* No. 614 (February 12, 1968), pp. 14-17. (Originally published in *Chieh-fang-chun wen-i,* Nos. 20-21. 1967.)

This article is on the early life of Mao Tse-tung.

Hsiao San. *Mao Tse-tung, His Childhood and Youth.* Bombay: 1953 n.p. (Originally published in *Mao Tse-tung t'ung-chih ti ch'u erh-t'ung shih-tai, ch'ing-nien shih-tai, yu ch'u-ch'i ko-ming huo-tung,* Peking, 1949.)

Huang, Yu-ch'uan, ed. *Mao Tse-tung sheng-p'ing tzu-liao chian-pian.* Hong Kong: Union Research Institute, 1970. 544 pp.

This volume provides an annotated chronological account of Mao's life from 1893-1969.

Li Jui. *Mao Tse-tung t'ung chih ti ch'u-ch'i ko-ming huo-tung.* Peking: Jen-min ch'u-pan she, 1957.

This is the only official biography of the life of Mao Tse-tung and contains some information not found elsewhere.

Mao Tse-tung yu hung-huo. Taipei: n.p., 1959. 560 pp.
This account of Mao and the CCP was prepared by the Central Executive Committee of the Kuomintang and represents an official Nationalist Chinese view.

Payne, Robert. *Mao Tse-tung*. New York: Weybright and Talley, 1969. 343 pp.
The book contains a fairly standard account of Mao's life with a useful chronology and index.

Rice, Edward E. *Mao's Way*. Berkeley: University of California Press, 1972. ix+596 pp.
A former American Consul General in Hong Kong, Rice offers a general account of Mao's rise in Chinese politics and especially his role during the GPCR.

Schram, Stuart. *Mao Tse-tung*. London: Penguin Press, 1966. 372 pp.
Schram provides one of the most comprehensive and analytical accounts of the life and work of Mao Tse-tung.

Shigeki, Kaizuka. *Mo Taku-to den*. Tokyo: n.p., 1956.
A popular account by a prominent Japanese scholar of traditional China.

Snow Edgar. *Red Star Over China*. 2nd. ed. New York: Grove Press, 1968. 543 pp.
This classic account given by Mao Tse-tung himself to the author still ranks as the best biography of Mao down to the Yenan period; the new edition contains some previously unpublished interviews with Mao.

IV. MAO TSE-TUNG'S EDUCATION THOUGHT: 1917-1949

Ayers, William. *Chang Chih-tung and Educational Reform in China*. Cambridge, Mass.: Harvard University Press, 1971. xiii+287 pp.
The author provides a probing view of educational reform attempted in China at the turn of the century by examining the life of one of the major promoters of reform.

Belden, Jack. *China Shakes the World*. New York: Monthly Review Press, 1970. 524 pp.
Originally published in 1949, this represents a classical account by a journalist who observed the last three years of pre-Communist China.

"Border Region Government Directive on Promoting the Study of Model Schools and on Experimentation with Popular-Management Primary Schools" [April 18, 1944], Translated in *Chinese Education*, IV, No. 4 (Winter, 1971-1972), 269-275.
This article is not attributed to Mao but appears in a Japanese collection of Mao's writings on education and seems to be in

Mao's style. Here it is cited as being a publication of the Civil Affairs Office of the Shen-kan-ning government.

"Chairman Mao's Activities in Revolutionary Practice," *Current Background,* No. 900 (January 30, 1970). 47 pp.

This pamphlet appeared possibly in 1966 under the title "Material for Study" and was probably intended as a source book for the Cultural Revolution.

Ch'en, Jerome. *Mao and the Chinese Revolution.* New York: Oxford University Press, 1967, 419 pp.

By far the most rigorous and objective account of Mao and his rise to power in China; it deals only peripherally with education and Mao's thought.

Chow Tse-tung. *The May Fourth Movement: Intellectual Revolution in Modern China.* Cambridge, Mass.: Harvard University Press, 1964. xv+486 pp.

Cohen, Arthur A. *The Communism of Mao Tse-tung.* Chicago: University of Chicago Press, 1964. 210 pp.

In this book the author presents a general summary of Mao Tse-tung's grasp of the fundamentals of Marxism—Leninism and attempts to show Mao's contribution to Marxism—Leninism.

Compton, Boyd. *Mao's China: Party Reform Documents 1942-1944.* Seattle: University of Washington Press, 1952. 278 pp.

This contains documents from an early reform movement including several documents by Mao appearing in translation for the first time; the introduction by Compton contains an illuminating discussion of the thought of Mao Tse-tung.

"Comrade Mao Tse-tung on Educational Work [Part I]." *Chinese Education,* II, Nos. 1-2 (Spring-Summer, 1969), 35-67. (Originally published by People's Publishing House, Peking, 1958. Pp. 1-3.)

"Comrade Mao Tse-tung on Educational Work [Part II]." *Chinese Education,* II, No. 3 (Fall, 1969), 37-57. (Originally published by People's Publishing House, Peking, 1958. Pp. 37-56.)

"Comrade Mao Tse-tung on Educational Work [Part III]." *Chinese Education,* II, No. 4 (Winter, 1969-1970), 63-72. (Originally published by People's Publishing House, Peking 1958. Pp. 57-64.)

"Comrade Mao Tse-tung on Educational Work [Part IV]." *Chinese Education,* III, No. 1 (Spring, 1970), 20-41. (Originally published by People's Publishing House, Peking, 1958. Pp. 65-85.)

"Comrade Mao Tse-tung on Educational Work [Part V]." *Chinese Education,* III, No. 4 (Winter 1970-1971), 265-282. (Originally published by People's Publishing House, Peking, 1958. Pp. 85-96.)

Dai, S. "Mao Tse-tung and Confucianism." Unpublished Ph.D. dissertation, University of Pennsylvania, 1952. v+455 pp.

An interesting comparison of major Confucian concepts with Mao's understanding of Marxism—Leninism.

Dow, T.I. "Neo-Confucian Philosophical Systems and Mao's Theory of Multiple Contradictions." Paper presented at the 10th Annual Southwestern Regional Conference, AAS, Winthrop College, Rock Hill, South Carolina, January 29-30, 1971. 14 pp.

Describes similarities between traditional Chinese thought and Mao's especially in the areas of theories of knowledge, dialectics, materialism, etc.

Getzels, Jacob W.; Lipham, James M.; and Cambell, Roald F., eds. *Educational Administration as a Social Process.* New York: Harper & Row Publishers, 1968. xx+420 pp.

"Hanrei kenkyu no teisho oyobi mintei shogaku shiko ni kansuru no tegami [April 18, 1943]." *Mo taku-to kyoiku ron.* Edited and translated by Saito Akio and Niijima Atsuyoshi. Tokyo: Aoki Shoten, 1957. Pp. 356-361.

The article goes into some depth regarding the operation and problem of primary schools in the Shanshi, Kansu-Ningsia border region.

Isaacs, Harold R. *The Tragedy of the Chinese Revolution.* 2nd revised ed. Stanford: Stanford University Press, 1961. xix+392 pp.

This book concentrates on events in China and the CCP from 1925-1927 with an appendix on the Kiangsi Soviet Period, 1928-1934.

Lewis, John Wilson. *Leadership in Communist China.* Ithaca, N.Y.: Cornell University Press, 1963. 305 pp.

An authoritative analysis of elites and leadership in China discussing such elements as philosophy of leadership, the mass line, cadre training, and urban and rural leadership.

Lindsay, Michael. *Notes on Educational Problems in Communist China.* New York: Institute of Pacific Relations, 1950. 195 pp.

A unique account of pre-1949 education in the communist held areas; some mention of Mao.

Mao Tse-tung. "Analysis of the Classes in Chinese Society." *Selected Works of Mao Tse-tung.* Vol. I. Peking: Foreign Languages Press, 1965. Pp. 13-21.

This article contains a section on the social class position of educational personnel as seen by Mao at this time.

———. "Ba hsien ch'u yi-shang ssu-wei-ai fu-tse jen-yuan ch'a-t'ien yun-tung ta-hui suo t'ung-ku ti chieh-lun." *Mao Tse-tung chi.* Edited by Takeuchi Minoru. Vol. III. Tokyo: Hokubosha, 1970. Pp. 251-264. Originally published in *Hung-ssu chung-hua,* No. 89, June 21, 1933.)

In this article Mao announces the results of the recently concluded educational investigation movement.

———. "Be Concerned with the Well-being of the Masses, Pay Attention to Methods of Work [January 27, 1934]" *Selected Works of Mao Tse-tung.* Vol. I. Peking: Foreign Languages Press, 1965. Pp. 147-152.

In this article Mao enjoins cadres to satisfy the educational needs of the poor peasants in the liberated areas.

______. "Cast Away Illusions, Prepare for Struggle [August 14, 1949]." *Selected Works of Mao Tse-tung.* Vol. IV. Peking: Foreign Languages Press, 1965. Pp. 425-432.

In this article Mao attempts to prepare those wavering intellectuals for the coming period of socialism and convince them that any ideas that the KMT and the U.S. influenced systems might return are illusions.

______. "Ch'ang-kang hsiang tiao-ch'a." *Mao Tse-tung chi.* Edited by Takeuchi Minoru. Vol. IV. Tokyo: Hokubosha, 1970. Pp. 125-174. (Originally published in *Ssu-ch'i nien pan Mao Tse-tung hsuan chi,* Vol. I, March 15, 1933.)

The progress of a district under the border government is analyzed including the progress made in the field of education. Mao has some interesting comments on truants in this article.

______. "Changsha [1925]." *Poems of Mao Tse-tung.* Translated and annotated by Wong Man. Hong Kong: Eastern Horizon Press, 1966. Pp. 2-5.

This poem by Mao recalls past exploits of he and his student companions.

______. "The Chiang Kai-shek Government is Besieged by the Whole People [May 30, 1947]." *Selected Works of Mao Tse-tung.* Vol. IV. Peking: Foreign Languages Press, 1965. Pp. 135-139.

Mao notes that the student movement is a significant force in alerting the rest of the populace to rise up and struggle against the KMT government.

______. "The Chinese Revolution and the Chinese Communist Party [December, 1939]." *Selected Works of Mao Tse-tung.* Vol. II. Peking: Foreign Languages Press, 1965. Pp. 305-334.

This represents a textbook compiled by Mao and other CCP members in 1939—a chapter by Mao gives his views on the social forces in China, revolution, and the role of students and intellectuals.

______. "Chih-hsing yu-tai hung-chun t'iao-li ti shih-shih pan-fa [February 1, 1932]." *Mao Tse-tung chi.* Edited by Takeuchi Minoru. Vol. III. Tokyo: Hokubosha, 1970. Pp. 87-92. (Originally published in *Ssu-wei-ai chung-kuo,* 1933.)

This article contains a regulation given by Mao on entrance policies for the border schools.

______. "Chung-hua ssu-wei-ai kung-ho-kuo chung-yang chih-hsing wei-yuan-hui yu jen-min wei-yuan-hui tui ti-er-ts'e ch'uan-kuo ssu-wei-ai tai-piao ta-hui ti pao-kao." *Mao Tse-tung chi.* Edited by Takeuchi Minoru. Vol. IV. Tokyo: Hokubosha, 1970. Pp. 219-283. (Originally published in *Chung-hua ssu-wei-ai kung-ho-kuo ti-er-ts'e ch'uan-kuo tai-piao-ta-hui wen-hsien,* January 26, 1934.)

In this report Mao discusses the progress in eliminating illiteracy and speaks of women's education.

———. "Chung-hua ssu-wei-ai kung-ho-kuo lin-shih chung-yang cheng-fu ch'eng-li liang chou-nien tui ch'uan t'i hsuan-min ti kung-tso pao-kao shu [October 24, 1933]." *Mao Tse-tung chi.* Edited by Takeuchi Minoru. Vol. IV. Tokyo: Hokubosha, 1970. Pp. 103-110. (Originally published in *Hung-ssu chung-hua,* No. 122, October 27, 1933.)

In this article Mao praises the developments in the field of education in the Soviet area and suggests that a desirable goal would be to develop a complete primary school to wipe out illiteracy.

———. "Chung-kuo kung-ch'an-tang hung-chun ti-ssu-chun ti-chiu-t'se tai-piao ta-hui chu-yi-an [1929]." *Mao Tse-tung chi.* Edited by Takeuchi Minoru. Vol. II. Tokyo: Hokubosha, 1970. Pp. 77-125. (Cited in a pamphlet by the same title and published in Hong Kong by Hsin-min-chu ch'u-pan-che, January, 1949.)

A segment of this article is devoted to the subject of Party educational policies primarily focused on the illiterate peasant soldier.

———. "Communism and Dictatorship [November, 1920; January, 1921]." *The Political Thought of Mao Tse-tung.* Edited by Stuart R. Schram. Revised ed. New York: Praeger, 1970. Pp. 296-298. (Originally published in *Hunan li-shih tzu-liao,* No. 9, 1959.)

In this excerpt from Mao's letters to Tsai Ho'-sen he takes issue with Bertrand Russell's contention that the ruling propertied classes can be reformed and made communist through education rather than revolution.

———. "Comrade Mao Tse-tung's Speech at the Opening Ceremony of the Women's University of China [July 25, 1939]." *Chinese Education,* II, No. 3 (Fall, 1969), 37-38. (Originally published in *Comrade Mao Tse-tung on Educational Work,* Peking: People's Educational Publishing House, 1958.)

In this statement Mao stresses the importance of women in education and the general liberation of women.

———. "Conclusions on the Repulse of the Second Anti-Communist Onslaught [May, 1941]." *Selected Works of Mao Tse-tung.* Vol. II. Peking: Foreign Languages Press, 1965. Pp. 463-468.

———. "Correct the 'Left' Errors in Land Reform Propaganda [Febru-11, 1948]." *Selected Works of Mao Tse-ting.* Vol. IV. Peking: Foreign Languages Press, 1965. Pp. 197-199.

In this article Mao again reaffirms the Party's position vis-a-vis the students and intellectuals as consisting of a united front.

———. "Culture and Education in Soviet Areas [January, 1934]." *Current Background,* No. 891 (October 8, 1969), 2. (Originally published in *Mao Tse-tung ssu-hsiang wan-sui.*)

Mao discusses the basic educational policy of the Juichin base area.

———. "Current Problems of Tactics in the Anti-Japanese United Front [March 11, 1940]." *Selected Works of Mao Tse-tung.* Vol. II. Peking: Foreign Languages Press, 1965. Pp. 421-430.

———. "Dialectical Materialism [April-June, 1938]." Translated by Dennis J. Doolan and Peter J. Golas. *China Quarterly,* No. 19 (July-September, 1964), 38-46. (Originally published in, "Pien-cheng-fa wei-wu-lun," *K'ang chan ta-hsueh,* Nos. 1-4 (April-June, 1938.)

The authors translate one of Mao's first Marxist theoretical documents and provide a commentary.

———. "Dialectical Materialism [April-June, 1938]." Translated by Stuart Schram. *The Political Thought of Mao Tse-tung.* Edited by Stuart Schram. Rev. ed. New York: Praeger Press, 1970. Pp. 180-190. (Originally published in "Pien-cheng-fa wei-wu-lun" *K'ang-chan ta-hsueh,* Nos. 1-4 (April-June, 1938.)

———. "Economic and Financial Problems in the Anti-Japanese War [December, 1942]." *Selected Works of Mao Tse-tung.* Vol. III. Peking: Foreign Languages Press, 1965. Pp. 111-116.

This article contains a short section on school financing.

———. "Essential Points in Land Reform in the New Liberated Areas [February 15, 1948]." *Selected Works of Mao Tse-tung.* Vol. IV. Peking: Foreign Languages Press, 1965. Pp. 201-202.

Mao discusses the role intellectuals were to play in the land reform movement.

———. "Fen-sui wu-ts'e 'wei-chiao' yu ssu-wei-ai ching-chi chien-she jen-wu [October 3, 1933]." *Mao Tse-tung chi.* Edited by Takeuchi Minoru. Vol. III. Tokyo: Hokubosha, 1970. Pp. 323-338. (Originally published in *Hung-ssu chung-hua,* No. 102 (October 16, 1933.)

In this article Mao discusses the relationship between education and economic development.

———. "For the Mobilization of all the Nation's Forces for Victory in the War of Resistance [August 25, 1937]." *Selected Works of Mao Tse-tung.* Vol II. Peking: Foreign Languages Press, 1965. Pp. 23-29.

Mao proposes an educational policy and curriculum to resist Japanese aggression.

———. "The Great Union of the Popular Masses [July 3, 1919]." Translated by Stuart R. Schram. *China Quarterly,* No. 49 (January-March, 1972), 76-87. (Originally published in *Hsiang-chiang p'ing-lun* (July 21, 1919.)

An early article by Mao in which he gives his views on the role of teachers and students in society and the state of education in China at that time.

———. "Greet The New High Tide of the Chinese Revolution [February 1, 1947]." *Selected Works of Mao Tse-tung.* Vol. IV. Peking: Foreign Languages Press, 1965. Pp. 119-127.

In this article Mao notes the high level of political activity among students in the KMT controlled portions of the country and considers this to be a positive factor.

———. "Hsing-kuo tiao-ch'a [January 26, 1931]." *Mao Tse-tung chi.* Edited by Takeuchi Minoru. Vol. II. Tokyo: Hokubosha, 1970. Pp. 185-252. (Originally published in *Nung-tsun tiao-ch'a.* Chieh-fang ch'u-pan-she, 1949.)

A portion of this article is devoted to describing educational conditions in the border regions and announcing limited governmental educational policies.

———. "Hunan tse-hsiu ta-hsueh chuang-li hsuan-yen." *Mao Tse-tung chi.* Edited by Takeuchi Minoru. Vol. I. Tokyo: Hokubosha, 1970. Pp. 81-84. (Originally published in *Tung-fang tsa-chih.* Vol. 20, No. 6, (March 1, 1923.)

This article describes Mao's "Self-Study University" for workers in the Ch'angsha area.

———. "In Commemoration of the Second Anniversary of the Death of An Wu-ch'ing [December, 1929]." *Current Background,* No. 891 (October 8, 1969), 1. (Originally published in *Mao Tse-tung ssu-hsiang wan-sui.*)

Mao expresses his support of students and youth.

———. "In Memory of Norman Bethune [December, 1939]." *Selected Works of Mao Tse-tung.* Vol. II. Peking: Foreign Languages Press, 1965. Pp. 337-338.

This article was written in commemoration of a Canadian surgeon who worked with the PLA and died in China. It was later utilized as a major textual item in education following the GPCR.

———. "Inscription for the Anti-Japanese Military and Political College [April, 1939]." *Current Background,* No. 897 (December 10, 1969), 5. (Originally published in *Jen-min jih-pao,* July 31, 1966.)

In this statement Mao identifies those qualities which distinguish revolutionary intellectuals from non-revolutionary intellectuals.

———. "Inscription in Memory of the Founding and Opening of the North Shensi Public School [October, 1937]." *Current Background,* No. 891 (October 8, 1969), 8. (Originally published in *Mao Tse-tung ssu-hsiang wan-sui.*)

In this article Mao describes the qualities young people should possess to become good revolutionaries.

———. "Instruction of the Military Affairs Committee of the CCP Central Committee on the Question of Consolidating the Anti-Japanese Military and Political College [July, 1939]." *Current Back-*

ground, No. 888 (August 22, 1969), 3-4. (Originally published in *Chairman Mao on Revolution in Education.* Peking: People's Publishing House, 1967.)

In this document Mao lists several objectives and goals for a correct educational policy.

______. "Instruction on the Question of Consolidating the Anti-Japanese Military and Political College [July, 1939]." *Current Background,* No. 897 (December 10, 1969), 10. (Originally published in *Chieh-fang chun-pao,* October 6, 1966).

Mao states that the main purpose of education at this time is to transform the students ideologically.

______. "Interview with British Journalist James Bertram [October, 1937]." *Selected Works of Mao Tse-tung.* Vol. II. Peking: Foreign Languages Press, 1965. Pp. 47-59.

Mao discusses reforming the educational policy in line with the "united front" policy of fighting Japan.

______. "Introducing the 'Chinese Worker' [February, 1940]." *Selected Works of Mao Tse-tung.* Vol. II. Peking: Foreign Languages Press, 1965. Pp. 403-404.

Mao introduces a new journal designed to raise the cultural and political level of new cadres.

______. "Kai-tsao wo-men ti hsueh-hsi." *Mao Tse-tung chi.* Edited by Takeuchi Minoru. Vol. VII. Tokyo: Hokubosha, 1970. Pp. 315-324. (Originally published in *Ssu-ssu nien pan Mao Tse-tung hsuan-chi,* Vol. V, May, 1941.)

This version contains a section which was omitted from the translated version in *Selected Works of Mao Tse-tung,* Vol. III, (1965), pp. 19-20 concerning the theory and practice of students who had come to Yenan.

______. "Kuan-yu chiao-yu kung-tso." *Mao Tse-tung chi.* Edited by Takeuchi Minoru. Vol. IV. Tokyo: Hokubosha, 1970. Pp. 29-32. (Originally published in *Chung-hua ssu-wei-ai kung-ho-kuo chung-yang jen-min wei-yuan-hui hsun-ling ti shih-ch'i hao,* September 15, 1933.)

Against the background of KMT military attacks Mao criticizes past educational work and suggests new guidelines for the future.

______. "Kuan-yu mu-ch'ien cheng-chih hsing-shih yu tang ti jen-wu chueh-yi [December 25, 1935]." *Mao Tse-tung chi.* Edited by Takeuchi Minoru. Vol. V. Tokyo: Hokubosha, 1970. Pp. 19-40. (Originally published in *Mu-ch'ien hsing-shih ti fen-hsi,* Li-lun yu shih-chien she, 1936.)

Following the completion of the Long March Mao suggests general policy guidelines including two points on education.

______. "Kuan-yu t'u-ti cheng-ts'e ti chih-shih [July 22, 1937]." *Mao Tse-tung chi.* Edited by Takeuchi Minoru. Vol. V. Tokyo: Hokubosha, 1970. Pp. 63-66. (Originally in *Shih-lun hsuan-chi,* Chih-hsin yin-shu chu, May 1, 1937.)

In this article Mao discusses the social class status of students and teachers in the land reform movement.

———. "Kuan-yu t'u-ti tou-cheng yi-hsieh wen-t'i ti chueh-ting." *Mao Tse-tung chi.* Edited by Takeuchi Minoru. Vol. IV. Tokyo: Hokubosha, 1970. Pp. 43-66. (Originally published in *Chung-yang cheng-fu kuan-yu t'u-ti tou-cheng yi-hsieh wen-t'i ti chueh-ting,* October 10, 1933.)

In this article Mao distinguishes the characteristics of good intellectuals and bad intellectuals.

———. "Kung-jen yeh-hsueh chao-hsueh kuang-pao [1917]." *Mao Tse-tung chi.* Edited by Takeuchi Minoru. Vol. I. Tokyo: Hokubosha, 1970. Pp. 49-50. (Original seen by author in Ch'angsha in 1972.)

In this short document Mao announces the opening of a night school for workers in the Ch'angsha area.

———. "Letter to Comrade Lin Piao [1936]." *Current Background,* No. 891 (October 8, 1969), 3. (Originally published in *Mao Tse-tung ssu-hsiang wan-sui.)*

Mao discusses curricular changes and urges the integration of theory with practice in the school curriculum.

———. "Letter to Venerable Comrade Hsu [February, 1937]." *Current Background,* No. 891 (October 8, 1969), 4. (Originally published in *Mao Tse-tung ssu-hsiang wan-sui.*

Mao praises his former teacher and in so doing describes his concept of the good teacher.

———. "Lun hsin chieh-tuan [October 12-14, 1938]." *Mao Tse-tung chi.* Edited by Takeuchi Minoru. Vol. VI. Tokyo: Hokubosha, 1970. Pp. 163-240. (Originally published in *Chieh-fang,* No. 57, October 25, 1938.)

In this article Mao makes an important statement with regard to the education of minorities in China.

———. "Manifesto of the Chinese People's Liberation Army [October, 1947]." *Selected Works of Mao Tse-tung.* Vol. IV. Peking: Foreign Languages Publishing House, 1965. Pp. 147-153.

In this important document Mao stresses the need for the PLA to unite with revolutionary intellectuals.

———. "The May 4th Movement [May, 1939]." *Selected Works of Mao Tse-tung.* Vol. II. Peking: Foreign Languages Press, 1965. Pp. 237-239.

Discusses the historical role of teachers and students.

———. "Methods of Work of the Party Committees [March, 1949]." *Selected Works of Mao Tse-tung.* Vol. IV. Peking: Foreign Languages Press, 1965. Pp. 377-381.

Discusses the organizational work-style of the Party committees which were in charge of the schools during liberation.

———. "On Coalition Government [April 29, 1945]." *Selected Works of Mao Tse-tung*. Vol. III. Peking: Foreign Languages Press, 1965. Pp. 255-320.

Contains Mao's program and the CCP's for a new government once the Japanese are defeated including clauses on education and culture.

———. "On Contradiction [August, 1937]." *Selected Works of Mao Tse-tung*. Vol. I. Peking: Foreign Languages Press, 1965. Pp. 311-347.

This is a basic theoretical document discussing Mao's conception of materialist dialectics, contradictions, unity of opposites, struggle, etc. It provides basic understanding for the importance of education as a part of the superstructure.

———. "On New Democracy [January, 1940]." *Selected Works of Mao Tse-tung*. Vol. II. Peking: Foreign Languages Press, 1965. Pp. 339-384.

Mao's blueprint for the new democratic stage of the revolution with a section on the new culture and education.

———. "On Policy [December, 1940]." *Selected Works of Mao Tse-tung*. Vol. II. Peking: Foreign Languages Press, 1965. Pp. 441-449.

This contains a section of the cultural and educational policy to be followed during the period of the war of resistance.

———. "On Practice: On the Relation Between Knowledge and Practice, Between Knowing and Doing [July, 1937]." *Selected Works of Mao Tse-tung*. Vol. I. Peking: Foreign Languages Press, 1965. Pp. 295-310.

This represents Mao's most serious exposition on the nature and essence of knowledge.

———. "On Protracted War [May, 1938]." *Selected Works of Mao Tse-tung*. Vol. II. Peking: Foreign Languages Press, 1965. Pp. 113-194.

Mao discusses the nature of the war against Japan and the role education can play.

———. "On Some Important Problems of the Party's Present Policy [January 18, 1948]." *Selected Works of Mao Tse-tung*. Vol.IV. Peking: Foreign Languages Press, 1965. Pp. 181-189.

Mao discusses the policy toward working with teachers and students.

———. "On Strengthening the Party Committee System [September, 1948]." *Selected Works of Mao Tse-tung*. Vol. IV. Peking: Foreign Languages Press, 1965. Pp. 267-268.

Discusses the organizational aspects of committee rule for various levels of control including the schools.

———. "On Tactics Against Japanese Imperialism [December 27, 1935]." *Selected Works of Mao Tse-tung*. Vol. I. Peking: Foreign Languages Press, 1965. Pp. 153-178.

Mao analyzes the role of teachers and students and their revolutionary potential for fighting Japanese imperialism.

———. "On The New Stage [November, 1938]." *Chinese Education*, Vol. II, Nos. 1-2 (Spring-Summer 1969), 62-63. (Originally published in *Comrade Mao Tse-tung On Educational Work*, Peking: People's Education Publishing House, 1958.)

In this excerpt Mao discusses the general policy of education during the war of resistance to Japan.

———. "On the People's Democratic Dictatorship [June, 1949]." *Selected Works of Mao Tse-tung*. Vol. IV. Foreign Languages Press, 1965. Pp. 411-424.

This important document on the eve of the establishment of the PRC is designed to describe the real role of Western educational and cultural policies in China—i.e., serving the needs of imperiism.

———. "On the September Meeting—Circular of the Central Committee of the Communist Party of China [October 10, 1948]." *Selected Works of Mao Tse-tung*. Vol. IV. Peking: Foreign Languages Press, 1965. Pp. 269-277.

In this document Mao notes the lamentable lack of trained personnel available to effectively operate the educational structures of the newly liberated areas.

———. "On the Spirit of Lu Hsun—Talk at a Meeting of the North Shensi Public School Marking the Anniversary of the Death of Lu Hsun [October, 1937]." *Current Background*, No. 891 (October 8, 1969), pp. 6-7. (Originally published in *July*, Semi-monthly, March, 1939.)

In this speech Mao notes the qualities of Lu Hsun which students should emulate.

———. "Oppose Stereotyped Party Writing [February, 1942]." *Selected Works of Mao Tse-tung*. Vol. III. Peking: Foreign Languages Press, 1965. Pp. 53-68.

This contains further comments on the style of study and communicating with the masses.

———. "Order to the Army for the Country-wide Advance [April, 1949]." *Selected Works of Mao Tse-tung*. Vol. IV. Peking: Foreign Languages Press, 1965. Pp. 387-396.

Discusses the methods the PLA must use when securing cities and taking over institutions such as schools etc.

———. "The Orientation of the Youth Movement [May 4, 1939]." *Selected Works of Mao Tse-tung*. Vol. II. Peking: Foreign Languages Press, 1965. Pp. 241-249.

Mao describes the responsibility and importance of youth in the anti-Japanese war and declares Yenan as the model for youth to follow elsewhere.

———. "Our Tasks for 1945 [December 15, 1944]." *Chinese Education,* Vol. II, Nos. 1-2 (Spring-Summer, 1969), 64-65. (Originally published in *Comrade Mao Tse-tung on Educational Work,* Peking: People's Educational Publishing House, 1958.)

In this section Mao outlines the policy that ought to be adopted toward intellectuals.

———. "Policies, Measures and Perspectives for Resisting The Japanese Invasion [July 23, 1937]." *Selected Works of Mao Tse-tung.* Vol. II. Peking: Foreign Languages Press, 1965. Pp. 13-21.

In this statement of measures Mao describes the role that should be taken toward intellectuals and the role the educational system should play during this period.

———. "Preface and Postscripts to Rural Surveys [March and April, 1941]." *Selected Works of Mao Tse-tung.* Vol. III. Peking: Foreign Languages Press, 1965. Pp. 11-16.

In this document Mao outlines his criticisms of some Party cadres and their style of work and study.

———. "Problems of Strategy in China's Revolutionary War [December, 1936]." *Selected Works of Mao Tse-tung.* Vol. I. Peking: Foreign Languages Press, 1965. Pp. 179-254.

In this classic of guerrilla warfare strategy Mao discusses the role of learning and the importance of practice in knowledge.

———. "Problems of War and Strategy [November, 1938]." *Selected Works of Mao Tse-tung.* Vol. II. Peking: Foreign Languages Press, 1965. Pp. 219-235.

Mao notes how red educational work can expand during the war of resistance to Japan.

———. "Proclamation of the Chinese People's Liberation Army [April, 1949]." *Selected Works of Mao Tse-tung.* Vol. IV. Peking: Foreign Languages Press, 1965. Pp. 397-400.

This proclamation included a directive to protect schools and teachers.

———. "Recruit Large Numbers of Intellectuals [December, 1939]." *Selected Works of Mao Tse-tung.* Vol. II. Peking: Foreign Languages Press, 1965. Pp. 301-303.

Mao suggests that the revolution cannot be won without significant support from the intelligentsia and urges stuffy cadres to attempt mass recruitment.

———. "Rectify the Party's Style of Work [February 1, 1942]." *Selected Works of Mao Tse-tung.* Vol. III. Peking: Foreign Languages Press, 1965. Pp. 35-52.

Mao notes the problems in the study habits and abilities of Party members and in the process states some of his general ideas on learning, theory, and practice.

———. "Reform Our Study [May, 1941]." *Selected Works of Mao Tse-tung.* Vol. III. Peking: Foreign Languages Press, 1965. Pp. 17-25.

In this article Mao criticizes those cadres who rely only on books, ignoring practical problems.

———. "Report on an Investigation of the Peasant Movement in Hunan [March, 1927]." *Selected Works of Mao Tse-tung.* Vol. I. Peking: Foreign Languages Press, 1965. Pp. 23-59.

In this article Mao discusses the educational needs of the rural peasantry and concludes that they want and need rural oriented educational enterprises staffed and operated by themselves.

———. "Report to the Second Plenary Session of the Seventh Central Committee of the Communist Party of China [March, 1949]." *Selected Works of Mao Tse-tung.* Vol. IV. Peking: Foreign Languages Press, 1965. Pp. 361-375.

With victory in sight Mao discusses the future goals of education.

———. "Resolution of the Ninth Congress of the Fourth Army of the Red Army of the Communist Party of China [December, 1929]." *Current Background,* No. 888 (August 22, 1969), 2. (Originally published in *Mao chu-hsi lun chiao-yu ko-ming,* Jen-min ch'u-pan she, 1967.)

Ten points are presented by Mao indicating guidelines for successful teacher performance.

———. "The Role of the Chinese Communist Party in the National War [October, 1938]." *Selected Works of Mao Tse-tung.* Vol.II. Peking: Foreign Languages Press, 1965, Pp. 195-211.

This document provides general guidelines for the second united front and specifically outlines study methods for Communist Party cadres.

———. *Selected Works of Mao Tse-tung.* 4 vols. Peking: Foreign Languages Press, 1965.

This selection provides a primary source of materials in English translation down to 1949.

———. "Shih-hsing kuang-fan shen-ju ti ch'a-t'ien yun-tung." *Mao Tse-tung chi.* Edited by Takeuchi Minoru. Vol. III. Tokyo: Hokubosha, 1970. Pp. 223-225. (Originally published in *Hung-ssu chung-hua,* No. 87, June 20, 1933.)

In this document Mao gives directions on the best method of carrying out educational investigations.

———. "The Situation and Our Policy After the Victory in the War of Resistance Against Japan [August, 1945]." *Selected Works of Mao Tse-tung.* Vol. IV. Peking: Foreign Languages Publishing House, 1965. Pp. 11-26.

In this article Mao notes some of the shortcomings of the cadres and mass organizations and urges further educational efforts.

———. "Some Questions Concerning Methods of Leadership [June 1, 1943]." *Selected Works of Mao Tse-tung.* Vol. III. Peking: Foreign Languages Publishing House, 1965. Pp. 117-122.

Mao advances some of his ideas on methods of school management and leadership.

———. "Speech at a Conference of Cadres in the Shansi-Suiyuan Liberated Area [April 1, 1948]." *Selected Works of Mao Tse-tung*. Vol. IV. Peking: Foreign Languages Press, 1965. Pp. 227-239.

Mao comments on the role intellectuals are to play in the nongovernmental organizations once the civil war terminates.

———. "Speech Delivered in November 1944 at a Conference of Cultural and Educational Workers of the Border Region." *Current Background,* No. 897 (December 10, 1969), p. 45. (Originally appeared in *Wen-hui pao,* May 4, 1968.)

———. "Spread the Campaigns to Reduce Rent, Increase Production and 'Support the Government and Cherish the People' in the Base Areas [October, 1943]." *Selected Works of Mao Tse-tung*. Vol. III. Peking: Foreign Languages Press, 1965. Pp. 131-135.

In this article Mao briefly discusses the necessity of self-sufficiency on the part of the schools.

———. "A Study of Physical Education [April, 1917]." Schram, Stuart R. *The Political Thought of Mao Tse-tung*. Revised ed. New York: Praeger, 1970, Pp. 152-160. (Originally published in "T'i-yu chih yen-chiu," *Hsin-ch'ing nien*. Vol. III. No. 2 (April 1, 1917).)

This early document by Mao reveals the importance he attached to the development of the body and the dislike he had for overemphasis on mental learning, in addition he reveals his rather eclectic knowledge at this time.

———. "Talk at Meeting of All Circles in Yenan Celebrating the 60th Birthday of Stalin [December, 1939]." *Current Background,* No. 891 (October 8, 1969), pp. 9-10.

———. "A Talk to the Editorial Staff of the *Shansi-Suiyuan Daily* [April, 1948]." *Selected Works of Mao Tse-tung*. Vol. IV. Peking: Foreign Languages Press, 1965. Pp. 241-245.

———. "Talk at the Second National Soviet Conference of the Central Executive Committee of the Soviet Republic of China [January, 1934]." *Current Background*. No. 891 (October 8, 1969), p. 2.

Mao articulates the first concrete educational policy for the Soviet base areas.

———. "Talks at the Yenan Forum on Literature and Art [May 1942]." *Selected Works of Mao Tse-tung*. Vol. III. Peking: Foreign Languages Press, 1965. Pp. 69-98.

The critical document which outlines Mao's approach on this subject and the nature of the arts.

———. "Tasks of the Chinese Communist Party in the Period of Resistance to Japan. [May 3, 1937]." *Selected Works of Mao Tse-tung*. Vol. I. Peking: Foreign Languages Press, 1965. Pp. 263-283.

The new class role of students and intellectuals is discussed briefly.

———. "Ten Demands on the Kuomintang [February 1, 1940]." *Selected Works of Mao Tse-tung.* Vol. II. Peking: Foreign Languages Press, 1965. Pp. 395-401.

This contains the contents of a telegram by Mao offering ten points for the KMT to follow to defeat Wang Ching-wei and his ideas.

———. *To Be Attacked by the Enemy is not a Bad thing but a Good Thing.* [May, 1939]. Peking: Foreign Languages Press, 1965. 5 pp.

A speech commemorating the Anti-Japanese Military and Political College in Yenan.

———. "To Hakuro Toten (Miyazaki Toten) [April, 1917]." *Mao Papers: Anthology and Bibliography.* Edited by Jerome Ch'en. London: Oxford University Press, 1970. Pp. 42-45. (Originally published in *Asahi Shimbun,* July 3, 1967.)

In this letter Mao expresses his desire to learn from a Japanese supporter of Sun Yat-sen.

———. "Turn the Army Into a Working Force [February, 1949]." *Selected Works of Mao Tse-tung.* Vol. IV. Peking: Foreign Languages Press, 1965. Pp. 337-339.

In this article Mao suggests that the PLA can assist and widen the administrative structure of the Party especially in the area of educational administration.

———. "The United Front in Cultural Work [October, 1944]." *Selected Works of Mao Tse-tung.* Vol. III. Peking: Foreign Languages Press, 1965. Pp. 235-237.

This article gives guidelines for educational facilities in the border regions.

———. "Urgent Tasks Following the Establishment of Kuomintang-Communist Co-Operation [September, 1937]." *Selected Works of Mao Tse-tung.* Vol. II. Peking: Foreign Languages Press, 1965. Pp. 35-46.

Mao criticizes the KMT for not adequately reforming the educational system in China.

———. "We Must Learn to Do Economic Work [January, 1945]." *Selected Works of Mao Tse-tung.* Vol. III. Peking: Foreign Languages Press, 1965. Pp. 239-245.

In this article Mao notes the differing situation between rural and urban economic and educational needs.

———. "Wei tung-yun yi-ch'ieh li-liang cheng-ch'u k'ang-chan sheng-li er tou-cheng [August 25, 1937]." *Mao Tse-tung chi.* Edited by Takeuchi Minoru. Vol. V. Tokyo: Hokubosha, 1970. Pp. 249-256. (Originally published in *K'ang-jih chiu-kuo shih-ta kang-ling,* 1937.)

This article contains information on the development of an educational program for those areas held by the CCP.

Selden, Mark. *The Yenan Way in Revolutionary China.* Cambridge, Mass.: Harvard University Press, 1971. xi+311 pp.

The author provides an exhaustive study of the Yenan period in China utilizing primarily original source material and including a provocative analysis as to the character of the "Yenan Way."

Snow, Edgar. *Red China Today.* Rev. ed. New York: Random House, Vintage Books, 1971. 749 pp.

This is a revised edition of Snow's *The Other Side of the River* and provides good background material necessary to understand conditions in China since 1949.

Takeuchi Minoru, ed. *Mao Tse-tung chi.* 10 vols. Tokyo: Hokubosha, 1970.

This collection of Mao's works is the most complete single source for the period down to 1949. The documents appear in the original Chinese and the original source material is also cited.

"The Thought of Mao Tse-tung." External Research Division Paper 138, Department of State, Washington, D.C., April, 1964. 73 pp.

This very useful bibliography of Mao's writings contains both those items appearing in English translation as well as original Chinese documents.

Wang, Y.C. *Chinese Intellectuals and the West: 1872-1949.* Chapel Hill: The University of North Carolina Press, 1966. xiv+557 pp.

The author traces the relationship between Chinese intellectuals and the West and provides a solid study of the transformation of China's educational system during the period under discussion.

Wittfogel, K.A. and Chao C.R. "Some Remarks on Mao's Handling of Concepts and Problems of Dialectics," *Studies in Soviet Thought,* III, No. 4 (December, 1963), 251-269.

Yen Chang-lin. *In His Mind a Million Bold Warriors.* Peking: Foreign Languages Press, 1972. 81 pp.

A former assistant to Mao relates his experiences on the Long March and discusses to some extent Mao's feelings and approaches to education.

V. MAO TSE-TUNG'S EDUCATIONAL THOUGHT: 1950-1973

Balazs, Etiene. *Chinese Civilization and Bureaucracy.* New Haven: Yale University Press, 1964. xix+309 pp.

Baum, Richard and Teiwes, Frederick C. *Ssu-ch'ing: The Socialist Education Movement of 1962-1966.* Berkeley: Center for Chinese Studies, 1968. 127 pp.

———. "Wen-chiao t'ung-yi chan-hsien fang-chen." *Mao Tse-tung chi.* Edited by Takeuchi Minoru. Vol. IX. Tokyo: Hokubosha, 1970. Pp. 133-138. (Originally in *Ssu-ch'i nien pan Mao Tse-tung hsuan-chi,* Vol. VI, October 30, 1944.)

This article contains a discussion on the need for workers and peasants to unite with progressive intellectuals.

———. "Yi-chiu ssu-wu nien ti jen-wu." *Mao Tse-tung chi.* Edited by Takeuchi Minoru. Vol. IX. Tokyo: Hokubosha, 1970. Pp. 141-154. (Originally published in *Ssu-ch'i nien pan Mao Tse-tung hsuan-chi,* Vol. III, December 15, 1944.)

Mao discusses the Party's position with regard to the intellectuals.

Nomura, Koichi. "Mao Tse-tung's Thought and the Chinese Revolution." *Journal of Social and Political Ideas in Japan,* V, No. 1 (April, 1968), 67-90.

The author discusses the origin of some of Mao's social and political ideas with particular reference to his period in the Ching-kang mountains.

"On Regulations and Curriculum in General Education [May 27, 1944]." *Chinese Education,* IV, No. 3 (Fall, 1971), 195-204. (Originally published in *Chieh-fang jih-pao,* May 27, 1944.)

This document outlines educational regulations and curriculum for border region schools; it was compiled by the Civil Affairs Office of the Shen-kan-ning Border Region Government.

"Regarding the New Curriculum for Middle Schools." *Chinese Education,* IV, No. 4 (Winter 1971-1972), 279-282. (Originally published in *Chieh-fang jih-pao,* May 27, 1944.)

This document outlines the actual curriculum for middle schools in the border region.

Rue, John. "Is Mao Tse-tung's 'Dialectical Materialism' a Forgery." *Journal of Asian Studies,* XXVI, No. 3 (May, 1967), 464-468.

Saito Akio and Niijima Atsuyoshi, eds. *Mo Taku-to kyoiku ron.* 2 vols. Tokyo: Aoki shoten, 1957. 287, 259 pp.

The two volumes contain selections of Mao Tse-tung's writings on education translated from Chinese into Japanese. For the most part they are selections that have already appeared in print previously but new material is also included.

Schram, Stuart. *The Political Thought of Mao Tse-tung.* 2nd ed. New York: Praeger Press, 1969. 479 pp.

This collection of Mao's writings is primarily oriented toward his political writings but several items appear which relate to education.

Schwartz, Benjamin I. *Chinese Communism and the Rise of Mao.* Cambridge, Mass: Harvard University Press, 1964. 258 pp.

A scholarly history of the development of the Chinese Communist Party and Mao's later leadership in it.

The authors provide an analysis with relevant translations of documents related to this important movement prior to the GPCR.

Boorman, Howard L., ed. *Biographical Dictionary of Republican China*. Vol. II. New York: Columbia University Press, 1968. 481 pp.

The Case of P'eng Te-hui: 1959-1968. Hong Kong: Union Research Institute, 1968. 515 pp.

"Chairman Mao on Revolution in Education." *Current Background*, No. 888 (August 22, 1969), 1-20. (Originally published in *Mao Tse-tung lun chiao-yu kung-tso*, Jen-min ch'u-pan she, 1967.)

This collection contains selected statements by Mao covering the period 1927-1967.

"Chairman Mao Runs a Worker's Evening School." *Survey of China Mainland Magazines*, No. 614 (February 12, 1968), 11-13. (Originally published in *Chieh-fang chun wen-yi*, Nos. 20-21, 1967.)

"Chairman Mao Tse-tung's March 7 Directive Concerning the Great Strategic Plan for the Great Proletarian Cultural Revolution." *Chinese Education*, No. 1 (Summer, 1968), 61-62. (Originally published in *Jen-min jih-pao*, March 8, 1968.)

This directive discusses the "three-in-one"committees for management of the schools and other institutions.

"Chairman Mao's Activities in Revolutionary Practice." *Current Background*, No. 900 (January 30, 1970), 1-47. (Originally published in booklet form with title "Material for Study,", 1966; no other publication data given. The document was received in Hong Kong and translated by the United States Consulate's office.)

This document reviews Mao's life up to 1966 and contains some statements on education not previously translated or available.

Ch'en, Jerome, ed. *Mao*. Englewood Cliffs, N.J.: Prentice-Hall, 1969. 176 pp.

This volume contains numerous statements and quotes by Mao translated into English for the first time.

———. ed. *Mao Papers: Anthology and Bibliography*. New York: Oxford University Press, 1970. 221 pp.

An invaluable source for post-1950 writings by Mao; also contains an extensive bibliography of Mao's writings arranged chronologically from 1917 to 1968.

Cheng, J.C. *Basic Principles Underlying the Chinese Communist Approach to Education*. Washington, D.C.: United States Government Printing Office, 1961.

This pamphlet provides a limited discussion of the basic theoretical tenets of Chinese education with only passing reference made to the works of Mao Tse-tung.

Chi Tung-wei. *Education for the Proletariat in Communist China.* Hong Kong: Union Research Institute, 1954. 73 pp.

This account contains a brief section on the theoretical foundations of Chinese communist education with brief mention made of Mao.

Chinese Communist Party Documents of the Great Proletarian Cultural Revolution: 1966-1967. Hong Kong: Union Research Institute, 1968. 692 pp.

This collection contains a large selection of important Party documents including twenty-five which appear in English for the first time.

Cohen, Arthur. "How Original is Maoism?" *Problems of Communism,* Vol. X, No. 6 (November-December, 1961), 34-42.

Combs, Arthur W. "The Human Factor in the Current Curriculum." *Curriculum Development in a Changing World.* Edited by Howard L. Jones. Syracuse, N.Y.: Syracuse University Press, 1969. 57-70 pp.

Elegant, Robert S. *Mao's Great Revolution.* New York: The World Publishing Company, 1971. 478 pp.

Forward Along the High Road of Mao Tse-tung's Thought. Peking: Foreign Languages Publishing House, 1967. 31 pp.

This Cultural Revolution document expresses the Party's position on Mao Tse-tung's thought at that time.

Fraser, Stewart E., ed. *Chinese Communist Education: Records of the First Decade.* Nashville: Vanderbilt University Press, 1965. 542 pp.

______ . ed. *Education and Communism in China: An Anthology and Commentary.* London: Pall Mall Press, 1970. 614 pp.

Knezevich, Stephen J. *Administration in Public Education.* New York: Harper and Row Publishers, 1962. xiv+554 pp.

Koopman, Robert G. *Curriculum Development.* New York: The Center for Applied Research in Education, Inc., 1966. viii+120 pp.

Li Teh. "Wu-ch'i kan-hsiao yu kung-kan lun-hsun." *Chung-kuo ta-lu yen-chiu,* No. 4 (April 25, 1971), 23-31.

Lipset, Seymour Martin. *Political Man.* New York: Doubleday and Co., 1963. xxxvi+477 pp.

Lun chiao-yu sheng-ch'an lao-tung hsiang chieh-ho. Peking: Chung-kuo ch'ing-nien ch'u-pan she, 1958. 263 pp.

This volume is a major pedagogical publication containing numerous articles by educational institutions, bureaus and governmental committees in support of Mao Tse-tung's educational thought; a lead article is entitled: "Hsueh-hsi Ma-k'e-ssu, En-ke-ssu, Lieh-ning, Mao Tse-tung lun chiao-yu" [Study Marx, Engels, Lenin and Mao Tse-tung on education], pp. 62-70.

Malraux, Andre. *Anti-Memoirs.* New York: Holt, Rinehart and Winston, 1968. 420 pp.

Malraux relates a 1965 meeting with Mao.

"Mao on Higher Education." *China News Analysis*, No. 723 (August 30, 1968), 1-7.

This document discusses Mao's post-GPCR program for higher education.

Mao Tse-tung. "Address to Regional Secretaries and Members of the Cultural Revolution Group Under the Central Committee. [July, 1966]." *Current Background*, No. 891 (October 8, 1969), 60-62. (Originally published in *Mao Tse-tung ssu-hsiang wan-sui.*)

In this discussion Mao comments on the role the Communist Party should play with regard to rebel students.

______. "The Anti-Japanese Military and Political University." *Mao Papers: Anthology and Bibliography*. Edited by Jerome Ch'en. London: Oxford University Press, 1970. P. 116. (Originally published in *Jen-min jih-pao*, August 2, 1966, p. 2.)

In this excerpt Mao is quoted from his Yenan days on the subject of the nature of higher education.

______. "Class Struggles." *Mao Papers: Anthology and Bibliography*. Edited by Jerome Ch'en. London: Oxford University Press, 1970. P. 116 (Originally published in *Jen-min jih-pao*, August 2, 1966, p. 2.)

Mao suggests that political education and vigorous political activities (class struggle) should be the primary ingredient in the curriculum of all schools.

______. "Comment on Courses of Study and Examination Method [March 1964]." *Current Background*, No. 891 (October 8, 1969), 45.

Mao suggests that the curriculum is too ponderous and should be reduced.

______. "Comment on the 'Instruction Concerning Learning to Strengthen Political Work From the Liberation Army' [1964]." *Current Background*, No. 891 (October 8, 1969), 48. (Originally published in *Mao Tse-tung ssu-hsiang wan-sui.*)

Mao suggest that all schools should learn from the PLA.

______. "Comment on Peking Normal College's Investigation Material Report [July, 1965]." *Current Background*, No. 891 (October 8, 1969), 50. (Originally published in *Mao Tse-tung ssu-hsiang wan-sui.*)

______. "Educational Revolution." *Mao Papers: Anthology and Bibliography*. Edited by Jerome Ch'en. London: Oxford University Press, 1970. P. 155. (Originally published in *Jen-min jih-pao*, August 27, 1968.)

In this statement Mao discusses the future organization of school administration in China.

______. "The Experience of the Liu-kou Village Branch of Chu-nan County Communist Youth Corps in Organizing Recording Work-Study Classes [1956]." *Chinese Education*, II, No. 3 (Fall,

1969), 54-55. (Originally published in *Mao Tse-tung t'ung-chih lun chiao-yu kung-tso*. Peking: Jen-min ch'u-pan she, 1958.)

In this article Mao stresses the idea of local control and initiative in education.

———. "Firmly Carry Out Chairman Mao's Latest Instruction and Rely on the Masses to Make Revolution in Education on a Large Scale." *Current Background,* No. 897 (December 10, 1969), 35. (Originally published in *Chieh-fang chun-pao,* November 6, 1967.)

In this instruction Mao gives the basic orientation to the PLA to restructure the educational system.

———. *Five Documents on Literature and Art.* Peking: Foreign Languages Press, 1967. 12 pp.

This pamphlet contains five short statements by Mao on culture and art in China; all statements date prior to the GPCR.

———. "Give Serious Attention to the Discussion of the Film *The Life of Wu Hsun.*" *Current Background,* No. 891 (October 8, 1969), 15. (Originally published in *Jen-min jih-pao,* May 20, 1951.)

Mao criticizes the approach of many intellectuals toward the fields of literature and art.

———. *The Great Power Struggle in Communist China.* Hong Kong: Asia Research Center, 1969. 503 pp.

This book contains numerous quotes and statements by Mao on a variety of subjects including education.

———. "His Wish." *Mao Papers: Anthology and Bibliography.* Edited by Jerome Ch'en. London: Oxford University Press, 1970. P. 115. (Originally published in *Jen-min jih-pao,* July 29, 1966.)

Mao states that he too must become a student again and learn from the masses.

———. "Inscription for the Anti-Japanese Military and Political College, April, 1939—'Take Chairman Mao's Works as Basic Teaching Material and Give First Place to Political and Ideological Education." *Current Background,* No. 897 (December 10, 1969), 5. (Originally published in *Jen-min jih-pao,* July 31, 1966.)

A 1939 statement by Mao is reiterated in the press urging intellectuals to "integrate" with mass organizations.

———. "Instruction Given on an Inspection Tour of Tientsin University (excerpts)." *Current Background,* No. 891 (October 8, 1969), 30. (Originally published in *Kuang-ming jih-pao,* August 19, 1958.)

In this instruction Mao urges schools to integrate theory with practice and comments on new organizational plans.

———. "Instruction Given on an Inspection Tour of Wuhan University (excerpts)." *Current Background,* No. 891 (October 8, 1969), 31.

Mao encourages students and teachers to take part in physical labor, September, 1958.

______. "Instruction on Part-Work, Part-Study [February, 1958]." *Current Background* No. 891 (October 8, 1969), 29.

In this document Mao suggests that all schools should introduce into the curriculum some form of part-work, part-study.

______. "Instruction on the Problems of Tsingtao, Changsha and Sian [September, 1966]." *Current Background,* No. 891 (October 8, 1969), 69. (Originally published in *Mao Tse-tung ssu-hsiang wan-sui.*)

Mao urges workers and peasants not to interfere with the student movement.

______. "Instruction on the Question of Consolidating the Anti-Japanese Military and Political College." *Current Background,* No. 897 (December, 10, 1969), 10. (Originally published in *Chieh-fang chun-pao,* October 6, 1966.)

A 1939 statement by Mao is reprinted in 1966 to give some general guidelines of the purposes of education.

______. "Instruction on the Question of 'Redness and Expertness' [January, 1958]." *Current Background,* No. 891 (October 8, 1969), 28. (Originally published in *Mao Tse-tung ssu-hsiang wan-sui.*

Mao discusses the relationship between political orientation and technical and academic expertise.

______. "Instructions Given at the Spring Festival Concerning Educational Work (excerpts) [February, 1964]." *Current Background,* No. 891 (October 8, 1969), 42-44.

This document contains a series of instructions on topics such as examinations, curriculum organization and administrative control of the schools.

______. "The Intelligence of the People." *Mao Papers: Anthology and Bibliography.* Edited by Jerome Ch'en. London: Oxford University Press, 1970. P. 103. (Originally published in *Hung-ch'i,* No. 2, 1966, p. 18.)

In this article Mao's statement reflects the Marxist relationship and analysis of education and social class.

______. "Introductory Note to the Second Lot of Material on the Hu Feng Counter-revolutionary Clique (excerpts)." *Current Background,* No. 891 (October 8, 1969), 19-20. (Originally published in *Jen-min jih-pao,* May 24, 1955.)

Mao discusses the issue of freedom of speech and other liberal issues under the dictatorship of the proletariat.

______. "Knock the Reactionary 'Authorities' Philosphy to the Ground." *Current Background,* No. 897 (December 10, 1969), 9. (Originally published in *Jen-min jih-pao,* September 11, 1966.)

Mao suggests that philosophy should be a subject for the masses and not one taught only in the formal schools.

———. "A letter to Kiangsi Communist Labor University [July 30, 1961]." *Current Background,* No. 891 (October 8, 1969), 36.

In this letter Mao discusses the idea of establishing part-work part-study schools at all levels of the schooling cycle.

———. "A Letter to the Red Guards of the Middle School Attached to Tsinghua University [August 1966]." *Current Background,* No. 891 (October 8, 1969), 63. (Originally published in *Mao Tse-tung ssu-hsiang wan-sui.*)

Mao urges rebellious students to form a broad united front with other sectors of the population including those who had "made mistakes".

———. "Military and Political Training is Good." *Current Background,* No. 897 (December 10, 1969), 17. (Originally published in *Jen-min jih-pao,* May 16, 1967.)

Mao suggests that the army play an active role in re-educating teachers and students.

———. "More on the Need for all Universities, Middle Schools and Primary Schools to Resume Class and Carry Out the Revolution." *Current Background,* No. 897 (December 10, 1969), 38. (Originally published in *Jen-min jih-pao,* November 26, 1967.)

Mao urges all students to return to classes and continue the GPCR in their schools.

———. "Notice on Forging Revolutionary Great Alliances According to Systems." *Current Background,* No. 897 (December 10, 1969), 34. (Originally published in *Jen-min jih-pao,* October 18, 1967.)

Mao outlines the preliminary organizational structure for administering the schools.

———. "On the Correct Handling of Contradictions Among the People [February, 1957]." *Four Essays on Philosophy.* Peking: Foreign Languages Press, 1968. Pp. 79-132.

In this document Mao notes that even under socialism class struggle continues to take place.

———. "On the Ten Great Relationships [April, 1956]." *Mao.* Edited by Jerome Ch'en. New Jersey: Prentice Hall, 1969. Pp. 65-85.

In this article Mao discusses the need to train skilled technicians from among workers in the plants.

———. "The Orientation of the Revolution in Medical Education as Seen From the Maturing of 'Barefoot Doctors'." *Current Background,* No. 897 (December 10, 1969), 49. (Originally published in *Jen-min jih-pao,* September 14, 1968.)

Mao urges all students of pre-GPCR schools to go to the countryside or factories to be re-educated by the workers and peasants.

——. "Outline for National Agricultural Development, 1956-1967 [1956]." *Chinese Education,* II, No. 3 (Fall, 1969), 53-54. (Originally published in *Mao Tse-tung t'ung-chih lun chiao-yu kung-tso.* Peking: Jen-min ch'u-pan she, 1958.)

In this statement Mao suggests long-term goals for rural education.

——. "The People's Liberation Army and the Schools." *Mao Papers: Anthology and Bibliography.* Edited by Jerome Ch'en. London: Oxford University Press, 1970. P. 2. (Originally published in *Jen-min jih-pao,* March 7, 1967.)

Mao instructs the PLA to play an active role in reopening the schools and reforming teachers and students.

——. "Place Mao Tse-tung Thought in Command of Everything." *Current Background,* No. 897 (December 10, 1969), 52. (Originally published in *Jen-min jih-pao* and *Chieh-fang chun-pao,* January 1, 1969.)

Mao in this statement reveals his faith in the enormous potential of education to transform society and man.

——. "Proletarian Dictatorship and Renegade China's Khrushchev." *Current Background,* No. 885 (July 31, 1969), 34. (Originally published in *Wen-hui pao* and *Chieh-fang chun-pao,* August 20, 1967.)

Mao discusses the relationship between dialectics and cognition.

——. "Quotation from Chairman Mao." *Current Background,* No. 897 (December 10, 1969), 45. (Originally published in *Wen-hui pao,* May 4, 1968.)

This statement originally appeared in 1944 and was reprinted to urge intellectuals to integrate with the masses and also to urge workers and peasants to have respect for intellectuals.

——. "Re-educating Intellectuals." *Mao Papers: Anthology and Bibliography.* Edited by Jerome Ch'en. London: Oxford University Press, 1970. P. 155.

——. "Re-Educating the Young." *Mao Papers: Anthology and Bibliography.* Edited by Jerome Ch'en. London: Oxford University Press, 1970. P. 157. (Originally published in *Jen-min jih-pao,* December 23, 1968.)
December 23, 1968.)

In this directive Mao specifically states that all educated young people must go to the countryside for re-education.

——. "Repressing Students [September 2, 1966]." *Mao Papers: Anthology and Bibliography.* London: Oxford University Press, 1970. P. 129. (Originally published in a pamphlet during the GPCR. The pamphlet was received in Hong Kong with no publication data attached.)

In this statement Mao warns Party members and others that it is incorrect to hinder the student movement.

———. "The Resolutions of the Eleventh Plenum of the Central Committee of the CCP—the Sixteen Articles." *Mao Papers: Anthology and Bibliography*. Edited by Jerome Ch'en. London: Oxford University Press, 1970. P. 117. (Originally published in *Jen-min jih-pao,* August 9, 1966 and *Peking Review,* No. 33, August 12, 1966.)

———. "Revolutionary Party." *Mao Papers: Anthology and Bibliography*. Edited by Jerome Ch'en. London: Oxford University Press, 1970. P. 148. (Originally published in *Jen-min jih-pao,* November 6, 1967.)

In this excerpt Mao notes that teachers often provide a negative model to their students.

———. "Scientific and Technological Training." *Mao Papers: Anthology and Bibliography*. Edited by Jerome Ch'en. London: Oxford University Press, 1970. P. 154. (This statement by Mao was monitored by the British Broadcasting Corporation on July 21, 1968.)

Mao states that higher education should be the responsibility of society and not just the formal educational institutions.

———. "Sixty Points on Working Methods—A Draft Resolution from the Office of the Centre of the CCP [February 1958]." *Mao Papers: Anthology and Bibliography*. Edited by Jerome Ch'en. London: Oxford University Press, 1970.

This document contains important points on polytechnical education and part-work, part-study education.

———. "Speech at a Work Conference of the Central Committee [October, 1966]." *Current Background,* No. 891 (October 8, 1969), 75-77. (Originally published in *Mao Tse-tung ssu-hsiang wan-sui.)*

Mao discusses with other Party members the rebellious student movement.

———. "Speech at Enlarged Work Conference of the Central Committee [1966]." *Current Background,* No. 891 (October 8, 1969), 65-67. (Originally published in *Mao Tse-tung ssu-hsiang wan-sui.)*

Mao discusses the policy of uniting with intellectuals.

———. *Speech at the Chinese Communist Party's National Conference on Propaganda Work*. Peking: Foreign Languages Press, 1966. 29 pp.

In this speech written in March 1957 Mao outlines the Party's position toward intellectuals and teachers.

———. "Summary of a Talk with Mao Yuan-hsin [July 5, 1964]." *Current Background,* No. 888 (August 22, 1969), 14. (Originally published in *Mao chu-hsi lun chiao-yu ko-ming*. Peking: Jen-min ch'u-pan she, 1967.)

In this discussion Mao criticizes the marking system, teaching methods and educational system in general.

———. "Summary of Talk to Heads of Education Departments and Bureaux of Seven Provinces and Municipalities [March 7, 1957]." *Current Background,* No. 888 (August 22, 1969), 7. (Originally published in *Mao chu-hsi lun chiao-yu ko-ming.* Peking: Jen-min ch'u-pan she, 1967.)

———. "Supreme Instructions." *Current Background,* No. 897 (December 10, 1969), 1-60.

This collection of Mao's statements down to March 1969 was published in booklet form and distributed in China during the GPCR; no publication date is known.

———. "Talk at a Meeting With Chinese Students and Trainees in Moscow [November, 1957]." *Current Background,* No. 891 (October 8, 1969), 26. (No original citation is available however the document is authenticated in *Quotations from Chairman Mao.* Peking: Foreign Languages Press, 1966. P. 288.)

Mao praises the Chinese youth and reveals his hope in their revolutionary potential.

———. "Talk at the Conference of Heads of Delegations to the Second Session of the Eighth Congress [May 18, 1958]." *Current Background,* No. 888 (August 22, 1969), 9. (Originally published in *Mao chu-hsi lun chiao-yu ko-ming.* Peking: Jen-min ch'u-pan she, 1967.)

In this statement Mao suggests that "the lowly are most intelligent while the elite are most ignorant."

———. "Talk at the Hangchow Conference [December, 1965]." *Current Background,* No. 891 (October 8, 1969), 51-55, (Originally published in *Mao Tse-tung ssu-hsiang wan-sui.*)

In this important document Mao makes concrete suggestions for reforming both secondary and higher education; many of the proposals are now in practice.

———. "Talk at the Reception for the Presidium of the Second National Congress of the Youth League (excerpts) [June, 1953]." *Current Background,* No. 891 (October 8, 1969), 16. (Originally published in Mao Tse-tung ssu-hsiang wan-sui.)

Mao discusses the qualities of revolutionary youth work.

———. "Talk at the Second Session of the Eighth National Congress [May 8, 1958]." *Current Background,* No. 888 (August 22, 1969), 9. (Originally published in *Mao chu-hsi lun chiao-yu ko-ming.* Peking: Jen-min ch'u-pan she, 1967.)

In this statement Mao urges young people to struggle against old authorities and not be afraid of speaking out.

———. "Talk at the Work Conference of the Centre [October, 1966]." *Mao Papers: Anthology and Bibliography.* Edited by Jerome

Ch'en. London: Oxford University Press, 1970. Pp. 42-45. (Originally published in *Mao Tse-tung ssu-hsiang wan-sui.*)

Mao discusses the GPCR and the student movement with Party members.

———. "A Talk Before the Central Committee Work Conference [August, 1966]." *Current Background,* No. 891 (October 8, 1969), 68. (Originally published in *Mao Tse-tung ssu-hsiang wan-sui.*)

Mao again supports the students and feels that the disturbances of the GPCR are minor.

———. "Talk Delivered in August 17, 1958." *Current Background,* No. 888 (August 22, 1969), 8. (Originally published in *Mao chu-hsi lun chiao-yu ko-ming.* Peking: Jen-min ch'u-pan she, 1967.)

Mao makes a short statement on the placement of agricultural colleges.

———. "Talk Delivered in 1958." *Current Background,* No. 888 (August 22, 1969), 7. (Originally published in *Mao chu-hsi lun chiao-yu ko-ming.* Peking: Jen-min ch'u-pan she, 1967.)

In this brief statement Mao urges the combination of education with productive labor.

———. "Talk on the Question of Education [June 8, 1964]." *Current Background,* No. 888 (August 22, 1969), 13-14. (Originally published in *Mao chu-hsi lun chiao-yu ko-ming.* Peking: Jen-min ch'u-pan she, 1967.)

In this statement Mao discusses reforming teaching method at the university level with special reference to the lecture method.

———. "Talk with the Guinean Educational Delegation [August 8, 1965]." *Current Background,* No. 888 (August 22, 1969), 15. (Originally published in *Mao chu-hsi lun chiao-yu ko-ming.* Peking: Jen-min ch'u-pan she, 1967.)

In this statement Mao suggests that a school can only be successfully operated if the political level of the leading cadres is high.

———. "A Talk with Mao Yuan-hsin [February, 1966]." *Current Background,* No. 888 (August 22, 1969), 16. (Originally published in *Mao chu-hsi lun chiao-yu ko-ming.* Peking: Jen-min ch'u-pan she, 1967.)

In this statement Mao discusses the need to streamline the curriculum to shorten the schooling cycle.

———. "Talk With the Nepalese Educational Delegation on Educational Problems [1964]." *Current Background,* No. 891 (October 8, 1969), 46-47. (Originally published in *Mao Tse-tung ssu-hsiang wan-sui.)*

Mao discusses a broad range of educational issues focusing primarily on curricular problems.

———. "Talks to Central Committee Leaders [1966]." *Current Back-*

ground, No. 891 (October 8, 1969), 58-59. (Originally published in *Mao Tse-tung ssu-hsiang wan-sui.*)

In this important discussion Mao throws his support behind dissident students at Peking University.

______. "Things are Changing [May 1957]." *Current Background,* No. 891 (October 8, 1969), 24.

In this article Mao criticizes the ideological problems of intellectuals.

______. "Under the Red Flag of Comrade Mao Tse-tung." *Chinese Education,* II, No. 3 (Fall, 1969), 44-45. (Originally published in *Hung-ch'i,* No. 4, July 1968.)

In this revealing statement Mao projects his vision of the society of the future.

______. "A Welcome Evening Agricultural Technical School [1956]." *Chinese Education,* II, No. 3 (Fall, 1969), 56. (Originally published in *Mao Tse-tung t'ung-chih lun chiao-yu kung-tso.* Peking: Jen-min chiao-yu ch'u-pan she, 1958.)

In this excerpt Mao suggests that individual villages take the responsibility of educating adults in night schools.

______. "Where Do Correct Ideas Come From [May, 1963]?" *Four Essays on Philosophy.* Peking: Foreign Languages Press, 1968. Pp. 134-136.

Mao concisely states the Marxist theory of cognition.

______. "Work Teams [August 16, 1966]." *Mao Papers: Anthology and Bibliography.* Edited by Jerome Ch'en. London: Oxford University Press, 1970. P. 128.

In this statement Mao prohibits governmental and Party work teams from interfering with the struggles of teachers and students in the GPCR.

Nee, Victor. *The Cultural Revolution at Peking University.* New York: Monthly Review Press, 1969. 91 pp.

The author concentrates on events leading up to and including the GPCR struggle at Peking University.

Oksenberg, Michel C. "Policy Making Under Mao: 1949-1968—an Overview." *China: The Management of a Revolutionary Society.* Edited by John M.H. Lindbeck. Seattle: University of Washington Press, 1971. Pp. 79-115.

Price, R.F. *Education in Communist China.* New York: Praeger Press, 1970. 308 pp.

Schram, Stuart R. *The Political Thought of Mao Tse-tung.* 2nd. ed. New York: Praeger Press, 1970. 479 pp.

Schurmann, Franz. *Ideology and Organization in Communist China.* 2nd. ed. Berkeley: University of California Press, 1968. lii+642.

Schwartz, Benjamin. "New Trends in Maoism?" *Problems of Communism,* VI, No. 4 (July-August, 1957), 1-8.

The author discusses Mao's method of rectification by education.

———. "On the 'Originality' of Mao Tse-tung." *Foreign Affairs,* XXXIV, No. 1 (October, 1955), 67-76.

Snow, Edgar. "A Conversation With Mao Tse-tung." *Life,* LXX, No. 16 (April 30, 1971), 46-48.

This is the most recent interview with Mao that contains published remarks some of which are on education.

Steiner, H.A. "The Curriculum in Chinese Socialist Education: An Official Bibliography of Maoism." *Pacific Affairs,* XXXI, (September, 1958), 286-299.

Townsend, James R. *The Revolutionization of Chinese Youth: A Study of Chung-kuo ch'ing-nien.* China Research Monographs No. 1. Berkeley: Center for Chinese Studies, 1967. 71 pp.

Tsang Chiu-sam. *Society, Schools and Progress in China.* New York: Pergamon Press, 1968. 333 pp.

The Whole Country Should Become a Great School of Mao Tse-tung's Thought. Peking: Foreign Languages Press, 1966. 19 pp.

This pamphlet contains some educational statements by Mao.

Wittfogel, Karl A. *Oriental Despotism: A Comparative Study of Total Power.* New Haven: Yale University Press, 1957. xix+556 pp.

VI. MAO TSE-TUNG'S EDUCATIONAL THOUGHT AND THE FUTURE DEVELOPMENT OF CHINA

An Economic Profile of Mainland China. 2 vols. Washington D.C.: Joint Committee of the U.S. Congress, 1967.

Eckstein, A. Liu, T.C. and Galenson, E. eds. *Economic Trends in Communist China.* Chicago: Aldine Publishing Company, 1968.

Liu, T.C. and Yeh, K.C. *The Economy of the Chinese Mainland: National Income and Economic Development 1933-1959.* Princeton: Princeton University Press, 1965.

Richman, Barry M. *Industrial Society in Communist China.* New York: Random House, Vintage Books, 1969.

Wheelwright, E.L., McFarlane, Bruce. *The Chinese Road to Socialism.* New York: Monthly Review Press, 1970.

Index

INDEX